JOURNEYS
WITH
PLANT SPIRITS

"The practices, meditations, and insights in *Journeys with Plant Spirits* expertly offer an accessible foundational practice that will help you deepen your relationship with spirit and nature. Emma shares grounded advice in a practical and generous manner that will not only help beginners on the plant spirit path but provide a supportive framework for those who have been connecting with the plant spirits for some time. Open this book on almost any page, and you will be invited through the portal into the Otherworld and feel the wisdom of the plants."

FAY JOHNSTONE, AUTHOR OF *PLANTS THAT SPEAK, SOULS THAT SING*

"Through shamanic exploration, historical relevance, and meditative connections, Emma shares the transmissions gifted through the ancient roots of plant spirit healing. This is a precious book in which she shares a passionate review of the restorative energies gifted freely by nature, so needed with pharmaceutical pressures and our current separation from the magic of the natural world. A must-read!"

SANDRA CORCORAN, AUTHOR OF *SHAMANIC AWAKENING*

"A beautifully written and highly practical guide to plant consciousness. Emma takes us on a wonderful journey into the realm of plant spirits, sharing her wisdom and offering effective tools to help readers have their own unique experiences with plants. She shows us how we can come into deep relationship with the plant world, ultimately helping us remember who we are and why we are here."

CAROLE GUYETT, AUTHOR OF *SACRED PLANT INITIATIONS*

"This is the first time in my 45 years of esoteric and spirit work that I have found a plant spirit guide that is holistic, authentic, disciplined, and ego free—based upon genuine personal experience by an authentic medicine woman who shares safe practice from deep, personal experience, taught by the plant spirits directly. I highly recommend this remarkable book."

DAVID LEESLEY, HIGH CHIEF IARUERI RAWI,
YERAMANU AND SKULL KEEPER

"An essential addition to the library of anyone working with spiritual healing and the alchemy of plant healing."

JON G. HUGHES, AUTHOR OF *A DRUID'S HANDBOOK TO THE SPIRITUAL POWER OF PLANTS*

"The plants are our elders. They are also master teachers if we but listen. In this practical, inspired, and no-nonsense guidebook, we are invited to do just that. Emma Farrell, through enduring tremendous hardship, takes the reader on a highly sophisticated journey to access the healing power of plant intelligence. At the outset, we meet Sekhmet and Iboga, who provide the wings for Farrell to fly over the vast physical, energetic, and intellectual landscape of the plants and bring us a treasure that is beyond compare."

BILL PFEIFFER, AUTHOR OF *WILD EARTH, WILD SOUL*

"An enchanting and accessible guide to healing our soul and ancestral trauma through relationships with the spirits of plants and trees. By generously sharing her personal story, as well as her extensive knowledge and healing practices, Emma Farrell shows us how to reclaim our ancient and magical relationships with plant spirits using methods that make sense to the modern mind. This fascinating book offers a pathway 'back to the garden,' where physical, emotional, and spiritual balance await."

ELIZABETH MEACHAM, PH.D., AUTHOR OF *EARTH SPIRIT DREAMING*

"We are in a time of human history when we will be tested as never before. As humans we need to develop a healthy relationship with nature and the spirits of nature to ensure our future as a species. This book provides a map of the journey—opening our hearts and minds to the sentience of Great Nature. Blessings on the voyage."

ELLEN EVERT HOPMAN, AUTHOR OF *SECRET MEDICINES FROM YOUR GARDEN* AND *THE SACRED HERBS OF SPRING*

"This book is a much-needed addition to the shamanic understanding of the importance of having plant allies in helping heal the deep spiritual maladies that plague us on the road less traveled on the path of the wounded healer."

MARTIN DUFFY, DIRECTOR OF THE IRISH CENTER FOR SHAMANIC STUDIES

JOURNEYS
WITH
PLANT
SPIRITS

Plant Consciousness Healing
and Natural Magic Practices

EMMA FARRELL

Bear and Company
Rochester, Vermont

Bear & Company
One Park Street
Rochester, Vermont 05767
www.BearandCompanyBooks.com

Text stock is SFI certified

Bear & Company is a division of Inner Traditions International

Cataloging-in-Publication Data for this title is available from the Library of Congress

ISBN 978-1-59143-407-8 (print)
ISBN 978-1-59143-408-5 (ebook)

Printed and bound in the United States by Lake Book Manufacturing, Inc.
The text stock is SFI certified. The Sustainable Forestry Initiative® program
promotes sustainable forest management.

10 9 8 7 6 5 4 3 2 1

Text design and layout by Virginia Scott Bowman
This book was typeset in Garamond Premier Pro with Hermann used as the display
typeface
Illustrations by Edward Foster

To send correspondence to the author of this book, mail a first-class letter to the
author c/o Inner Traditions • Bear & Company, One Park Street, Rochester, VT
05767, and we will forward the communication, or contact the author directly at
www.plantconsciousness.com.

For my ancestors

Acknowledgments

With deepest gratitude to my best friend, guardian, and husband, Davyd, without whom this book could not have been written.

I would not be here today were it not for my husband and all my beloved teachers who have gifted me the light of awareness into new realms and possibilities.

Great thanks to my parents who have always supported me, whichever path I have chosen in life.

Thank you to Inner Traditions/Bear & Co for taking a chance on a new author.

And gratitude to all of my spirit team who have been among my greatest teachers, who have held me, guided me, and shown me that life is full of magic.

A Caution and Disclaimer
for the Reader

I make no judgment regarding psychoactive plants that, at the time of writing, could be illegal. In my humble opinion, it is absurd that certain plants and fungi are illegal or that people campaign for them to become legal. Plants and the natural world should not be subjected to the jurisdiction of the government, which decides what is legal and what is illegal. Nature is also our nature, and we do not have to be scared of it, unless we are fearful of ourselves, which many people are. We, of course, need to be discerning and practice common sense. With that in mind, any plant, tree, or mushroom is taken at your own risk. I or the publishers of the book cannot take responsibility for the decisions or actions you take as a result of reading the words here or performing the meditations.

Contents

PART 1

Entering the World of Plant Spirit Healing

PART 2

Thirteen Plants and Tree Spirits

Foreword

Pam Montgomery

I MET EMMA FARRELL several years ago in London at Plant Consciousness, a conference that she and her husband, Davyd, were hosting. I was so honored and excited to be a part of such a gathering that brought together plant lovers, land stewards, and those striving to expand their consciousness to the point of embracing all life, both the seen and unseen, while recognizing their place within this vast interconnected web.

Since that first event years ago, I have taught at subsequent conferences, run plant spirit healing apprenticeships, and brought plant initiations to the British Isles, all because Emma and Davyd recognize the powerful transformation both personally and collectively that can happen when being in cocreation with nature, especially with the plants and trees. As Emma says, "Plants can help us transform from an isolated, scared, and conditioned individual to a sovereign, soul-conscious being in alignment both with Mother Earth and with higher purpose." What I found in Emma was a soul sister who deeply embraces raising consciousness to achieve one's higher purpose and who acknowledges that plants and trees can serve as guides on this journey.

Through intense exploration, from an early age, into her own spiritual awakening, Emma has emerged as a beacon lighting the way for those wanting to participate in the telling of a new story to shift the paradigm into a world of cocreation and unity. Her avenue has been via a dedicated meditation practice and her profound love of nature, which includes plants and trees.

Drawing on the foundations of magical spirituality of the British Isles, the Celtic medicine wheel, and various meditation practices, Emma presents a profound, yet practical guide where the plant-human matrix of sentient consciousness merges and our original way of being blossoms. In the second half of this book, Emma brings alive the plants as magnanimous beings with her in-depth dive into plant and tree spirits who can guide us in our evolution.

Even though the arena of plant consciousness is mostly uncharted territory, Emma's extensive experience in plant research through dieting, meditation, and essence making has made it possible for her to share a clear path to healing and wholing both personally and planetarily. *Journeys with Plant Spirits* takes us on a voyage of self-discovery and collective remembering by making us aware of our inherent kinship with nature. As Emma says, "We can reveal our true nature and within it is the seed of mystical unity with all that is. As we are truly not separate from nature and never have been, it is nature itself that can guide us back to aspects of ourselves long forgotten. The plants and trees can remind us of our spiritual connection in order for us to recognize and live the great paradox, recognize ourselves as a drop in the ocean that is both the drop and the ocean, living lives where we are both the dreamer and the dream."

What rings loud and clear throughout *Journeys with Plant Spirits* is that cocreative partnership is an aspect of the new paradigm with plants and trees as ready, willing, and able partners. Cocreative partnership with nature and by extension plants and trees is a topic near and dear to my heart, which I have been exploring for over three decades. Just like all partnerships, the ones you have with plants and trees grow and deepen with time. You begin as acquaintances, move into friendship where the plants act as allies, and eventually you become beloveds. You may wonder how you could experience deep love with a plant, but as you read this book and delve into the plants and trees Emma shares with you, a door begins to open where you can envision a whole new world that is possible. You are being invited into the vision of cocreative partnership where we support one another to be all we possibly can be through cooperation, loving kindness, consciousness raising, and balanced spiritual ecology.

One of the key ingredients in an effective cocreative partnership is good communication. What we know is that our ancient ancestors understood the language of nature and communication was innate. As Emma so wisely suggests, we begin our communication by listening. Quieting the mind through meditation then tapping into the vibratory resonance of the plants, our "big ears" open and communication begins to flow. This communication is part of our birthright since we are a part of nature, and our symbiotic relationship with plants and trees makes access possible. Since we are all unique individuals, the form our communication takes may be different from another's, but it is no less valid.

As we build our relationship with the plants and trees into a cocreative partnership where the spirits of plants give us their healing gifts, a path to well-being emerges. As Emma discusses plant spirit healing, she suggests that "it evolves and changes with each person who engages consciously with the plant spirits and blends them into his or her own healing modalities, spiritual path, or way of being."

As this new wave of engaging with plant consciousness and working with plant spirits washes over us, hope rises as we tell a new story of cocreative partnership. What a blessing to have a pioneer such as Emma Farrell, who rides the crest of this wave, bringing us *Journeys with Plant Spirits* to serve as a way finder. This is a book whose time has come, for the great awakening is upon us.

PAM MONTGOMERY
OCTOBER 2020
DANBY, VERMONT

PAM MONTGOMERY is an herbalist who has passionately embraced her role as a spokesperson for the green beings and has been investigating plants and their intelligent spiritual nature for more than three decades. She is the author of two books, one of which is the highly acclaimed *Plant Spirit Healing: A Guide to Working with Plant Consciousness*. She teaches internationally on plant spirit healing, spiritual ecology, and people as nature evolutionaries. She is a founding member of United Plant Savers and more recently the Organization of Nature Evolutionaries or ONE.

My Plant Story

I ONCE READ THAT A YOGI leaves no trace. I don't know where I read it, but I remember being in my early teens, and the phrase stuck with me purely through my intrigue of what it meant. Many years of spiritual seeking and inner work have led me to a more and more profound understanding of this enigmatic concept. On a basic level it conveys mindfulness, ensuring that you leave a place in nature exactly how you found it. On a metaphysical level it is about traveling so lightly upon Earth that you don't interfere, change, or disturb anything on any energetic level because your actions of body, speech, and mind are in total alignment with unconditional love, with the purest energy in the universe. I aim to be that yogi, and after many years of study and application, I have identified a potential route to achieving this level of self-mastery through liberation from suffering. Naturally, it is a cocreative rebirth with our mother, Earth, and one that, therefore, anyone can follow.

～

I grew up in a beautiful community in Yorkshire in the United Kingdom. During my childhood I suffered from severe asthma and hay fever and spent many summers on the sofa, unable to even feed myself for lack of energy. The summer I was eleven, the pollen count was especially high, and I became very ill. That summer, the child of friends of my parents died from the same condition I had, and on a particularly difficult day, it was thought I, too, was in my last hours. The priest was called, and my last rites were read to me as I lay on the sofa, wondering what all the fuss was about. During that difficult summer, as my mother sat up with me night after night, it dawned on her that to give me a full and healthy life, we would have to move to where the air was clean and I could be a normal eleven-year-old.

So we headed off to St. Ives, to the farthest southwest toe of the British Isles, to live in an old granite house overlooking the beach. It was during my time in St. Ives, an old hippie and artists' colony, that my interest in spirituality and meditation was sparked. Not only was Cornwall full of legend and folklore of mermaids, giants, and witches, but my best friend for quite a while was the stepdaughter of Keith English, the now-departed and celebrated artist of mystical and transcendental imagery. He and his wife introduced us to meditation, and I would spend hours looking through their magical book collection, learning about the chakra system and the beings that inhabited altered states of consciousness.

I excelled at school and headed to Penwith College in Penzance and later spent a year at Paul Valéry University in Montpellier, France, or rather I was meant to be at university but spent much of that time on the beach and traveling, soaking up the new culture and landscape. Upon my return to Cornwall before my final year, I became incredibly sick again with asthma and hay fever, similar to when I was a child. For some reason my mother decided to take me to an energy healer. I walked into her healing space and was greeted by a picture of Sai Baba with his crazy hair and orange robes. I cannot remember the name of this healer, but she told me her story of how through visitations from this famous yogi, whom she had never met in the flesh, she left her role as a schoolteacher and went to India to train with him. That day she healed my torn and distorted energy field, returning my life force to me, and I floated out of that place, determined to return to learn her art. But the healer left, and I never saw her again.

Seventeen years later, after living for nine years in Dubai and becoming depressed and disillusioned with life, my husband, Davyd, and I moved to India and took two years off to find ourselves. Despite generous salaries we could not tolerate the soulless life of the corporate world, the backstabbing and duplicitous behavior of people in that world. It's a classic story, but I needed more from life. Little did I know that the spiritual and shamanic worlds are just as deceptive and deluded as the mainstream, just with the added bonus of an integrated system of self-liberation, which the world of money does not offer.

En route to India we decided we could not leave the Middle East without visiting Egypt and booked ourselves onto a tour with the author of an alternative history book I had bought Davyd. That trip changed our lives forever. Private access into temples before dawn allowed the power and majesty of these places to awaken aspects of ourselves that we had long forgotten. An initiatory experience in the Great Pyramid at dawn on the spring equinox brought my deepest wound of abandonment gushing to the surface.

We had spent two hours in the King's Chamber, each lying in the stargate sarcophagus for a few minutes. I was the last to enter, and when I emerged, everyone had disappeared. I went to the Queen's Chamber, thinking everyone had gathered there, but it was empty. I peered down the shaft to the subterranean chamber, but I could not see even one of the sixty people I was with. I left the pyramid thinking perhaps everyone had gone to watch the sunrise, and I walked the entire circumference of the pyramid but found no one. I was lost, alone, and quite afraid. Everyone had forgotten me, left me, and gone somewhere else. I sat and cried until sorrow was overtaken by anger, and I stormed to the front of the pyramid again, and there emerging from the doorway was my husband. I was furious that I had spent the last hour searching for him when he was inside all the time, and as it was time to leave, I was unable to visit the subterranean chamber. My spoiled and angry abandoned inner child threw a tantrum on the Giza Plateau! That morning marked my initiation into the inward journey. Something so shocking as being abandoned in the Great Pyramid had to happen to awaken me from the sleep of my deluded mind that was preventing me from seeing truth.

The next part of my initiation took place in the small temple of Sekhmet at the Karnak Temple Complex, usually closed to the public, but some baksheesh and the cover of darkness permitted us entry. We entered in pairs to a small chamber with one end filled by a large, dark, and ominous statue of the lioness goddess illuminated by candlelight. As I stood awkwardly in front of the statue not knowing what to do, I suddenly felt a strong resonating energy rising from my feet up through my legs. Ancient and deep, I had never felt anything as holy. It crept over my whole body, as tears rolled down my face and the man next to me fell to his knees. Sekhmet, the initiator of healers, made herself known to me, and as I left her temple and sat on a rock outside to meditate on this energy, she told me that I had to subdue my ego, that it was out of control due to childhood and past-life traumas and I had to see through its illusions if I was to find my inner truth.

Egypt marked the transition point between leaving the Middle East and moving to India. After some time in Goa, we headed to McCleod Ganj in the foothills of the Himalayas in Dharamasala, home to the Dalai Lama, where we spent time doing meditation retreats and studying at the Dialectic School at his temple. Farther up the mountain sits a ramshackle but endearing village called Bhagsu and the tiny Maa Asho Healing Center. As soon as I looked into the gentle and transparent eyes of Supriti Sood, one of the two healer-teachers at the center, I knew I had found the teacher I had been searching for since my return from France, seventeen years previous. I spent weeks with Supriti, learning energy healing and psychic surgery. She helped to remove all of the pain and suffering I had endured during nine years in Dubai and into a new way of being, my mind being blown wide open at the same time by the Buddhist concepts and practices of emptiness and dream yoga that I was learning at the temple. Something old and familiar was awakening within me, and I knew my life would be spent in service to the spiritual dimension of life. I would never be the same again.

On the way back to the UK, we decided to spend more time studying Buddhism and meditation, so we headed to Italy and the rolling hills of Tuscany to enroll at the Istituto Lama Tzong Khapa and the University of Pisa Higher School of Social Service (Università degli di Pisa Scuola Superiore di Servizio Sociale), where I undertook a two-year master's degree in the preservation and development of wisdom culture and the art of liberation. It was during this time that the plant spirits made themselves known to me. While living and studying in Italy, we decided to run events in London to increase awareness of all the wonderful spiritual practices we had encountered and that we thought others would be interested in, such as lucid dreaming, out-of-body experiences, and other forms of consciousness expansion. In 2012 we launched Gateways of the Mind, and during that first conference, the concept of plant medicine was mentioned to me on several occasions.

We were also invited to a private ceremony with the African root and psychedelic medicine *Tabernanthe iboga,* and so a few months later, I was back on a plane heading to a sacred ceremony that would change my understanding of life, spirituality, consciousness, and healing at a fundamental level. It was during the most beautiful two days that I sat for hours having a direct conversation with a spirit. I had never done this before and didn't even know it was possible, yet I asked the spirit of Iboga many questions about myself and about life, and I was given straightforward and truthful answers. That weekend gave me a road map for the rest of my spiritual unfoldment. After encounters with the dynamic spirit of Ayahuasca, I realized that, while I was indebted to these powerful plants for the healing and gifts they had given me, I couldn't continue a long-distance relationship with spirits that did not feel that familiar to me. Although I was aware that there perhaps was a karmic connection of some kind to iboga and ayahuasca, I needed to get to know the native plant spirits of my own land.

It was through undertaking research for a new large conference in London, Plant Consciousness (an event that the spirit of Ayahuasca told my husband to organize!), that we came across Pam Montgomery and her book *Plant Spirit Healing.* We knew she would have to be the keynote speaker at our event. I also knew that she would be my teacher and guide to the language of the plants of my own land, and I spent five wonderful years with her, learning about plant diets and plant communication. My husband also went to study for two years with medical herbalist Carole Guyett in Ireland, and together we undertook years and years of plant diets. I can't say this ten-year period was fun; it was the most grueling and challenging period of my entire life as the plants took me deep into the soul traumas of this life and past lives to recognize these traumas, bring them to the surface, and release them to free myself from the stone walls I had built around my mind and which had manifested as various kinds of autoimmune issues. It took many different plants to get to the root cause of my emotional and physical issues, and I had to be taken to the brink of death a few times to release deep-rooted fears and anxieties. Yet I became my own physician and healed myself of illnesses for which modern medicine still has no cure.

It was not until I read R. J. Stewart's *The Underworld Initiation* seven years after my initiation in Egypt that my spiritual journey started to make sense. By sheer coincidence I came across the book in a second-hand bookshop, and as I have enjoyed his other works, I purchased it and took it to Ecuador with me. As I sat in the Amazon jungle reading a book about Merlin's seven-year journey through the Underworld, I saw how the previous seven years of my life had mirrored his story in many ways. The painful and dark experiences I had had and that I had taken a long time to emerge from started to make sense as a process of inner unfoldment and illumination. I realized I had been initiated as a healer in Egypt by Sekhmet and had to be taken to the edge of death and through the halls of the hell realms to emerge transformed and able to assist others on their paths. Five months in the Ecuadorian Amazon exposed me to such darkness and black magic that I had never witnessed before. I had to experience the underbelly of the human psyche to awaken the warrior healer spirit within me and be able to assist others in their darkest moments. It was the plant spirits who showed me how to walk the middle way and hold the light and the dark in balance and nonpolarity within. It was the yew tree that stripped away the last major aspects of my fictional self and assisted me in becoming the healer and teacher that I am today.

INTRODUCTION

A Guide to the Path
of Plant Consciousness

THIS BOOK IS A PRACTICAL GUIDE to the method of plant spirit healing and the use of natural magic that I have crafted in partnership with my husband, Davyd, and in cocreation with the plants and trees spirits themselves. It is a methodology that sets out a therapeutic way to communicate with plants for emotional and psychospiritual healing. This book sets out a progressive path through which the practitioner can weave his or her own unique journey toward emotional balance and self-realization. The wisdom contained herein is not only my own; it has flourished through contacts from the Otherworld, through the medicine wheel, through teachings from our incarnate and discarnate elders, and through the insightful perceptions of meditation, all held and guided by the plant spirits themselves. It is the path of plant consciousness.

As humans we have developed a worldview or perspective that we exist as individual selves, separate from the rest of our species and separate from the world. We live within the illusion that the rivers, forests, and mountains that make up our planet and even the planets that make up our solar system are all separate, discrete objects. Our struggle to be successful and recognized by others and our misguided search for happiness outside ourselves have led us into the trap of disconnection and ultimately isolation. In the Buddhist and Hindu traditions, the self does not exist as a separate entity with its own inherent existence; as long as we identify ourselves in this way, we are caught in *samsara* or *maya*, a version of the world based on deluded perceptions. While we associate with this delusion, we create many kinds of blockages within ourselves that result in personal crises, imbalances, and illnesses. This perceived disconnection from the world, from nature, from our true existence is the basis of most mental and physical illnesses. To transcend our misperceptions, it is necessary to penetrate the nature of reality and understand the paradoxes of life that lie therein. To experience oneness with the universe, we must first discover our unique self, a fundamental paradox that has led us astray for millennia. In the words of psychotherapist M. Scott Peck, "an identity must be established before it can be transcended."[1] We need to uncover the truth of our existence before we can relinquish it to the great overarching story of life on this planet. Within our true nature is the seed of mystical unity with all that is. As we are truly not separate from nature and never have been, it is nature itself that can guide us back to long-forgotten aspects of ourselves. The plants and trees can remind us of our spiritual connection so that we can recognize and live the great paradox: recognize ourselves as drops in the ocean, that we are both drop and ocean, living lives as both the dreamer and the dream.

"We're made of star stuff" is another quote, from Carl Sagan, that I have heard many times. We emerge from the eternal source and will return to it one day, but in between, we create complex and elaborate experiences, stories, and games to keep us entertained. All the while we are pushed onward from an unknown source deep within the psyche, wanting us to find our way home. So we search for experiences of God, in our quest to solve the great mystery of life, and have created untold numbers of religions, philosophies, and schools of wisdom to help us do this. Although all these spiritual endeavors have served humanity, providing solace and guidance, they have also gotten us to where we are today—in a state of separation from the source. So while I am deeply grateful for the great wisdom held within the essence of many of these traditions, and they do indeed assist us on our path, we need to come back to basics with our practice, to the fundament underlying most of these mystery schools and ancient practices—back to nature.

The ancient traditions of the British Isles recognized the spiritual aspect of plants, and the Druids created elaborate rituals to cross the divide between the physical and spiritual realms for their own and others' healing and spiritual advancement. Jon G. Hughes, a fifth-generation practicing Druid of genealogical lineage, states that "the Druidic tradition has retained the union between the physical and the mystical in the belief that the two are inseparable and that neither may be effectively employed without the other. While accepting the physical curative properties of the plants it employs, it also believes that the physical (chemical) benefits of potions and remedies can reach their full potential only if they are prepared and administered by mystic ritual."[2] By crossing the bridge between the physical world and the spirit world through ritual and, as outlined here in this book, the working of the medicine wheel, the healing potential of plants is increased.

I do not claim to be an expert in Celtic shamanism, Buddhist philosophy, or plant lore; however, I have spent many years immersed in these worlds, studying them, undertaking many plant diets, and communing directly with the Otherworld and the plant spirits through ritual. This book is a result of that direct experience. The map is not the terrain itself, and so this book is a series of guiding words, but it is not the healing process itself. This book is meant to be worked with—not only read and learned in the mind but put to practical application. The words in this book provide a doorway to new paradigms: enter and learn for yourself what truly lies within. Don't take my word for it: discover your own inner wisdom and balance through your own connection and experience of the inner realms of nature. Inner balance is required to move forward effectively in life. Sovereignty over our inner world and energy field is an essential aspect of this, yet our society deems this aspect of ourselves irrelevant, especially in modern medicine. Just like the chariot card in the tarot, a black-and-white horse is required (balance of opposites) to steer and move the vehicle onward; we need both to become one. We need balance of our inner elements, our emotions, and our energies to stand as strong as a tree in our external world. We then come into balance between our individual self and the collective of humanity, of which we are an integral part. So don't hold back: be brave and open your heart to the living wisdom of nature.

This book explores ways to experience the multidimensional aspects of reality through cocreational healing with plant consciousness. It will show you how to effectively work with the plant spirits for emotional and spiritual healing, moving you into a new relationship with yourself and the world around you. Today, many are recognizing that emotional and spiritual healing produces the physical healing we need. The way that plant consciousness is becoming common knowledge is a staggering shift in recent years and one that is very welcome, and just in time. The ultimate objective of plant spirit healing is this level of personal remembrance, a deep awakening to the wisdom of the soul and the eternal spirit. Practiced at its deepest level, this book can open you to the majesty of the natural world both within and without; it can bring lasting meaning into your life through shifts in consciousness, insights, and empowerment.

In part 2, descriptions of thirteen plant spirits are provided. These are not exhaustive, describing all the healing qualities of the plants, but rather introduce you to each plant and its potential, from which you can dive into the unknown depths of your psyche with their guidance and protection. Each plant spirit is a treasure chest of divinely and earthly inspired wisdom, which can assist you on your soul path and inward journey.

If we combine internal plants (medicine) and external plants (our surroundings) within the nurturing womb of meditation, we maximize the potential for healing, inner transformation, and spiritual development. This book sets out a series of progressive meditations to take you deeper into the plant realm and deeper into yourself in order to awaken your inner senses to the subtle and the unseen therefore bringing the potential for psychospiritual healing.

PART I

Entering the World of Plant Spirit Healing

The first half of this book sets the foundation for your work with the plant spirits. Part 1 outlines aspects that require consideration and practices to bring awareness to the unseen parts of yourself and the world around you and provides a framework to allow the organic process of inner work to unfold safely and effectively. Take your time reading this first part: there are meditations and points to consider over and over again, techniques that will help you effectively cocreate with the plant spirits and achieve your intentions and goals. The container for our work here is the Celtic medicine wheel; however, any medicine wheel can be worked with. If you have a different one from your own land and indigenous traditions, that is absolutely fine; you will simply be working with the correspondences of nature that work for you. This book is a guide, a signpost along the way; it is not the path itself. Only you can walk and experience your inner landscape; only you can understand your divine essence and your own unique connection to the spirits of the plants.

1

Returning to the Plant Spirit Path

THERE WAS A TIME when the entire British Isles was covered in trees, from John O'Groats to Land's End, and the ancestors would say that a squirrel could run from one end of the country to the other without touching the ground. Imagine living among so many trees, in an unpolluted environment with pure air. During the era of the original wildwood, the ancestors of the current residents of the British Isles lived in much closer proximity to nature—much as the rest of humanity once did. This must have shaped their consciousness in a very different way from ours, their worldview more in alignment with the archetypal forces of nature and their sense of self being a lot more group-centric or tribal than our individual orientation today. Our ancestors likely lived their lives in a much more symbiotic way with Earth.

We do not want to turn the clock back and live exactly as our ancestors did; their worldview was not perfect either. It is they who undertook the large-scale clearance of trees to make way for agricultural land, creating a very denuded landscape in places. We cannot romanticize about the past when it is clear that the forces of good were nearly always corrupted by opposing forces, and so nothing of our history is clear-cut. We can learn from wrong turns, however, and blend the more positive qualities of that ancestral perspective with the modern mind.

It is known that our predecessors at a certain point in time had an animistic view of the world, seeing spirit in all things, in the rocks, trees, rivers, and streams. They recognized a creative force that animates everything in existence, with all phenomena being expressions of one pervading consciousness or spirit. Immanence survived in various guises throughout the epochs, such as the medieval alchemists and gnostics, although they, too, became corrupted.[1] Everything has shadow when we work in this dualistic realm. Animism as a way of being can bring a lot more meaning, consideration, and compassion into our lives, however, and open our senses to the wonders of the multiverse. Communicating with the spirits of plants and trees would have been part of our ancestors' daily life, rather than an obscure phenomenon as it is viewed today. At one time they believed that their thoughts came from nature, arose within their mind, and went back to nature. There was much less separation between the individual and the environment, and perhaps their thoughts would have been more fluid rather than static as they appear to us today.

Consciousness is constantly evolving, and thanks to the groundbreaking work of natural world researchers such as Suzanne Simard, there is, once again, more of a Western mainstream understanding and acceptance of the sentience of plants and trees. Thanks also to the work of plant spirit healer Pam Montgomery and author Stephen Buhner, the wisdom of the plant spirits has been kept alive, bubbling in the background in the West until now, when human consciousness is ready to receive it again on a collective level. We owe much of the knowledge that is available to us today to those who have walked before us.

We have a lot more in common with plants than you would suspect, blood and chlorophyll being very similar in molecular structure. The physical plants themselves do not perceive; they are the receptive organs for Earth. Similar to our ears, which receive sound vibrations but do not interpret them, plants are the receptive organs for the consciousness of Mother Earth, capturing and emitting frequencies to perpetuate the cycles of manifest life. The observer within, the consciousness of Gaia, translates the frequencies into coherency for survival and inner balance and to assist life-forms in fulfilling their purpose. The consciousness of the plants is the consciousness of Earth; the plants work to bring balance to all aspects of Earth, including us, her children.

Just like us, plants and trees have a metaphysical counterpart to their physical body, an astral aspect through which their souls can work. Plants can be studied and understood from a botanical and herbal perspective as well as from a shamanic and esoteric level. And just like us, each plant or tree is an expression of the soul force of Mother Nature and carries her unique medicine to heal on the physical, emotional, and spiritual level. The plant spirits are unique emanations of the Divine, spirits within physical carbon-based bodies. It is easy to anthropomorphize human traits onto nature and that can be of both benefit and hindrance: the latter because we are then limiting our understanding to that which we already know and a benefit because it helps us understand the qualities of the plants and trees in relation to ourselves. The plant spirits are more evolved than us, having awakened their eternal self, and it is the awareness of this aspect of plant consciousness that can assist our own advancement. We need to acknowledge that we are dealing with conscious spirits who work outside time and space and are not bound by their physical body; they have already transcended it, not in a rejection of it but as a realization of the true nature of reality, that spirit and matter are one. They therefore do not experience the same emotions and demands that physical life asks of us. When we connect to these spirits, we are tuning in to their frequency like a radio and asking for a cocreative process to take place. These conscious spirits are not restricted like us (before we fully awaken); they can be in many places at once, which is why many people can work with the same plant spirit at the same time.

Plants carry their medicine at varying levels of density from the chemical to the etheric, all aspects resonating in unison as the plant but expressing its diversity through these overlapping dimensions. These frequencies of nature can be beneficial to the beings who are out of alignment with the pulses and resonances of Earth. For humans who have many mental, physical, and spiritual maladies due to their self-differentiation from the world, plant and tree spirits can be our personal inner health service. Through their union with us on all levels they can realign us back to our natural way of being. Because they are structured in the same way as us and because we are all made of the same elements, they can heal us while at the same time teaching us how to heal ourselves and be our own physician. Plants can help someone transform from an isolated, scared, and conditioned individual to a sovereign soul-conscious being aligned with both Mother Earth and a higher purpose.

When we observe plants from an energetic perspective, each has its own unique bioresonance, its own animating life force that some refer to as spirit. It was Sir Jagadis Chandra Bose (1858–1937), a genius in both physics and botany, who first studied the behavior of plants as early as the nineteenth century, demonstrating through scientific experimentation that plants have a nervous system: they have memory, can make decisions, and therefore have consciousness. Subsequent studies within this field have brought the heartbeat of the trees and the dream life of the plants to the mainstream, but is anyone really listening?

Plant spirit healing, as it was taught to me by Pam Montgomery, is not a healing methodology with a specific set of definitions and protocols; it is organic and alive. It evolves and changes with each person who engages consciously with the plant spirits and blends them into their own healing modalities, spiritual path, or way of being. Within the foundations of its wisdom, however, lie processes passed down through the generations of how to communicate with the plant spirits and how to understand their healing qualities on a physical, emotional, and spiritual level. When indigenous peoples of the Amazon are asked how they learn about medicines with complex plant combinations, they say the plants told them directly how to combine them and make the medicine. They listened. Communication with plants is essential to survival in some parts of the world, and indigenous cultures have kept the wisdom of the plants sacred and alive, despite great opposition and oppression from the capitalist and Western worldview. As our entire survival depends upon plants, perhaps it is wise for us Westerners to start to listen too. Indigenous cultures understand that within each plant or tree is the spirit through which its higher intelligence works. Many of our indigenous brothers and sisters have retained their metaphysical senses;

they can still perceive beyond the physical plane and so recognizing nature spirits is easy when you can simply see them.

Our obsession with the surface, material world has shut off these innate human senses within us, yet we need to reconnect with the deepest aspect of ourselves that trusts our subjective experience and awakens the inner knowing that has been suppressed under years of societal conditioning. Many of the world religions teach that extrasensory perceptions are gifts bestowed upon those that walk the path of the ascetic or the holy person, and while this is true, it is also true that we are born with these gifts, and through working with plants we can reawaken them from their dormancy. Continuous work with wild plants, turning to them for medicine and consuming them over a period of time, will open the doors of perception and allow our true nature to shine through. As our mind becomes less rigid, as our energy field becomes clearer, and as we come into emotional balance, the metaphysical side of our senses comes online.

These precious gifts of insight and illumination elevate traditional herbalism to a more dynamic and powerful method of healing and can bring deeper awareness to other practices, such as yoga or bodywork therapy. The plant queendom is vast and ever evolving; it exists within a universal consciousness alongside a human collective consciousness, which is also in a constant state of flux and evolution. By expanding our consciousness into the inner realms of nature, we are opening ourselves up to a deeper level of our selfhood, and therefore all of our mundane and spiritual pursuits are enlivened. We are bringing life force into areas of the body and mind that need healing in a conscious way, not in an unconscious allopathic quick-fix way but in a way that embraces our own inner wisdom and vitality so that we can become our own physicians and be empowered to take responsibility for our own health and spiritual well-being. As Pam once said, the ultimate goal of plant spirit healing is to remember who we truly are. This is a gentler more humble way of expressing the aim of all the great mystery traditions throughout the ages, from the Eleusinians to the Druids—that of consciously awakening our eternal spirit and remembering aspects of our essential being so that we can bring balance and healing impulses from higher and deeper dimensions of life. In this way we can step outside the labyrinth or cycles of unconscious death and rebirth to become the architects of our own fate.

I have worked with plant spirit healing within the ancient traditions of my own land to cure my illnesses, establish emotional balance, and awaken my own eternal spirit to consciously live my life purpose. In order to work with the plant spirits for personal healing, we need to have a basic knowledge of the physical plants. We will touch on the basics of herbalism in part 2 to ground the healing gifts of the plants in the physical realm. Plants do not grow in isolation; the forces and spirits of land also work within and through them. This form of plant spirit healing sits within a contextual framework of the Celtic traditions of the British Isles, rich in folklore, magic, and wisdom, which has not been lost over time but still resides within the trees, rivers, plants, and spirits of the isles.

To witness and experience the healing forces of nature, we need a consciousness capable of it; meditation and training the mind is essential to our practice as we seek to expand our awareness beyond the confines of the boxes we have bound ourselves within as a result of conditionings, trauma, and the stresses of life. To awaken the magic within once again, we need to learn about energy and how it moves, transmutes, and evolves. Natural and universal laws play their part in forming our understanding of the healing powers of nature and the unseen world. By bringing together the powerful forces of the energies and spirits of the land we live on (through the plants) with the principles of natural magic (through correspondences) and the mind training that meditation offers, we create a powerful path to liberation from suffering and disease. This process combines the wisdom of the ancients with the wisdom of Earth to illuminate our own modern inner sage. The plant spirits are our guides during this process, and we turn to them as the wisdom keepers of Earth to remind us of our own sacred purpose and of our eternal self. It is a process of inner inquiry that many have called the hero's or heroine's journey.

The plant spirits are guides to healing; they are not fixers. When we refer to healing, we are not only referring to the physical relief from pain or disease but the awakening to spiritual awareness, which is one and the same thing. The body and emotions are expressions of the soul; their imbalances are clues to aspects of our consciousness that are repressed or suppressed. To suppress an emotion or thought is to push it to the back of the mind or sweep it under the carpet, which equates to pushing it into part of the body and energy field to store it because we feel we cannot deal with it. To repress emotions denies them any acknowledgment at all, and so these imbalances are completely unconscious. All energy needs to move; static energy becomes stagnant and builds in pressure if it is not permitted expression. Eventually, it will need to be released somewhere, often either through emotional outbursts or illness and pain in the body. By using our unhelpful emotions and imbalances in the body as our compass, we bring wholeness to our consciousness, integrate our shadow aspects, and work through emotion and disease to recognize the parts of ourselves long forgotten. We heal.

Of course, everything must be held within balance; even our drive to be healed, if we are not careful, can become fanatical. Desperation to improve our life drives us to latch on to that which makes us feel better, and we strive to hold on to the light, while continuing to deny the shadow. Love and compassion for ourselves as well as for others is key to self-empowerment. Without holding ourselves in a gentle and kind way, we can push ourselves into further psychoses and desperation. Take your time as you work through this book and with each plant or tree. We all heal at our own pace; there is no set time frame for healing and self-development. We are all beautifully unique; you will find your way if that is your desire.

Plant spirit healing can also be viewed as a response to the ecological crisis that is taking place in all corners of the world right now. When Charles Darwin published his doctrine of natural selection and physical evolution, *On the Origin of Species,* in 1859, our connection to nature and our umbilical cord to Mother Earth was severed as, according to John Daniel Morell, British educationalist and Congregational minister, he "determined to banish *spirit* altogether from the universe and make infinite and omnipresent Mind itself synonymous with the all-pervading powers of an impersonal nature."[2] In other words, he became a coconspirator to the controlling religion of the time, Christianity, and determined that humankind cannot know the ultimate nature of reality, while at the same time stating that we have been gifted with a superior intellect that can dominate and control the natural world. Considering this today, it sounds absurd, but when the general populace was indoctrinated with this belief in the nineteenth century, and it was compounded by the church, which played a more active role in society than it does today, the notion stuck and became the mother of capitalism. This way of thinking destroys our world through linear exploitation of Earth's resources. A very sad situation, indeed, when you understand that Earth creates oil, minerals, and metals as part of herself. She needs them, they are a part of her own sacred body, and we just take them and give nothing but pollution in return.

Plant spirit healing offers a methodology of direct perception of and connection with the spirit realms once again and to our own divine spirit within so that we can remember and experience our profound relationship to Mother Earth, to the one who gives us life. Our perceived disconnect is constructed through childhood, as a response to societal conditioning, trauma, and ancestral and soul karmas. Healing with the spirits of the natural world helps us remember our original way of being: that we are all made of the same elements, that we are all part of this great song. We are not parasites upon this Earth; we are her children who have forgotten a sacred and blessed relationship that we have been gifted. Plant spirit healing helps us develop compassion toward ourselves and others and in doing so brings self-awareness so that effective inner change can take place. We are taken back to an honest, clear, and loving way of being in alignment with the truth of who we are. Our issues, hang-ups, and illnesses are transformed into wisdom and inner strength; they become our friends and aspects of our inner sage. The depth of this kind of healing is far more than allopathic symptom treatment; it is an investigation into the origins of imbalance, and quite often we are led right down to the traumas of the soul. Instead of looking at the evident symptoms of an illness or disturbance, we can go to the origin. This form of healing has not been adopted by the mainstream because it deals with the unseen and not necessarily what is measured by scientific means. Modern medicine deals with pathology, *pathos* means "suffering" and determines the type of suffering through diagnosis. *Dia* means "across" or "through," and *gnosis* means "knowing." The word *diagnosis* means "through knowing." Once we know what it is, we can deal with it. All seemingly good and logical so far. The knowing in this case, however, refers strictly to the symptom. Allopathic means treating a symptom with its opposite, *allo* meaning "opposite," and *pathic* meaning "suffering." This approach ignores the source of the symptom, forcing the symptom to stop (and very often only temporarily) or pushing it back into where it came from. This approach is suppressive.

When we work with plants and their spirits for healing, we create the causes and conditions for the body and mind to naturally bring itself back to balance without force. We allow the natural course of a symptom to run, knowing that it will be eased once the underlying catalyst has been supported and given a helping hand in realigning itself. These underlying causes can be in the form of conditioning, trauma, misunderstandings, or ancestral inheritance, for example. The plants and their spirits gently remind us of parts of ourselves that are unconscious or missing. Through the revealing of our inner selves, through the awakening of the soul and what moves us, we are offered a way to bring balance to all areas of life, both within and without, through the awareness of our traumas and the transmutation of their wounds.

Through creating a relationship based on reciprocity, respect, and trust with the plants, we can heal the psychological, emotional, and spiritual wounds from our past, which in turn heals their resultant illnesses in the body. What begins as an affection for certain plants and trees can develop into a cocreational and transformational relationship that is life changing. As our relationship with one plant or tree spirit deepens and grows, we reach a point where we no longer need to take the physical part of the plant as medicine; simply by working with the spirit directly, we can heal and bring balance to our body, psyche, and soul. We carry the spirit of the plant within us, and so we can attune to its frequency at any given moment to evoke its healing response within us. This form of healing moves us toward an active form of sacredness, a nondependence on taking plants from the wild, and therefore contributes to the vast environmental regeneration that needs to happen. There is also mounting evidence that the more that people feel connected to nature, the less they want to destroy it, which seems obvious, but it took scientific studies to make these concepts mainstream. A recent study published by the National Trust, UK, with the University of Derby, found that "people who regularly notice and connect with nature are far more likely to act to help tackle the crisis facing wildlife." Professor Miles Richardson, from the University of Derby, said: "This report for the first time demonstrates that simple everyday acts of noticing nature that build a closer connection are key to people taking action for nature."[3]

When humans lose their connection to nature and to spirit, they destroy their environment as well as each other. It is imperative that we heal our connection to the natural world in order to effect change on a societal level, as well as a planetary one.

The Path of Awakening

Most people today are familiar with the chakra system, and it is a useful system to know, giving us a structure within which to understand the shifts taking place within us during our meditations or healings with the plants. The human body is the outer expression of the intricate layers of etheric bodies that exist within and around it. These metaphysical bodies are commonly known as the auric field or the aura, and their existence is scientifically validated not only through modern technology but through the ancient science of yoga, a system of vital life originating in the Vedic scripts. The human energy field is nourished and enlivened by *pranas* or different types of life force, providing all the necessary requirements for full health, longevity, and spiritual illumination. The chakra system is a series of vortexes of these energies aligned along and connected into the central channel or pranic tube, which runs through the center of the body, emerging through the crown and through the perineum to connect us to divine consciousness and earth consciousness, respectfully. I primarily deal with the seven chakras located within the realm of the physical body: from the root chakra to the crown chakra plus the earth star chakra, positioned approximately a foot below your feet, and the soul star chakra, located a foot above the head. This energetic structure connects our inner world to the external world through our senses, thoughts, and emotions. All interconnect and weave through the auric or energetic field to make impressions and influences upon the mind.

From a physiological perspective the human body's seven chakras correspond to the seven main nerve ganglia that branch from the spinal column and each chakra holds the energy key to its associated area of the body.[4] By bringing energy into each of the seven chakras, one is able to unblock and release life force. We will be working with the various plant spirits to bring cleansing and healing to the chakras and therefore to aspects of the mind.

One of the secrets to awakening our inner senses and communicating with plants is the heart. Known as a second brain, the heart has over forty thousand neurons of its own, and through an expansive field of resonance, which is bigger than that of the brain, it can perceive in ways that our conceptual mind cannot.[5] The brain is polarized within its structure and how it works, the left and right sides of the brain differentiating and labeling things as either good or bad, black or white. The heart is not polarized; it works within a unity consciousness. It is the first organ to develop in the embryo, and with its fiery rhythm, it pumps life into every other part of the body. The heart perceives by way of entrainment, aligning you to your environment so that you can understand it on an energetic level. We have all felt an oppressive atmosphere when we walked into a certain building or room; this is heart-body perception, not perception of the mind. The heart perceives the patterns and connections within the energetic framework of our reality; it is therefore our second brain (or perhaps the first one) and our second sight, which are aspects that we can exercise and strengthen not only through meditation but by working directly with the plants and trees who hold many keys to unlocking the deeper aspects of this awareness.

It can be a long road for some from the head to the heart, and to truly live from heart consciousness can be a lifetime's work. It is possible, though, to step into this awareness and achieve symbiosis and communication with a plant quite easily; we just need to meet it on its level. The heart chakra is traditionally green (there's a clue!), and we need to rest our awareness in the heart center to start to perceive through the heart and to shift our consciousness into the realm of the plant spirits. One of the first teachings that we receive when we enter the unseen realm is the notion of reciprocity: we must give in return and in whatever way we can for that which we receive from Earth. The mind-set that nature exists solely for our own use and is there to be dominated is a destructive pattern that has resulted in the catastrophic state of the planet today. Nature deficit disorder is now a labeled condition along with nature blindness and both are known to result in behavioral problems and mental health issues. Our identification with extreme individuation has disconnected us from nature and from our soul and has contributed to the extremely high levels of mental health issues that we are experiencing in our society.

Walking the nature path as a means to our awakening requires us to approach ourselves holistically, from the perspective of mind, body, spirit, and soul. It requires the understanding that the mind, body, and energy field are one; they are not separate. By healing the body we heal the mind. By cleansing the energy field, we heal the body. By meditating we heal the energy field and so forth. Our objective is to have a healthy vitality, a compassionate heart, and a clear mind.

Dropping the Mind into the Heart Meditation

There are countless forms of meditation, but the underlying objective of many is the taming of the mind. This is not a controlling taming, as this can be counterproductive, but it is a calming taming so that our conceptual mind can be quieted and we can start to understand which thoughts are ours and which arise from conditionings, habit, and trauma defense mechanisms. Most people believe the majority of their thoughts to be true, leading them into delusion and unhelpful situations. Most of our thoughts are about the past or the future, coming from memories or from worry; again, these are unhelpful, and we waste a lot of our energy in this way. By moving the mind toward the peace of the present moment and back toward alignment with nature and Mother Earth, we reveal aspects of ourselves that have remained hidden for years under the conditioning and distraction of modern life. We start to awaken our metaphysical senses and start to perceive the subtler dimensions of life. The plants and trees can be our guides along this path that is fraught with wrong turns and self-deception, standing as beacons of truth to help lead us home.

The first place to start on your journey into the inner realms of the plants and trees is to learn a technique to drop you out of monkey mind and into the heart and to increase alpha brain waves, paving the way for the theta frequency of inner vision. This meditation can be done before each of the meditations in this book to bring you into the state of grace necessary for communicating with plants. It is an ancient technique from the Dzogchen Buddhist tradition and can be performed indoors or outdoors, any time of day or night, and during any normal daily activity to assist with disturbing emotions.

Sit cross-legged on the ground or on a chair with your feet flat on the floor and your back straight. Take three deep breaths, and on each exhalation release any tension held in your body, paying more attention to the jaw, shoulders, and stomach.

Find a place of stillness within your body or mind among all the movement taking place. Allow your awareness to gently rest on this stillness, allowing stillness to permeate throughout your body. If the mind is moved by thought, just notice this and bring it back to the stillness.

Notice that within this stillness is silence. There is not as much space for the chattering mind in silence, but if it does wander, just gently bring it back to the stillness within the silence. You will notice how vast and spacious stillness and silence are. Rest in the peace and this expansive state of awareness for five to ten minutes.

Once you feel calm and centered in your awareness, sometimes you can feel a shift in your internal energies as your brain waves move from beta to alpha. Bring your attention down to the heart. Feel the warm glow from your heart chakra. Bring to mind something that you are grateful for in your life and allow that state of gratitude to permeate your body from the heart. Focus on this inner smile for a few minutes.

It is from this state of grace that you can proceed into the meditations, presented in the following chapters.

2

The World of Spirit

IT IS DIFFICULT TO PUT INTO WORDS something that is ineffable, etheric, and unseen by most people. While I love the English language, trying to express experiences of transcendence or of the unseen realms is more challenging because it lacks the vocabulary for such experiences. Irish Gaelic has a very nature-based vocabulary, with many words, idioms, and phrases that have no English correlative. Ancient languages such as Sanskrit and certain forms of Tibetan are called sacred because they were devised to express forces and concepts of the spirit realm. One Tibetan word needs a whole paragraph of explanation in English simply because our language is fixed to a one worldview rather than encompassing the multidimensional universe that we actually live in. The reasons for this are debatable, but from my perspective, this narrow framing of our world keeps us locked into an industrial and material mind-set. So to understand the plant spirits, who they are, where they reside, and how they work, it is therefore useful to place them into a cosmological framework such as the medicine wheel, an ontological mechanism that can be visualized as well as expressed through words. We will encounter this method of working in the following chapters.

The Three Realms

The spirit world can be a complicated and confusing place if you are not used to consciously being with it, which is why most spiritual traditions work around a central cosmology through which all experiences can be navigated. In Celtic shamanism, with its correlations to both the Norse and Scandinavian traditions, we see a beautiful yet practical depiction of the levels of consciousness that we encounter through our meditations and inner work. The Upper, Middle, and Lower Worlds are not unique to Celtic and Norse lore, but they eloquently express the overarching planes of existence for both physical and nonphysical beings. The concept of the three worlds is not only very useful and simple to understand, it is also the container for the range of frequencies in our universe and forms the basic cosmology of many shamanic and mystical traditions.

The Upper, Middle, and Lower Worlds encompass all the realms of light and dark (not necessarily positive and negative) that we can experience and all the planes of existence for many types of physical and nonphysical beings. The Upper World is the divine end of the spectrum with high vibrational states and the location of light beings. It encompasses the cosmic star families as well as the gods and high elven realms. It is the place of the shining ones, the enlightened beings who are perhaps the angels of the Judeo-Christian tradition. Mercury and the elements of air and fire are the communicators and messengers between the Middle World and the Upper and Lower Worlds. The Middle World is the embodied realm, where we now stand and where objects are manifest yet imbued with spirit.

The Lower World is the watery Underworld or Otherworld where the *sidhe,* the fae or fairies, and the ancestors reside. The beings who live in this place are also known as the Pale People in British pagan traditions, referring to their association with the land of the dead and their nonsolar existence. The primal force or power of this place is the Great Mother herself. In Welsh mythology it is known as Annwn, the chthonic and primal forces dreaming, informing, and reflecting the Middle and Upper Worlds, providing the life force for all of nature. It is therefore known not only as the land of the dead but also of life. These three worlds are not separate but overlap and intertwine with one another so we can encounter the Otherworld as a land existing on the etheric and astral levels, with our physical realm being a reflection of it. The Upper World, which encompasses the cosmic forces, overlaps the Middle World, as the planet we live on is also part of the cosmos. These other dimensions of reality are accessible through our imaginal faculties, the inner doorways, and through the gateways of the plants.

More about the Otherworld

The Otherworld is the repository of the original wisdom and magic of the British Isles: it is a realm of myth, legend, and beings of many lineages. These spirit beings populate the mythic realm of our ancient past and are as alive today as they were then. They carry the archetypal forces of the cosmos, yet they are also fully conscious beings who potentially stand as sentinels, initiators, and guides on our path, as they remind us of our true origins, our emergence from the soul of Earth. In this great transition of the ages, the ancient kings and queens of the British Isles are rising once again to reclaim the sovereign Mother Goddess, who was usurped many lifetimes ago. The ground stirs as the Otherworld also evolves into a new consciousness; they are not left behind but become allies on the path to a new way of living in cocreation with Earth. We are not devolving back to her-story; we are moving through his-tory into our-story. Human consciousness has evolved to the point where we can understand our individuality within the collective and recognize we are one integral nodal point in the great web of life.

Although the Otherworld is a fundamental aspect of the traditions of the British Isles, it is not exclusive to the isles. Underworld traditions exist in indigenous cultures around the world, with each tradition varying in its cultural wrapping and its setting within the unique topography of its land. When I visited Iceland I experienced the Otherworld there as very similar to the British Isles, with the same themes, gods, goddesses, and spirits. They might be called different names, but they are the same beings living within a familiar energetic architecture. I have not, however, encountered similiar Underworld traditions in other countries and cultures; elsewhere, they have been very different and unfamiliar.

An exception to this can be found in the history of one of my teachers, David Leesley, whose full title is High Chief Iarueri Rawi (White Serpent), a position he was endowed with after years of ceremony and initiations with High Chief Wai Wai Rawi of the island of Tanna in the Republic of Vanuatu, South Pacific. During his initiation process he learned about the creation story and cosmology of this ancient tribe and discovered that their main god is called Majikjiki, the very same presiding deity of his own birthplace and home, the Isle of Man or the Island of Manannan Mac Lir. Manannan is the Celtic god of the seas, of warriorship, and of magic. He protects the shores and coastlines of the British Isles. According to the creation story of the tribe of Tanna, Majikjiki sailed across the ocean during the time of the great flood and landed on a powerful island off the coast of England, where the descendants of the White Serpent would live. Majikjiki became known as Manannan, and David's synchronistic arrival on Tanna in 2003 fulfilled an ancient prophecy for the tribe, the reunification of the Black and White Serpents. David reconciled with his spiritual twin brother, the high chief of the tribe.*

Denizens of the Otherworld

The Green Man, the Morrigan, Ceridwen, and Taliesin are some of the beings who can make themselves known through direct experience or through archetypal forces when we walk on the Otherworld path of the ancestors. This book is not a compendium of the populace of the Celtic world, but I would advise you to familiarize yourself with the characters who could be your guides and helpers during your inward journey.

This plane of existence has a hierarchy (for want of a better word) of dimensions and levels, each a residence for different types of beings. The faery realm is one such place in the Otherworld, where the British Isles' legends of the little people, nature spirits, and goblins come from. There is much confusion as to how this multitude of beings exists due to a

---

*To read more about this inspirational and magical story, see Leesley's books: *Kassoso: When Myth Becomes Reality* and *Return of the White Serpent*.

lack of written evidence from our ancient past, mistranslations, overlays by Christian clerics, and the human disconnection from nature. Over the centuries, as we have lost the ability to perceive these beings and elves have become confused with dwarfs and genius loci have become confused with sprites, the understanding of their abilities has become lost in the mistranslations of the Middle Ages. The study of European folklore is fascinating yet misleading; it is always best to rely on direct experience. Through working with certain plants and by cleansing our doors of perception, we can find out and experience them for ourselves.

The myths and folklore of the faery realm were molded into caricature and cartoon by the Victorians, who, on the one hand, managed to preserve the wisdom of the fae within children's stories but, on the other hand, reduced them to pesky little beings flitting around and sitting under toadstools all day. There has been a huge disservice done to the vast diversity of life-forms in the Otherworld. The variety of beings in the spirit realm is staggering, and many do not interact with humans for obvious reasons, but others are happy to make themselves known and seen. Just to clarify, though you will encounter them on inner planes, it is very rare for these beings to manifest on the outer plane before your open eyes. You could be lucky enough to experience this but do not expect this to happen; otherwise, you will be setting yourself up for disappointment. We perceive other worlds through the faculty of the inner eye.

Although realms of the fae and the nature spirits have been confused over the centuries, their existence has been documented by the Egyptians, Greeks, Indians, and Chinese in antiquity. The fae were once thought to exist as part of the air elementals, but in reality, they exist on a plane of existence of a much more substantial nature. Nature spirits are the elemental beings that live within the subtle forces behind the physical manifestation of the four elements: their bodies are made of the element within which they live and so they are restricted to their specific realm. Gnomes are the earth elementals, nymphs are of the water, sylphs of the air, and salamanders of fire. Within each category there is a diverse range of inhabitants, all with various names attributed to them: for example, fauns, dryads, and hamadryads all inhabit the earth element. It was the great philosopher and healer Paracelsus who named the nature spirits within the elements; literature and wisdom traditions have perpetuated their existence, even to modern times. Whereas the elementals consist of only one etheric body, other beings have both spiritual and astral bodies. The elementals should not be confused with beings such as the fae, the elves, and the merfolk; these beings exist within the elements but are masters of them. The only difference between us and them is that we also have an earthly, manifest body, whereas those who exist in the spiritual realms do not. Races of beings such as the elves exist within a hierarchy of beings, from those deep within Earth known as the dark elves (but not dark as in sinister or negative) right up to the light elves of the higher realms in Norse mythology; these beings are, I believe, equivalent to the Judaic system of angels.

The Otherworld as Home of the Plant Spirits

British folklore refers to the Otherworld as existing either across the sea, under the sea, or beneath Earth, but it really exists as an overlap or interweave of our physical world and cannot be pinpointed to a physical location. It exists alongside our physical world and receives its watery connection from the nature of its energy, it being more etheric and fluid. Just as our world is very outward-facing, a masculine expression of consciousness, the Otherworld is the inner watery world of deep femininity from which the life force emerges into our world through the light of nature. Portals, gateways, and access into this realm can be found in special places on the land and within our own interiority. We will be exploring this concept and its practical application later in the book. For now, we need to formulate an idea or picture of what this other realm is as it is fundamental to working with the plant spirits; it is where they and their spiritual forces come from.

The Otherworld is where nature evolves and where she returns. It's where the soul of the Mother Goddess of the land resides and from which healing energies emerge. It is almost impossible to expand your consciousness into the inner realms of native plants and trees without encountering aspects of the interiority of the land. Plants do not sit in isolation but within all of the forces of life that emerge from Earth; we therefore cannot avoid the origin of the life force that runs through them or the telluric energies that inform them when we work with plants. The ecosystem does not only encompass the physical and manifest elemental aspects of nature but the unseen realms and beings also, a vast and complex place housing many kingdoms or realms within itself, including the land of our ancestors, the land of the fae, the elven realm, and the rainbow bridge to the divine realms. The plant spirit approach is holistic not reductionist. Our world and the Otherworld are reflections of one another with distinct similarities as well as differences. As your work progresses and you increase your experience of and familiarity with the Otherworld, it will increasingly manifest through you, but its deeper teachings will not enter your awareness until you are ready.

An academic snobbery pervades the Western mentality: if something is not verified by the scientific method or presented as a solid fact, it is disregarded and discounted as primitive or at best fanciful. This attitude squashes our innate intuitive ability. The scientific method of analysis and measurement breaks everything down into parts, thus creating separation within everything, including our own bodies. This compartmentalization has almost eradicated the sense of a unifying spirit from our worldview and left us washed upon the shores of meaningless lives that we desperately try to fill with entertainment and new things. Science is not sophisticated enough to grasp the subtle realms we refer to here; it is only through the most advanced technology on the planet, the natural mind, or natural intelligence (and I include the consciousness of Earth and all of nature as well as our own) are we able to journey to the inner realms so that our spiritual selves can be understood. Quantum mechanics is bridging the gap between science and spirituality, but its findings are only now starting to filter down into everyday reality, and even its name, mechanics, feels rather devoid of spirit. Those who remain stuck in realism limit their world so much that real meaning and understanding are usurped by functionality and ego.

If it were not for the elders of our society such as John and Caitlin Matthews and R. J. Stewart, the wisdom of the Otherworld might have been lost to us today. Its knowledge and connection have been suppressed over the centuries by the church and industrialization. We are indebted to those who are the wisdom keepers and have sacrificed much to keep the foretime and the secret commonwealth alive.

Spirit and Soul

At this point, we should dive into the difference between spirit and soul, a contentious subject over the millennia and one that has elicited multiple theories and assertions from philosophers of all cultures and spiritual traditions. There are many interpretations and misinterpretations of these words mainly due to the superficial level of theological inquiry taught in our education system, if it indeed exists at all in some schools, and also due to a lack of available metaphysical words in the English language. These two words are today used interchangeably but perhaps that is because we have forgotten what differentiates them or because we have been confused by overlays of religion. The Christian doctrine states that the soul is the intellectual and moral eternal aspect of the individual that survives the body after death and moves on to either heaven or hell. This soul, also called the spirit in this religion, refers to the animating force of the body, which returns to God when the body dies. The Tibetan Buddhist perspective does not entertain the notion of a soul but teaches that from the objective substrate or void emerges a subjective substrate consciousness, the fundamental ground of awareness. This consciousness arises as a radiant stream that underlies all perceptions from lifetime to lifetime, but it does not carry any personality nor intellect as it moves from one incarnation to the next.

In our own pagan past, it was believed that the human being was composed of three aspects: a body, a soul force, and a spirit; however, the meaning of soul and spirit here are quite different from the Christian understanding. In pagan anthropology, the soul is the life force of the body and is provided by Mother Earth; this soul force is the same as that of nature. Soul is downward-moving energy; it is the yin of Taoist philosophy and what makes us human. It carries the personality and connects the spirit with the physical body. The spirit is upward-moving energy; it lifts us and has a yang expression. According to Robin Artisson, as spirit takes form, it is "a mysterious 'other' being, a divine being that acts as a 'follower' or 'double' to the living human being, but, from the perspective of the living human, seemed to be an autonomous, independent being."[1] Artisson is referring to what the ancient Greeks called the *daimon* and for which many cultures and philosophies have their own terminology. This is the unborn eternal spirit. Through inner inquiry and immersion in the natural world, we can awaken this higher self aspect of our being to full consciousness and this is the great work (*magnum opus*) of alchemy and the true meaning of immortality. By awakening and functioning from our eternal spirit during our life on this planet, we step outside the confines of linear time and potentially out of the cycles of reincarnation. When we work with the plant spirits, we are working with the same divine guiding aspect that works through their own soul force and physical body. Just as in Tibetan tantra, we can align our consciousness to something greater than our limited selves so that we eventually become it. This unity of mind, body, soul, and eternal spirit is the true gift of being human.

Working with Plant Spirits

So how and where does the eternal independent spirit reside? Perhaps on the same plane as the plant spirits. According to Rudolf Steiner and Theosophy, the devic plant spirits live on a plane of existence called Devachan. Higher in vibration than the astral and sitting beneath the realms of the Buddhas and ascended masters, this land of gods and goddesses sits on the edge of the space-time continuum and so appears to be almost timeless. The religious overlay through Steiner's work complicates what is essentially a logical concept. The world of causality and duality that we live in is ruled by space-time and is a reflection of the Otherworld, a timeless dimension from which all nature emerges. Our dualistic world has to have its opposite, a realm of the ethereal as opposed to a realm of physical objects. Yet as mentioned, they are not separate; we just have to remember how to blend them together within our understanding of reality. This Otherworld is the home of the plant spirits. It is not restricted by the same laws of physics and time as we are. It is a much more thought-responsive realm, and moving between elements and transforming energy is a much quicker process. This is also where our own eternal aspect exists.

Working with plant spirits has the potential, therefore, to be a much deeper and more powerful healing experience than just working with their physical parts such as in everyday herbalism. As master elementalists, plant spirits can heal on a physical, emotional, and spiritual level, a truly holistic experience that gets to the root cause of issues. Often these issues go back to past-life or soul trauma that has carried over into this life and manifested in a different but similar form. Karmic cycles repeat similar motifs within differing circumstances and time lines. For example, the experience of losing a child in a past life can create deep-rooted soul trauma, preventing the expression of unconditional love in the current lifetime, a blockage that can result in physical heart issues. Or being on the losing side of a battle in a past life can manifest as conflict trauma in the present life, creating relationship and self-sabotage issues. The range of causes for present conditions is as varied as we are, and it requires a consciousness less limited than ours to discover the root.

Time is not linear, as we are led to believe, but cyclical. The great calendars of the ancient world worked on rotation and calculations of the stars or the position of Earth against them. Nature progresses through cycles, and as we are also a part of nature, we also exist upon and within cycles of time and space. Our past lives therefore cannot be ordered in a nice thread of one leading into the next one; the concept of past is misleading. As we work on issues within ourselves that seem to have an origin outside our current lifetime, that issue is very much still alive within us and, therefore, so is that past life; it is not past but still very present. In the Buddhist tradition it is not considered helpful to go into past lives because we are the result of everything that we have ever been: all our karmas are facing us right now in the mirror. All our past lives are alive within us now. Perhaps a better analogy of how past lives work is if we imagine our physical body in the center and all our other lifetimes radiating from us into different time lines and dimensions, creating a web rather than one thread. We are a complex interweaving of many threads. We can tap into specific parts of our trajectory to the root cause of an illness by following along a particular thread or part of the web to facilitate healing and rebalance in a past life, which will resonate through our web into our current lifetime. It is a case of thinking in spheres rather than lines.

When we are working with the spirits of plants, we are working outside normal space-time; therefore, time lines and dimensions can be accessed from the present moment. Our plant allies can follow the energetic thread of a disease from the present moment right back to the moment of inception of the trauma, whichever lifetime that occurred in. The plant spirits can read our energetic state of being and can therefore know us better than we currently know ourselves. Patterns of thought or behavior that are still unconscious for us can be brought to our awareness via the consciousness of the plants. Plant spirit healing works on the understanding that illness and disease have an underlying emotion and trauma that needs to be addressed before curing can take place. This, however, requires that we face the stuff we have, until now, preferred to sweep under the carpet or box away, hoping it would be gone forever. Fears and shadows need to be addressed, and not everyone is prepared or ready to do that. Yet if we are to truly know ourselves and if we are to evolve as humans and spiritual beings, we have to shine the torch of awareness into the darkest corners of our psyche to uncover forgotten aspects of our self that usually reveal our unique gifts. We can turn our lead into gold, our weaknesses into strengths. The inner light of the plants can be our guides and protectors on this path. What a gift.

Who Are the Plant Spirits?

The plant spirits themselves are as diverse and multifarious in their quintessence as their physical counterparts. Within the common native plants and trees, their spirits range from elusive and mercurial, such as herb-Robert (*Geranium robertianum*), right through to benevolent ascended masters, such as *Angelica archangelica,* teaching through gentle yet profound and heart-conscious ways. When we move into the realm of the poisonous plants, these spirits clearly have a stronger connection to the land of the dead and are a lot more unpredictable. With these plant spirits there can be a wrestling of will as the spirits work in a psychological way. Within the poisonous spectrum, *Artemisia absynthium* (wormwood) is classed as poisonous and is a very powerful witch yet is amenable to cocreation. At the other end of the poison spectrum, we have plants spirits who should only be called upon by experienced plant shamans, such as the Brugmansias, wild and possessive sorcerer spirits who bring extremely powerful medicine of protection but only if you acquiesce to their will. There is always a way to work with these types of plant spirits, but again I emphasize that only very experienced shamanic practitioners should even consider it. Once we move into the sphere of the psychoactive or teacher plants, there is also a spectrum of spirits that heal in a more dramatic, karmic, and sometimes even brutal way. These plant spirits offer a baptism of fire into the world of spirit, opening our doors of perception into other dimensions. From the heart-opening and protective San Pedro cactus (*Echinopsis pachanoi*) to the karma-ripening *Tabernanthe iboga,* these plant spirits should also be approached with extreme caution as they are complex and require an understanding of the nature of the mind and reality in order to navigate their world effectively. Healing can become a counterproductive and retraumatizing experience with these plants if the space in which they are worked with is not held effectively.

When we start to work with the plant spirits, we quickly realize that there is the animating spirit of the individual plant or tree, which has its own unique expression within its species, and then there is the group spirit of the species. You can connect to the spirit of the beautiful oak in the park or you can connect to the Oak spirit. The chief overarching spirit of each species is called its deva or *apu*. It is simply through intention that we can choose which aspect of the plant or tree spirit we wish to work with.

When we behold these spirits, we perceive them through our own cultural and phenomenological filters. This is the texture and shape of the background we were raised in from childhood—the cultural narrative of the period, the accepted norms, the archetypes most predominant, and the characters present in our stories. All of these influence our worldview and what we accept as reality or not. By perceiving plant spirits, we are translating energies into recognizable visuals through a specific filter that is unique to us. They may take on a humanoid shape or other familiar appearance, which is both our way of understanding and making sense of the new energies we are encountering and may also be a response from the spirits themselves—a way to make themselves recognizable to us. Many of the native plant spirits of the British Isles appear as witches because in the Otherworld of the isles incarnated witches are reflections of and receptacles for healing energies from that world. For example, the spirit of Wormwood is often personified in the tradition of the British Isles as a witch in a flowing green garment, but someone from India would likely see a very different morphology of this spirit. These humanoid shapes are generally not their usual forms, if indeed they have one at all.

From my experience plant spirits are generally shape-shifters: they can appear to us in many different ways according to situation and circumstance. I have seen the spirit of Mugwort appear as an elemental wizard wearing a multicolored robe, as a wrathful witch ready to take on opposing forces, and as a motherly figure with protective arms around me as I fell asleep. Some plant spirits are more elusive, especially those that rarely work with humans, and so their appearance can be more difficult to apprehend. Some plant spirits appear as undefined shapes of colored energy, sometimes with sacred geometry within them; others appear as characters from mythology and folklore, and perhaps they are indeed those beings. Plant spirits in general can manipulate the elements and emphasize particular frequencies within their own resonance to bring it forward when required; in this regard, we need to keep an open mind as to how a plant spirit will appear to us within our inner landscape and our mind's eye.

A realization that I have had over my many years of working with the plant spirits is that they are powerful beings and in the native common plant realm are comparable to bodhisattvas in the Buddhist tradition, enlightened beings who choose to reincarnate to help all sentient beings achieve enlightenment. By incarnating as plants these high beings can populate whole countries and continents with their healing gifts, thus reaching far more beings with their kindness than they could do in one body. It is no surprise then that many plant spirits appear as goddesses and noble teachers. In the Vedic scripts the plant medicine known as soma was described as hosting the goddess of the same name. We do not know what plant the soma medicine came from, but we do know the prodigiousness of its spirit. The Hawthorn and Sacred Basil spirits are also goddesses, and the Angelica and St. John's wort spirits emanate as ascended masters. Existing almost entirely outside time and space, their mastery of the elements is god-like and their wisdom far greater than ours. The gods and goddesses are the beings already aware of all that is, the level of consciousness that we are working toward as mortal humans.

The Lookie-Likies of the Spirit World

One aspect that I think needs mentioning here is that when we are venturing into the spirit world, not just plant spirits reside on these dimensions but many types of beings also live there, all with their own agendas, some complementary to humans and some not. Varying planes or dimensions exist in this world, with many types of energies. It is important to understand and be thoroughly familiar with the energetic frequency of a plant and how it feels for you. Without this baseline of familiarization, it is much more difficult to recognize the footprints or the new characteristics of your ally as it assumes its various guises. You risk being fooled by a spirit that pretends to be the plant spirit you are working with. This interplay between human and plant spirit is one of the most enjoyable yet potentially risky aspects of working shamanically with plants. Many disincarnate spirits crave a physical body due to the vast range of opportunities available on an emotional and spiritual level and they will try to take advantage of your inexperience. We have our own spirit ally team who looks after our well-being, but we also have free will, which they respectfully do not override, so if we choose to interact with a nonphysical being who is not who they claim to be and who transgresses our energetic boundaries without permission, then unhelpful situations can arise.

I call these spirits lookie-likies and have experienced them both within my own inner travels and through feedback from students. One of the rules of working in the spirit realm is that when we encounter a spirit for the first time to always ask three times if it is truly who it claims to be. By the universal law of three, on the third inquiry the spirit must reveal its true identity or true intentions to you. This is not to instill fear into you but to empower you and strengthen your ability to operate with discernment on these planes. It is for this reason that it is essential that you are familiar with the frequency of your plant ally; you must know it intimately so that you can recognize it instantly. Taking your time with the inner sensation meditation, provided in chapter 5, will help you to develop your unique connection to a plant spirit and to know it both within your body and your mind. But first, in the next two chapters, we explore the fundamentals of meditation and shamanic journeying.

3

Meditation and
Shamanic Journeying

TRAINING THE MIND is fundamental to inner work. We need a calm mind to work through our issues rather than be overwhelmed by powerful emotions and traumas, which keep us locked in loops. Understanding how the mind works from both a personal and collective perspective facilitates our evolvement, enabling us to operate from a state of balance and awareness. Types of consciousness and perception need to be considered alongside an honest and self-reflective attitude. When we are navigating the spirit world we need to be sharp, aware, and clear in order to understand the landscape within which we find ourselves.

The Nature of Consciousness

Central to all wisdom teachings is the role of the mind. Without understanding how the mind works both for and against us, we cannot evolve or heal. Without an understanding of the various levels that the mind operates at and where our central axis is, we can get lost in a maelstrom of confusion, not knowing what is us and what is not us.

The practice of the true nature of the mind or the Great Perfection in the Buddhist tradition is called Dzogchen. The teachings that make up this body of work are much older than Buddhism. The tradition is also known as *atiyoga* (utmost yoga) and is considered a higher practice than tantra as the teachings have the perfect view or the most profound perspective and are the most direct path to liberation. The Dzogchen perspective on the true nature of the mind is that it is like a mirror, it reflects. To these experts the natural state of the mind is a unification of emptiness and clarity. We can understand this as clear, silent, and spacious. The conceptual mind reflects what our five normal senses perceive, and the higher mind reflects the universal, the collective, and the Divine. The Hindus explain consciousness as reflections of the moon in different buckets of water. They are all different reflections of the one moon just as our minds are all reflections of the one universal mind. For many Eastern meditators, peaceful contemplation is a way to connect to the Divine and to discover the same divine nature reflected within oneself. These qualities of the mind are always present but our unhelpful emotions, conditionings, and busy modern lifestyles all cloud and inhibit the awareness of this level of consciousness.

Lama Yeshe who founded the Buddhist Institute where I studied in Italy stated that spirituality was simply understanding the mind. Meditation developed in the Hindu and Buddhist cultures because it was believed getting to the core of consciousness, understanding the true nature of our consciousness would help us to connect to the universal mind, the creative force that manifests and underlies all there is. By investigating our thoughts—where they come from, how they arise, and what effect they have on us—we can start to break down the walls we have built around the mind to set it free and to be our friend rather than our ruler. We can liberate our soul from the constraints of trauma and conditioning and bring the light of awareness into deeper aspects of our self. We can find our way out of the labyrinth of duality. This is the true meaning of spirituality. As Lama Anagarika Govinda states, we must work to integrate our experiences at the deepest level.

> If we do not dissolve or integrate the creations of the mind, we will get attached to them and become their prisoners, as a man who becomes possessed by his possessions. If, on the other hand, we remain in a state of irrevocable finality, we will be frozen in a state

of complete stagnation. Every experience has to be integrated in our deepest consciousness or in the totality of our being, until we have reached the state in which our consciousness has become an exponent and meeting place of all living forces of the universe, and our body the multistoried temple and mandala of these forces.[1]

The materialist and mainstream worldview is that consciousness is a product of the activity of the brain. This view says that if you feel an expansion of consciousness, a deeper sense of connectedness during or after meditation, it is simply a change in the nervous activity in the brain. Yet all the wisdom traditions of the world, all the indigenous cultures and our own direct experiences through meditation or shamanic practices, demonstrate something very different. In the alchemical system of emergence through the unification of spirit (masculine) and matter (feminine), consciousness arises. Bringing together these two fundamental forces that form our world opens a portal through which the light of the Divine, consciousness itself, can arrive. In the Celtic tradition and indeed in many indigenous cosmologies, the human body is the unification of all of the five elements (earth, air, fire, water, and space) and is the gateway to infinity due to our capacity to experience and understand all that is.

For anything to manifest on the physical plane, the phenomenal world, there must have been a previous series of causes and conditions. There is a process of involution into manifestation from the subtle and nonphysical to the dense and solid. This law of nature takes place across everything that manifests, including illness and disease. The body is therefore an expression of consciousness, and consciousness simply cannot arise from the brain itself; it is impossible. The body is the result of our auric field, not the cause of it. The body is the expression of the consciousness of the soul and the mind of the Divine. John O'Donohue beautifully summarizes how we ourselves, mind and body, express the infinite:

There is the infinity of space that reaches out into the depths of the cosmos; the infinity of time reaching back over billions of years.

There is the infinity of the microcosm: one little speck on the top of your thumb contains a whole inner cosmos, but it is so tiny that it is not visible to the human eye. The infinity in the microscope is as dazzling as that of the cosmos. However, the infinity which haunts everyone and which no-one can finally quell, is the infinity of their own interiority.[2]

Shifting Our Perceptions into the Inner Realms of Nature

In order to facilitate effective inner work and efficient healing, we need to shift our awareness away from the physical world to the nonphysical, from the outer world to the inner world. We release our thought consciousness from its attachment to the rigid, dense, and seemingly static world and orient it toward a free-flowing and spacious realm. So that we can function effectively in the world, our general daily perspective operates from an outward-facing yang orientation, at the detriment, perhaps, of our inner life, our emotional and psychic consciousness. We were never taught to balance the two. Yet by awakening more of the yin within we can operate from a much more holistic and therefore realistic and balanced perspective.

There are three main types of perception that we need to understand to differentiate between our various experiences during meditation and journey work. Gareth Knight in *Experience of the Inner Worlds* lays them out very clearly as physical world, inner world, and spiritual world, which correlate respectively to physical perception through the five senses of the body, psychic perception of the inner world plane of the soul through our inner senses, and mystical perception of the "heavenly world which is of God" or the spirit.[3] Even though we have to differentiate between these states of consciousness for our understanding, we also have to remember that everything is interrelated and comprises aspects of the whole. This is not an escapist route out of the pains of the external world but an expansion into a deeper understanding of reality, incorporating everything we experience. We can open the door to these new inner states of consciousness by becoming more aware of the energies moving through our body. Meditating on the emotions, pranas, thought responses, and even body pain awakens our inner senses and attunes them to the subtle world.

The predominant type of perception that we are working with in this book is psychic perception of the inner realms. This does not mean that you have to be clairvoyant or psychic to experience the inner planes; this is simply the standard terminology used for this type of perception, which works with our inner senses. Our five senses all have inner reflected counterparts: where our physical eyes perceive the outer world, their etheric aspect (everything physical has an etheric or energetic aspect or double) perceives the inner worlds. Just as plants and trees have a metaphysical level of existence so do our eyes, ears, and nose. The more we flex the etheric muscles of our spiritual or shamanic senses, the stronger and clearer they become as they attune to the new realms they're operating in.

Throughout your journeys with the plants, you will also be strengthening your intuition. As we cleanse our karmic baggage and clear the blockages in our energy fields, we start to know and understand ourselves better; we start to recognize what is our own emotion and what we may have acquired or learned from someone else. Access to our intuitive mind gradually opens up, and as it does so, our body wisdom also comes online. The body knows better than the conceptual mind what it needs. It has an innate wisdom and consciousness of its own. The sciences of kinesiology and craniosacral therapy both work with this body-mind awareness to bring healing and relief. We, too, can tap into this inner gnosis directly by cultivating an awareness of our inner planes and cleansing the body and mind of toxicities and unhelpful energies. For those whose intuition is already strong, the plants will take your connection to newfound levels of perception.

As our consciousness expands into new aspects of ourselves, we start to dismantle our sense of separation. The plants teach us about the dualistic nature of our world and our perception of a constant battle between the light and the dark. They teach that we actually live in a triality rather than a duality, as there is also the consciousness that perceives the opposites of duality. There is black and there is white, but there is also the witness of both. Or perhaps it is consciousness itself that has created the black and the white. Either way, there are still three awarenesses or perceptions here, and perhaps this is one of the reasons why the number three holds such sacred power for many wisdom traditions.

As human consciousness evolves, we are moving into what is being called fifth-dimensional consciousness. Higher thinking or fifth-dimensional awareness removes blame or bias so that we can see both sides of the argument and accept that others have their own truth from which they live. This balanced way of perceiving is a blissful state as it keeps you on the middle path away from the dramas of polarity. This state is vast in its nature as it has no bounds or prejudice; it is in alignment with the true nature of the mind and with nature itself. Ultimately, we are working toward a perspective that is nondualistic and nonpolarized in order to achieve self-mastery. This is the state where we are no longer ruled by our emotions and we remain in equipoise when any situation arises in our life. We can walk the fine line between nihilism and eternalism and navigate paradox with ease. Meditating on duality and its consequences allows realizations of our own inner conflict.

What are we still fighting? Who are we still fighting? And why? If we were born through the natural process and not cesarean, we had to fight our way into this world, and so exerting our will to achieve something is in our nature. Yet have we misinterpreted our traumatic struggle to be born and turned it into a lifetime of fighting against the world? Answering these questions can be painful yet liberating. People and situations that triggered us no longer do so as we process and work through our traumas and conditionings that pull us into dualistic or polarized views. A dualistic view pits us against others; it sees right and wrong as either black or white. We are literally dueling and dualing with something. A polarized view takes a biased position as the truth. When things are polarized they are not necessarily in conflict but are separate, and we cling to our position for various reasons—which are for you to work out. The middle path offers the escape route from both of these delusions and takes us to a place of acceptance of all that is. This is the ultimate teaching of all the plants and trees, so it is good to know where we are heading on our journey.

As we work through the meditations in this book and start making connections and relationships with different plants and trees, we become aware of the various ways in which the spirits of nature communicate with us. We each also perceive in different ways, as outlined in chapter 5. Some of us have more affinity with aesthetics and so our eye consciousness and consequently inner visions are clear. Others find their body awareness is stronger so will perceive through sentience and feeling. There is no right and wrong way to perceive; there is no hierarchy within the senses, although most people have strong affinity with either their eye or body awareness. This also does not mean that our other senses do not work in the inner realms either; let's not box ourselves into any one way of perceiving. All of our five inner senses and our intuition are required to navigate the inner planes effectively.

Through the meditations provided in this book and the methods of approach toward the plant spirits, you will start to receive imprints or impulses from the inner world of the plants that will need interpreting. Perhaps these insights come in the form of symbology, which will have specific meaning for you. Perhaps they will come as feelings or moments of inspiration. Whichever form the inner world speaks to you, there are often layers of meaning that reveal themselves over time. The plant spirits live outside time and space, so there is a chance that you may not understand the meaning of a particular symbol or message until some time later. It is helpful to keep a journal during your plant diets and meditations to record what you have experienced so that you can return to these observations at a later date when your awareness and perceptions have deepened and changed position. Retrospection has particular value for understanding interrelatedness. Very often insights that come to us have a certain familiarity to them as if we are simply remembering something we had forgotten long ago or we are reminded of a dream we had. This type of insight can be an awakening of cellular memory passed down through the twin communication channels of ancestral and soul lineage or the link to some useful information that was already on the periphery of our awareness. This form of perception is not concerned with the divination of the future but simply a deeper understanding of our inner landscape and an awakening to who we truly are.

Training the Mind through Meditation

From the perspective of mind, the objective of meditation is not to control the mind; trying to do this will create unnecessary tension and aversion to your practice. Control is an exertion of the ego and counterproductive to the goal of discipline and calm. We cannot control the arising of thoughts in the mind; however, we can watch them rather than participate in them. Through meditation we can create distance between our thoughts and the observer of our thoughts, the self. In this way, we start to recognize the fallibility of thoughts, that they are not arising from our true nature but from habit, conditionings, and perhaps false beliefs. We become more accustomed to questioning the provenance of the thoughts that shape our mind and drive our behavioral patterns.

There are benefits to meditation no matter what your beliefs, and a plethora of research has been done into its ability to reduce stress, foster greater creativity, and support mental health issues, which is why movements such as mindfulness and Transcendental Meditation have become so popular in recent years. What becomes mainstream tends, however, to get watered down to a digestible form for the masses. We have to go back to the true forms of meditation and the origins of thought to access a deeper understanding of meditation to reap the benefits of true inner joy, wisdom, healing, and connection to Mother Earth.

Various spiritual traditions, including that of the British Isles, offer methods of meditation that are transformative and support the expansive quality of the mind. There are countless forms of meditation for all types of minds and persuasions, so we need to define what form of meditations we will be working with in this book and why. In this book we will apply traditional forms of meditation along with shamanic journeying and even dream work to create the structure through which the organic process of awakening and healing can take place. Some of the meditations have been given to me by the plants themselves and others have been adapted from tried and tested wisdom traditions. By applying a variety of techniques, we will train the mind toward balance and open the doorway into the imaginal realm and other dimensions of reality that exist alongside this physical realm. We will place our life and existence into a more universal context, supporting spiritual development and connection with the deepest aspects of the self, with the heart, and with the consciousness of the natural world. We can free ourselves of societal conditionings and outdated modes of thinking that are not serving us or humanity any longer.

One effective form of meditation, which I do not include in the book but which is very useful for those with an excessively erratic mind, is walking meditation, which I learned at Plum Village in France with the wonderful Thich Nhat Hanh. Resting the mind in the connection between your feet and the earth is profoundly liberating and life affirming. Our consciousness is rarely in our body because we spend most of our time in the future or the past, which shifts our energy body out of alignment. By bringing ourselves into the body as it moves over the earth, we come back to the present moment, back to our body, and we calm the constant stream of thoughts. Working with something physical such as the movement of the breath or the body gives the mind something more tangible to anchor to, and it can quickly become more restful. Progressing from walking meditation to resting the mind on the movement of the breath continues the process of unification with reality as we seemingly become one with each inhalation and individualized from life and the world around us with each exhalation. Continued practice of mindful breathing dissolves the barriers between the internal and external worlds, fostering unity, the ultimate goal of meditation.

Bringing plants into our meditation practice offers us support, guidance, and insight in a much more tangible and accessible way than if we practice solo. By applying tried and tested techniques and working with guides such as plant spirits, as well as our own inner discernment, we can create the causes and conditions for the true nature of the mind to arise within us. It is through clarity and calmness, through touching into the deep void within that we can understand our true potential and awaken our senses to new levels of reality.

That is not to say that traditional methods of meditation without the aid of anything outside ourselves are not effective; they certainly are. However, just like bells and music have been meditational supports in many traditions, so can plants be. Our conditionings and obscurations of the mind can create blind spots of awareness. When we're scrambling in the dark and becoming discouraged, sometimes a meditation support can show us the way forward.

To understand the mind and see its shadows requires a process of self-reflection supported by meditation and journey work. At the same time, we can also draw upon the knowledge of the human energetic and chakra systems to illuminate unseen aspects of ourselves. Working shamanically with plants requires a holistic perspective of human existence—physical, emotional, and spiritual. One cannot be truly healed or brought into balance without consideration of the other. We need to create a safe space from which to work to ensure we protect the nervous system. Make a commitment to yourself, but don't push yourself too hard and stay present for whatever arises within you. Remain connected to your body at all times; meditation is not about escaping to another reality but about navigating aspects of the mind safely and creating transformational space for ourselves. All emotions and thoughts are valid; no part of you is denied. Every part of you is welcome in this healing space.

Shamanic Journeying

Within the context of this book, there are two types of shamanic journeys that you will encounter and work with. The first is the traditional practice of journeying through the inner planes and inner worlds. According to the *Encyclopaedia of Celtic Wisdom,* "the shamanic journey may be defined as a non-physical journey in which the riocht or soul-shape of a shaman travels from earthly reality into many other-worldly regions."[4]

The true shamanic journey is a journey between worlds, where the consciousness is projected (a process explained by metaphysics) into different realms and dimensions of reality. In the tradition of the British Isles and Celtic practices, these realms are within the Otherworld, the inner realms of nature and the source of life and death for us mortals. By traveling to this world, we can retrieve information and receive healing and guidance from the ancestors and spirits who live there. We can also discover a lot about ourselves and what we truly carry in our heart. Visiting the Otherworld through shamanic journeying is like a remembrance; we know this place like a forgotten dream yet navigating its terrain needs guidance and practice. Some shamanic practitioners have power animals or a body protector spirit to accompany them on their travels in this realm; we have the partnership of the plant spirits.

Beginning a shamanic journey will need the employment of the imagination to begin with until the process and points of access become more familiar to you. Like jump-starting a car, we allow the imagination to activate the journey into which we surrender and allow to unfold. Over time, the more familiar we are with the process, the more we allow the inner space of the journey to expand and speak to us.

The imaginal realm is both the Otherworld and our inner landscape; it is the creative source of the mind through which we interact with both this world and other dimensions. The imagination is not simply part of our consciousness that we daydream with; it is the driving force of our life. We cannot access these realms without it, and so through it we become both a guest and a participant in these realms. The misunderstanding of this powerful aspect of our consciousness prevents realists from awakening into the magic of life.

As we start our journey, we invite our plant spirit with us to lead the way and protect us as we traverse new landscapes. The Otherworld has many realms, and beings of all types and persuasions live there. So while we surrender to the process, we also stay alert and aware of what is happening and where we are. To return from a shamanic journey, it is imperative to retrace the path that led you in and emerge from the entry point back into the Middle World. Returning instantly from the Otherworld back to this world can result in leaving soul fragments or some of your energy behind, negating the objective of the practice and potentially causing you more harm than good.

The second type of shamanic journey is a longer expedition that you take with your chosen plant. This journey could last a lunar cycle or a revolution around the medicine wheel; the time frame is the container that you have chosen to work with your ally. Within this container everything that happens to you and for you is viewed through the perspective of the plant spirit. You have made an agreement, whether it be for healing or teachings, with your ally to take you on a journey of discovery. This type of shamanic journey is not about the destination but all about the inner pilgrimage itself. Keeping a journal of this process over the days, weeks, or months that you have chosen for your protocol is very useful as we can have realizations and insights when we consider in retrospect what has happened over that time period. When our students attend a training module weekend, their shamanic journey starts as soon as they leave their front door: on their trip to Wales, the journey includes the people they meet along the way, the obstacles they encounter, and their state of mind. All are a reflection of the teachings of the plant spirit.

Psychic, Energetic Hygiene

The fundamental requirement for a solid meditation practice, good health, and spiritual development is having a clean energy field. The energy field or aura is the bubble of electromagnetic frequencies that are layered around us at varying levels and dimensions and through which energy is drawn into and out of the chakra system. It is the bridge between our inner and outer world, yet it is only our perception that sees inner and outer as separate; they are in fact one. We experience reality through the interplay between the inner world and the energy field. Understanding the energy field and learning how to manage it is crucial to maintaining the sovereignty of our body and mind. Once we start to understand our energy field, it becomes apparent how much of our energy we give away by having poor boundaries: we pick up toxicity from our environment and are susceptible to other people's energies and emotions.

Our modern world is full of toxicity, from the food we eat to the air we breathe and the water we drink; chemicals and distortions of the natural state have slowly crept into everything we put into our body. This is the first place to start when it comes to cleaning up your auric field. Take a good look at the water you drink. Is it from plastic? Is it from the tap? How good is your filter? Unless you are blessed to have your own well of spring water, more than likely you are drinking and bathing in water that contains toxic chemicals, metals, salts, hormones, and pesticides. The pipes that deliver the water to your house will also contain bacteria and toxic psychic debris as they may run under the houses of sick and angry people before they deliver water to your sink. Having a good quality filtration system for the water you drink and cook with is essential. The state of the water that comes out of the tap is shockingly poor. Its molecular structure and that of bottled water is fragmented: when viewed microscopically, their appearance is shattered; the molecules have lost their integrity, which makes it difficult for the body to absorb the water. This is unstructured water. The water in our body is the same water that is in the seas and clouds. When we drink poor quality water we are telling our body that we do not love it, that we do not respect it or the whole body of water on the planet. We are disconnected from the waters of life. Our disconnection from nature has also led to the abuse and disregard for our seas and waterways.

Taking time to consider the type and provenance of the food you eat is also fundamental to your physical and spiritual health. If you cannot afford organic or biodynamic produce, eat food as close to its natural state as possible. Whole grains, plenty of green vegetables, and a good source of local protein form a good basic diet. Every day I eat something wild: nettle tea, Jack-by-the-hedge (*Alliaria petiolata*) pesto, dandelion coffee, various spring flowers in salads, hawthorn tincture, and cleavers (*Galium aparine*) juice are just some of the ways to get wildness into your body. Wild plants offer a more dynamic range of vitamins, minerals, and frequencies of nature, which are not present in cultivated foods. Over a long period of time, the effects of eating wild every day are palpable. The mind loses rigidity as does the body, and the more flexible we are, the healthier and more vital we remain. Wild plants also have the added benefit of being medicinal and contribute to keeping our energy field clean and at a high vibration. We rewild ourselves.

Television is the real hallucinogen of our era: it's primarily a mouthpiece for the authorities and a conduit for brainwashing that suppresses selfhood. The many forms of toxicity that we see and hear on the TV screen can manifest in our energy field through thoughtforms fueled by emotions. If we are not aware of these destructive thoughtforms in our energy field, they can grow over time and be more oppressive and influential on our mind. They create shadows in the energy field that therefore reflect as shadows in the mind.

Everywhere we turn in our modern life we are confronted by toxicity and misplaced energies. It is hardly surprising that as a species we are now dealing with a dramatic increase in undiagnosed illnesses and a mental health crisis. A huge burden would be lifted from our health services if we simply learned how to manage and maintain a healthy energy field.

By maintaining a good psychic hygiene practice, we are implementing preventive medicine and supporting our healing process, meditation practice, and spiritual development. The clearer our energy field becomes, the clearer our mind becomes, and the less likely we are to become sick in the future. By working with plants we can cleanse our energy field, strengthen it, infuse it with high vibration life force, invite more vitality into our spiritual practice, improve our inner vision, and sharpen our extrasensory perceptions. We also start to address the underlying traumas and conditionings that affect our thought processes and emotional balance. By allowing ourselves to merge with the plant spirits, we are releasing ourselves from self-imposed isolation. Human nature is sociable, and believing ourselves to be individual, isolated people is contrary to our fundamental nature.

Psychic Hygiene Techniques

Below are a few examples of ways you can work with the plants and trees to cleanse and purify your energy field. This list is not exhaustive and there are many techniques held within the many wonderful *curandero* (healer) traditions of our indigenous brothers and sisters. Below I am presenting a few that I find effective.

Plant Limpia

Limpia means "clean" in Spanish and refers to the cleansing of toxicities from the energy field. This tradition comes from the Americas; however, I am sure this tradition also exists in the British Isles as it is both obvious and evidentially beneficial. Collect a bunch of plants from your garden or anywhere in nature that is clean and free from chemicals or pollution; ideally, these plants should be pungent and have medicinal qualities. Speak with the plants: ask their permission and tell them what your intention is. Have a bowl of fresh (not tap) water present. Dip the bunch of plants in the bowl and gently sweep the plants through the energy field of yourself or a friend. As you sweep downward toward the earth, speak gently to the plant spirits asking for their healing and for them to remove any unhelpful toxicities in the aura and to heal any holes that might exist. Our energy field can split and holes can manifest in it through either our own doing or from an outside influence. The bunch of plants will collect the toxicities. Once all the energy field has been swept and adequately cleansed, give the plants to the person who has had his or her aura cleansed and ask him or her to give them back to the earth by burying them or, if this is not possible, placing them in a paper bag and disposing of it in an outside bin.

Auric Sprays

Spritzing the energy field with a premade combination of plants, flowers, and even gemstone elixirs is another way to quickly freshen up your field. This is only a quick fix and should not be relied on for deeper cleansing, as received by working directly with the plant spirits or with the other protocols outlined here. There are many auric sprays on the market, and they are easy to find.

Smudging

This cleansing technique is well known and involves the burning of dried plants and resins on hot coals, the smoke of which purifies both the air and the energy of space, whether it is the space of a room or the personal energy field. Different plants and resins cleanse in different ways. Rosemary, for example, will purify toxic bacteria in the air as well as its energetic counterpart. Mugwort will transform psychic debris into a higher vibration. It is worth getting to know how each plant works so you can apply the correct remedy to any given situation and clearing requirement.

Magic Baths

One of the most enjoyable ways to keep the energy field clean and clear is taking a magical bath. It is also one of the most thorough and effective ways to help release trapped emotions, toxic energy, and thought-forms. These baths can be taken at any time of the year but using spring plants seems to add an extra zing to them.

Collect a large bunch of leaves, stems, and flowers from wild plants, medicine plants from your garden, or trees. Possible plants are dandelion, mugwort, angelica, meadowsweet, primrose, hawthorn, beech, oak, and birch. Only use plants that are edible, and do not take more than a third of any one plant. Ensure to ask permission before you take the plant, and it's always a good idea to state why you are collecting the plant so that you and the spirit of the plant can work with you toward your intention.

Place the plant parts in a large pot of approximately three liters (about three quarts) of filtered or stream water; cover and bring to a boil. Turn down the heat and simmer for thirty minutes. Turn off the heat and leave in the pot with the lid on overnight. The next morning, drain off the strong infusion and add most of it to a warm salt bath that evening. Put at least 100 grams or one-half cup of salt in the bath. Soak in the bath for a minimum of thirty minutes, frequently submerging your head and face. Once finished, thank the plants, the water spirits, and the mineral kingdom for the cleanse.

The remainder of the infusion can be placed in a spray bottle and sprayed around your house to cleanse and lift the vibration. Again, this is particularly effective in spring after a deep spring clean.

To amplify the magic of your bath, use plants from each of the five elements, for example, dandelion for air, angelica for fire, mugwort for water, and oak for earth and space.

Other Energy Hygiene Practices

The practice of arts such as qigong, tai chi, yoga, and *pranayama* all support the clearing and movement of energy, while training the consciousness to reach subtler levels of awareness. To truly heal, it is advisable to approach the healing path from many tried and tested angles; incorporating a physical practice plays an important role.

4

The Way of
the Ethical Warrior

FACING OUR FEARS, our destructive habits and their underlying blockages, and our shadowy aspects is challenging for most of us. We need to cultivate a new attitude of inner strength based in truth and self-love to establish inner peace. Our innate inner warrior is an ancient archetypal aspect of the self, and when we tap into it, we become stronger so that we can effectively apply ourselves to our spiritual path. As always, this process starts in the mind.

The Importance of Ethics

The place to start calming the mind is through understanding ethics and applying them to your life. This was the first truth bomb that changed my life considerably when I began studying meditation. Generally, most people live ethical lives: we are good citizens, we help others when needed, we love our family if we're lucky, and we try to do our bit for the planet. But think about a time when you have lied about something. How did you feel afterward? How long did it play on your mind? Did you have to repeat the lie to solidify it? How did you justify the lie to yourself? Did it start to feel familiar, and did you eventually start believing the lie?

Perhaps you believe that you don't lie. Are you sure about this? Are you not just lying to yourself right now? If you stop and think about how much you lie, even small white ones, how much you distort the truth to suit your aims, you will be surprised. But don't feel too bad about it; the ego in its efforts to keep us alive plays one-upmanship with our thoughts and creates very convincing justifications for our illusory words. Meditating on our lies and their effects on us is a great meditation within itself and one that I encourage everyone to do. It can show us how anxious or ungrounded lying makes us. It can reveal the toxic thought patterns that are the result of lying and the shadows that we create in our world. Lies are not comfortable, and their effects are destructive. How can you evolve and understand your true self if you think that it's OK to lie to others and to yourself? Oh, it won't matter, just this once, you may think. But lies create shadow, and each time you lie, you push your inner truth further and further into the darkness. By making a commitment to yourself not to lie (and I appreciate it is very difficult when lies have become a commodity in today's world), you are instantly releasing yourself from all the anguish and mental torment that comes with lying, and you are freeing your mind without even having to meditate. Over time, your radar for untruth also sharpens, and you become much more discerning about what and who you trust, where you put your faith. Life becomes easier and less confusing. Supported by a meditation practice and deep inner work with plant medicine, we become more aware, awake, and in alignment with the truth of existence.

This principle also applies to all areas of ethics concerning the right actions of our body, speech, and mind. Many wisdom traditions offer lists of right and wrong deeds, which can be helpful but whose meanings have also been distorted over the centuries to suit the aims of the leaders of those religions. To achieve self-liberation, we have to apply self-governance. If we cannot be responsible for our own actions, then we will remain unawakened to our own unique individuality and power. By recognizing all of the ways in which we outsource blame or place authority outside ourselves is an empowering act within itself. Taking our power back means taking responsibility for everything in our life, both within and without. If we assume responsibility for our lives only when things are going well but blame outside forces when things go awry or others hurt us, then we are in a delusional state of mind. Either we are active creators of our lives or we are not. If we live from the perspective and understanding that we *are* our life, that it is not simply something that happens to us, then we are empowered to cultivate both inner and outer change, and we can make better choices. In the West we are used to exerting effort to control our lives and save ourselves from the suffering of uncertainty, but it is often in vain because nothing is certain and everything can change in an instant. So how resilient are we to that change? If we have outsourced all our power, the answer is not very resilient at all. If we don't know the full extent of our power, we will not recognize it when we need it.

When it comes to interacting with others, the simple overriding principle of right action is whether we are trying to influence them without their permission. This is operating from shadow and goes against the principle of natural law, which states that all individuals are sovereign. Disrespect this law and even your good deeds can result in psychic attack within the energy field of the other. Sending healing to people without their permission is a classic example of this. This not so coincidently is the line between light and dark magic, healing and sorcery.

Unethical actions generate unhelpful emotions, which are the foundation for all manner of misery and suffering. Effecting positive inner transformation cannot happen when you are acting from selfishness, greed, hatred, and jealousy. It is these destructive patterns that are the underlying causes of many issues in our life as we get caught up in our own illusions and lose ourselves to unreality. His Holiness the Dalai Lama states that "our state of mind and how the mind perceives things greatly affects us. Because of the control they have over their minds, some people are little disturbed by failure or adverse circumstances. This is a clear example of why taming, or training, the mind is so important."[1] Meditating with plants helps to weed out these behaviors and thought patterns to support our journey toward self-realization. Plants reflect our thought and behavioral patterns back at us and facilitate moments of inspiration where the light of truth penetrates the clouds of illusions around us. They are very useful tools to awaken our own inner counselor. In this way, we can familiarize ourselves with both our shadow and with our true nature in order to become the person we were meant to be.

Facing the Shadow through Myth

Myth deepens our connection to the underlying forces of nature and offers alternative narrative to the common modern culture, which is moving further into the world of virtual and fake, where meaning is lost and the heart is usurped by the fear and avoidance of death. The education system suppresses creativity, our authorities undermine the arts, and the imaginal realm is forced into the background of a hypnotized race. Myth offers a more sophisticated understanding of the balance between dark and light, between the opposing forces of this dualistic world. Myth helps us face the shadow and accept it as part of our journey. Just as Gandalf the Grey would not have become Gandalf the White in *Lord of the Rings* without facing the Balrog, each of us cannot step into our true majestic greatness without defeating the shadowy aspects of our personality. If we do not face and accept the hidden sides of ourselves, those sides will consume us as we become lost in their unconscious embrace. The struggle between the forces of dark and light are within and are reflected into our external world, as within, so without. This fundamental wisdom has the potential to resolve all of the world's problems if it is only recognized. Inner worlds and outer worlds are one and the same.

Mythical stories present images and archetypes that reside at the deepest levels of our psyche and within the collective unconscious according to Jungian psychology. Deities and mythical characters therefore personify human aspects and attributes. Taliesin, for example, is the illuminated shaman and bard in the Celtic mysteries, a shining one who demonstrates the heights to which the human spirit can soar on the wings of our creativity and inner light. Yet at the same time, mythical characters do not simply derive from the human psyche. When we encounter these beings on the inner planes they are alive and well; they are conscious and existent in and of themselves. They can be our teachers and our guides if we approach them with humble and open hearts rather than reducing them to static human concepts.

Our inner world has been forgotten just as mythos has been usurped by the logos mind. The common and modern definition of mythos is that which pertains to a story and the unreal world, a profound disservice to this primal and integral aspect of the cosmos, for which we are paying the price today. Mythos refers to a level of consciousness that expresses imagery and the urge of the soul to create and connect. The mundane chores and functions of life have caused us to lose our connection to mythology. Logos has overtaken mythos in importance in our patriarchal world, much to the detriment of the human spirit. The plants with their correspondences of archetype and deity can awaken these mythical aspects of our eternal spirit from the depths of the unconscious and reestablish our connection to both our ancient past and our evolved future. Everything has shadow from the human perspective; we therefore have to be careful not to become lost in mythos when we start to reawaken it within ourselves. There is a balance that can be struck between imaginal and substantial, between the human and the Otherworld. We all carry the archetype of paradise lost, a hankering back to the Shire. We need to balance both mythos and logos just as we need to balance the left and right hemispheres of the brain for optimal navigation through life.

Awakening the Warrior Within

To truly live in alignment with noble ethics is challenging. If it was an easy endeavor, we would live in a very different world than we do today. People have persistently compromised their ethics and principles to further their ambitions or to survive, so much so that they have lost sight of the true nature of ethics and therefore have lost the inner strength and conviction of a life based in true right action. It is easy for authority and government to erode human rights when we do not have much sense of their meaning. Our human rights can be taken from us, as they have been over the last few years, and hardly anyone does anything about it. So eroded is our sense of selfhood that we are unaware of the consequences to future generations when we acquiesce to laws that permit someone else more rights over our own and our children's bodies. Those who do stand up for our rights are scorned and vilified or squashed so they are not heard. And we allow it.

Let's not be too hard on ourselves, though, because the indoctrination into the belief in a soulless world starts in school. Our education system is so narrow in its worldview that life essentials such as understanding and managing our emotions or the power of the natural world for healing are deemed unnecessary. Children are pitted against one another in a culture of competition, nurturing self-criticism, feelings of inferiority, and shame, all of which disempower and make them more obedient to industrial life. Since the nineteenth century, psychology has studied how competition can motivate people to achieve. But these studies are based on the assumption that winning is the ultimate objective and don't take into account that instilling a belief that we must strive to be better than our neighbor creates separation and is detrimental to human goodness and the cultivation of a soulful life. Creating a hierarchy and encouraging people to aspire to something outside themselves and to be seen by others as the best or the most special is counterintuitive to natural law. Competition pulls us away from the nature of our evolved consciousness, encouraging us in the false belief that if others see us as better then we must be better. Yet a higher perspective is available to us, of valuing individuality within the collective whole. We master skills and develop our intellect not with the objective of dominating others but with the desire to be of service, to help others align with their inner goodness. There is no higher calling in life than to serve others—not through fear but through unconditional love fueled by inner freedom.

A Kichwa elder I know calls this a prison planet, and from one perspective he is right. The only act of free will that we have left is whether we choose to walk a path in alignment with our base instincts or one attuned to the higher forces of human goodness, whether we choose the path of shadow or light. The latter is the concern of our work here. To achieve any level of liberation we must turn toward the light until we can hold both our light and our shadow in balance. We are not chasing the false light of spiritual bypass, denying our shadow, but looking toward the inner light of truth, wherever that takes us. This is the nondual middle way where everything is accepted as it is; nothing is judged or pushed away; all is in balance and harmony.

Because it is not easy to stand in complete sovereignty in all its depth of meaning, the warrior within must be awakened. We are conditioned to hide from our fears, to establish behavioral and thought patterns that prevent our fears from getting close to us, yet the grace and power of the warrior is already seeded within us, as all archetypal forces are. The plants and trees teach us how to awaken this power within us, to hold our center when our external world conspires to pull us into polarity and separation, to stand with strength as we turn toward our shadows. To navigate between resistance and acceptance, fighting and peace, subjective and objective takes inner strength and a clear mind. Nature doesn't lie, so as our work with the plants and trees progresses, our attachment to beliefs diminishes and the barriers we have built up around our heart and mind start to crumble. Not everyone wants or even cares to take this journey. That is their free will, and we must accept that this is their choice; we cannot coerce people into coming with us. It is an arduous road, and after placing just one foot on it, there is little chance of turning back. We cannot unsee what we have seen. So it is advisable to cultivate fearlessness—not recklessness but a strong sense of your inner bravery.

How could anyone be a healer without traversing the darkest depths of their own psyche and integrating their own shadows? To be a true healer, we have to know all aspects of the human psyche and hold both the dark and the light in balance and nonpolarity within. This is the middle path. Our task as shamanic healers is to know the spirit world so intimately that we bring the healing impulses and frequencies through from that realm into this one, from the plant spirit realm into this physical realm to invite change and healing to occur without judgment or attachment. We are the bridge between worlds. We can discover our own inner healer and shaman in order to bring physical, emotional, and spiritual healing to ourselves and therefore the world around us.

The noble warrior of old embodies the qualities we need on this path if we are to truly know thyself: strength, courage, nobility, and honor, which really are the basics of ethics. Being able to make decisions from the heart and take decisive action with the humility to admit mistakes and be able to learn from them makes us better human beings. Warriorship is an internal state directed toward our own inner demons; it is not about pushing your "truth" or authority onto others, thinking you know best. The fearful seek to master the world, while the fearless seek to master themselves.

The inner warrior has the determination to overcome destructive behaviors, the fortitude to establish emotional balance, and the wrathfulness to vanquish the demonic forces that plague the depths of the psyche. We can tap into this pool of power to make the changes we feel are required within. The motivation to continue on the path of awakening can be challenging to maintain when we are the midst of a healing process; therefore, inner strength and determination for the highest good of all are essential.

Repressed toxic emotions cause and attract physical toxins in the body, which result in disease, sickness, and mental issues. Remembering the hermetic principle of "as above, so below" or "as within, so without," we can also see that what is happening in our external world is a result of our inner world. This is then reflected into the macro. The evil and darkness in the world comes through people, through us. The only reason there are evil forces on the planet is because we allow them. We have to take responsibility for this, and most people do not want to, preferring to leave it to others to deal with the conflicts and problems. Most do not even acknowledge that the darkness in the world is also in them. How could it? You may be thinking. I'm a good person! Perhaps this is true, but perhaps you are also suppressing early traumas through drugs, such as antidepressants and alcohol, or other diversions. Why not take a look at them?

Healing can be as simple as bringing to conscious awareness the initial instance that caused trauma or emotional imbalance in the first place. When we push the painful causative experience to the dark recesses of the mind and avoid its deeper meaning, we deny ourselves freedom from the resulting unhelpful emotional and behavioral patterns that emerge. We develop these thought patterns to protect us, but they also obscure the truth and a higher perspective. Many people believe that by denying negative feelings they are making themselves better, and they can stay positive. What they don't understand is that they are building more and more barriers between themselves and inner freedom. They are creating blind spots in their consciousness and pushing emotions into the realm of the subconscious, where they will fester and emerge later in life as illness and disease. By allowing the negative feelings to flow and sitting with them for just a short while allows the body to change; it can be that simple. A few moments of feeling the doubt, grief, or hurt without holding on to it, just permitting it space, offers us the chance to evolve, and even though the trauma or sickness does not leave immediately, it can be the catalyst for transforming us, for carrying us to the next evolutionary part of our journey. Keeping things static and being fearful of change locks us into destructive patterns. To progress on the path of liberation, we have to evoke the warrior spirit within to face and feel into that which up until now we have not dared to look at. Every time we employ inquiry and exploration as opposed to suppression and running away, we are changing the very essence of how we impute meaning to things, and therefore the true nature of how things exist will become evident to us. The more we get in touch with our body consciousness, the more we learn about the causes of our ailments. Pain is in reality neither good nor bad within itself; it is simply nature's way of informing us that something needs to change, whether physical or emotional. The more we learn about ourselves, the more we are making the unconscious conscious. Because you are reading this now suggests that you are ready to be released from the binds you have created around your mind. The truth quite literally can set you free.

When you know who you truly are, when you know the trajectory that your soul has taken to bring you to this present moment, and when you know why you are here on Earth at this point in time, all worries about direction in life and any feelings of disempowerment and fear dissolve. To get to this point is not easy, though, and requires a huge amount of courage. To conquer the heart, tame the mind, and achieve emotional balance requires radical honesty and dedication. It also requires a belief in the first place that this is even possible. If we do not step up and take responsibility for the sovereignty of our body and mind, and therefore the body and consciousness of Earth, who will? We are the ones that we have been waiting for. There is no second coming of the messiah, no benevolent intergalactic race coming to save us. We can only save ourselves.

To truly know ourselves and reveal inner aspects hidden and forgotten by trauma, to go into the pain, to face our unhelpful thoughts, to heal and release, we need to awaken the warrior spirit within. To confront our inner demons and accept all past transgressions, we need to find a certain inner strength. We all carry this spirit; the seed of every archetype is contained within the mind. Warriorship means commitment—commitment to your cause, commitment to the path of authenticity and integrity, and commitment to help humanity, including withstanding change, hardship, and discomfort, and to be able to endure all of that and still be able to give to others from the heart. As Chogyam Trungpa states, the way of the warrior means being open and living in the present:

> The challenge of warriorship is to live fully in the world as it is and to find within this world, with all its paradoxes, the essence of nowness. If we open our eyes, if we open our minds, if we open our hearts, we will find that this world is a magical place. It is not magical because it tricks us or changes unexpectedly into something else, but it is magical because it can *be* so vividly, so brilliantly.

However, the discovery of that magic can happen only when we transcend our embarrassment about being alive, when we have the bravery to proclaim the goodness and dignity of human life, without either hesitation or arrogance. Then magic, or drala, can descend into our existence.[2]

Thankfully we have the powerful plant spirits to help guide and strengthen our resolve.

Awareness of Awareness Meditation

To establish inner balance and to cut through the illusions that life presents us, we need to understand the true nature of the mind, what exactly we are working with, and how it works. To gain a grounded understanding of our true self and to establish our sovereignty, it is valuable to contemplate the nature of the mind and therefore the nature of our reality. The only way to know the mind is to look at it directly.

At first, you might think this sounds absurd and that looking at the mind makes no sense when it is not a solid object and does not seem to have any distinguishing features. I am not referring to thoughts: they are the movements of the mind and therefore are intrinsically part of it, but they aren't the mind itself. Thoughts are like ocean waves, and I am referring to the ocean, to consciousness and cognition. The mind has no discernible form, yet it is right there with us all the time. By looking directly at the mind—how it moves, where thoughts arise from, and where they go after passing through our mind—helps us to distinguish between reality and fiction in our belief systems, thought patterns, and emotions. It is challenging to see reality in its starkness and be confronted with the understanding that most of our perceived enemies are simply of the mind; they are our own doing. To practice awareness of awareness, we have to be strong and dedicated to truth, drawing on the strength of the inner warrior.

The following meditation is a variation on the advanced Buddhist practice of *mahāmudrā,* meaning the "great seal," and most traditions of this practice can be traced back to Tilopa who taught it to his disciple Naropa on the banks of the Ganges a thousand years ago.[3] The realization of this meditation practice is the direct experience of Buddha nature or the true nature of the mind, which has no inherent existence but arises from the great void. In shamanic traditions this great void is the Great Mother, the portal of creation. Do not think nihilistically and feel that the void means that nothing exists. The void is quite the opposite; everything exists in it, just not in the way we think it does. The void is luminous and holds the potential and the creative forces of all that exists on both the seen and unseen planes.

The beauty of this meditation is that it can be performed anywhere both in formal meditation and in between meditation sessions, such as when you are washing the dishes, cooking dinner, or engaged in a task that does not require interaction with other people. I recommend performing it inside to start with, where external sound and disturbance can be limited somewhat. Once you feel you have grasped the meditation's rhythm, meditating out in nature is ideal.

The objective of the practice is to rest the mind in its natural luminous clarity. I cannot deny that this is not an advanced practice and therefore challenging. Persistence, however, delivers profound results. Underneath and within every thought is the observer of that thought, the mind that is observing and that seems to be powered by its own light of awareness. Resting in the ground of awareness and simply observing anything that arises without changing it or getting involved in it is the essence of this practice.

When you practice this meditation, you quickly start to understand just how powerful the mind truly is as you release it from the habitual burden of having to solve, create, or understand. Creating space between the observer and the observed mitigates the power that the external world has over us. We are releasing powerful internal energy as we disconnect ourselves from the bounds of the conceptual mind and the trappings of samsara.

Find a comfortable place either on your meditation cushion or out in a safe place in nature where you will not be disturbed. Turn off the Wi-Fi and your phone. Set a strong determination within that this is your time to just be; nothing else needs to be done or attended to.

Using the first three stages of stillness, silence, and spaciousness from the dropping the mind into the heart meditation in chapter 1, rest your mind here in its natural state. Make sure both the mind and the body are fully relaxed into this state. Do not hold on to it too tightly; just rest here.

As you rest in this peace, you will notice that it does not last for long as noises, thoughts, and emotions arise that want your attention. Simply notice them without labeling them and allow them to pass. They will not stay if you do not grasp on to them. The mind wants to possess and understand things by naming them: watch as it does this and notice how it does this.

Each time you get lost or caught up in a powerful thought or distraction, simply and gently bring your awareness back to the natural state of observing. If you suddenly start thinking about your body, notice and rest in observation. If you suddenly start thinking about your parents or partner, notice and rest in observation as that thought passes. If you hear a car door slam outside, notice but don't generate a story to fit the noise, such as your neighbor arriving home from work. Just allow the noise to be as it is, simply noise that passes.

Observe where your attention goes, but do not try to control your attention or direct it. Allow it to rest in its natural state of observing without judgment or qualification.

You may find that five minutes of this is enough to begin with. Over time, build this meditation up to ten, then fifteen and twenty minutes.

5

The Plant Spirit Path to Self-Realization

TO AWAKEN OUR ETERNAL SPIRIT must be a gentle process; it is not something that can be forced. That spirit does, however, already express itself through our creativity: we simply need to recognize its language, get to know its uniqueness, and accept its wisdom into every moment of our lives. Easier said than done, as it also takes great bravery to overcome our shadows, the blockages between us and our eternal spirit. We need a self-reflective mind capable of understanding and integrating paradox, willing to make the required sacrifices, and motivated to find the pearl hidden in the depths of the mud. Most wisdom traditions and magical systems are all devised to move us toward this consciousness of our divine nature, to awakening the inner kingdom. Plant consciousness healing is no different; healing takes place at the soul and spirit level, which then, through the natural process of manifestation, effects healing on the physical plane, which is in the body.

Many people can already connect with their higher self and have had experiences of nondualistic perception, yet when issues arise or when confronted with challenges, the connection gets severed again, and they fall back into places of fear and confusion. We must learn to walk this tightrope with grace if we are to become fertile ground for the divine forces to become manifest, for healing to take place. We must learn to allow our eternal self to express itself through the heart.

The soul is moved by the heart and the mind and so cannot be seen as separate. When the heart and mind carry imbalances and manifest as distortions in our inner elements, then soul loss can occur. This is a state of fragmentation of our soul forces, which prevents us from operating from wholeness and disconnects the lines of communication between us and our divine aspect. When we do not work through our issues and integrate our shadow or refuse to acknowledge that we are anything other than a random occurrence on a piece of rock circling around a ball of fire, then our soul forces are going to have very limited channels of expression and wholeness cannot manifest. If we are ruled by our animalistic tendencies and are only concerned with survival and having a good time, we reduce the capacity of our greater mind to reveal a wondrous multidimensional world where the heart is king and where we no longer need to operate within limited constructs.

Plant spirit healing is a path of illumination through a balancing of the emotions, the inner elements, and the nurturing of our divinity. The disturbing emotions and elemental imbalances are the clues to the spiritual healing that needs to take place. The plants become our mediators and our guides back to equilibrium, ensuring we are the fertile ground for the divine forces to work through us. It is a process of inner unification to transform our shadows into the pure gold of wisdom and our limitations into liberation through the guidance of the plants. Plants have been on Earth approximately 120 million years longer than us; they are very evolved and advanced beings. Their own spirit forces have had much longer to master the elements and this realm. Trees are tantric masters, the flowers are the sexual organs of the gods, and the plants are the physical expression of ascended masters and bodhisattvas. Plant spirit healing helps us cut through the conditioned illusions of how we believe our world works and helps us to live a life fully present within our multidimensionality.

The Native Healing of the British Isles

The Celtic shamanic traditions of the British Isles have many influences. (The word *Celtic* has been used here due to its popular understanding; in reality, Celtic is a relatively modern term in relation to the traditions referred to here.) To help us along the nature path, perhaps we can learn something from the ancient mystery schools, which came before the disconnection between religion and science. These schools evolved from the observations and direct experiences of the forces of nature. There isn't one mystery school tradition within itself that originates from the British Isles; however, the isles have ancient traditions, oral transmissions, and a deep Otherworld initiatory path, which are equivalent to the highest teachings and essence of Buddhism, Taoism, and Hinduism of the East. I am indeed blessed to live on islands that are not only steeped in mythology and legend but that also have a strong undercurrent of natural magic. Various mystery schools have influenced the Otherworld traditions, and many spiritual and magical groups have emerged out of them, such as the Druids and the original witches' covens. The Eleusinian mysteries, the hermetic tradition, and the Platonian system have all played a major role in shaping the consciousness of the inhabitants of the British Isles, both past and present, and provide a fundamental structure to self-healing and self-liberation.[1] The paths that these schools and traditions taught were not easy, and they safeguarded their most sacred wisdom lest it land in the wrong hands or be received by a mind not ready or capable of understanding it.

When wisdom lands on infertile ground, it cannot grow: it dies. Entropy creeps into the core of the wisdom and dilutes it; we lose sight of the truth over time, and this in turn dims the light of the soul. We therefore need a mediator between the light and the dark to show us the way, to guide us along the path and ensure that we are ready to receive the ultimate truth, that our nervous system and mind have been prepared, cleansed, and healed sufficiently to be a vessel for higher consciousness because all of the mystery schools have one fundamental theme at their core: the search for ultimate truth within.

In these traditions the acolyte is working toward liberation from all conditions of the mind to a state of self-mastery and unification of the lower mind with the consciousness of his or her divine nature, the eternal spirit, the daemon, or the higher self. Until we transcend the great paradox of life, when duality is balanced within us and the spirit is made conscious, it remains asleep to some extent, although many people can identify with the experience and feeling of a higher power watching out for them as they have a near miss of disaster or always seem to land on their feet. This all-knowing aspect of self seems disconnected from the day-to-day self, from the conceptual mind that is fixed in orientation upon the surface and physical world. The lower mind perceives time as linear and objects as separate from the self. The higher mind exists outside time and space; it is all knowing of all time lines and dimensions and dwells within unity consciousness. It knows much more than the "meat-bag at the end of the telephone line," as mist-walker David Leesley says. It is our eternal spirit self, and we can open the lines of communication with it so that it functions through us every moment of every day, as many wisdom traditions of the past have taught.

In the Celtic tradition, the soul, heart, and mind are sacred in their union; they work in harmony as an expression of the Divine. The body is the expression of the soul, and through our five senses, we can taste, touch, smell, hear, and feel the sacredness in all experiences of life. The body is made from the same stuff, the same soul forces and elements as all of nature, as everything on Earth. When the body dies, those same soul forces go back into nature. There was no separation between the senses and the soul in the minds of our ancient ancestors, and despite the Christian mind-set forcing barriers between the mundane and the Divine, we are still acutely aware that the eyes are the doorway to the soul. The truth of our existence cannot be squashed for too long; its memory is in the very cells of our being.

From a practical perspective we will work with the Celtic medicine wheel (chapter 6), which creates a dynamic, profound, yet practical container for all of our healing work, holding us within a structure of natural law, and which assists in aligning us back to our natural human self in cocreation with Earth. It is through the medicine wheel we can apply the power of natural magic to our healing process and apply the doctrine of correspondences to effect inner change.

Natural Magic

It is difficult to be in the world of plants for a long while and not come across or directly experience magic: a result that sits outside the normal acceptance of how we perceive things work. The *Cambridge Dictionary* defines the word *magic* as "the use of special powers to make things happen that would usually be impossible, such as in stories for children." Indoctrination into a particular society and way of being is done through the language of the people. Denigrate the words we use or the meaning of words, which build the world we experience, and you condition the mind-set, perceptions, and abilities of the people. Our acceptance and understanding of magic have been taken to the realm of special powers and degraded to superstition when it quite simply is a matter of training focused consciousness to particular frequencies. Remembering that we can all perform magic—and do so every moment of every day as we bring thought into manifest action or form—reminds us of our individual power and sovereignty, quite a dangerous thing to authoritarian rule.

The practice of magic takes many forms, from the outdated grimoires of old spells and incantations to the chaos magic of today. Some magical arts have survived into the modern era simply because, if used correctly, they work. Others have died out due to their low level of effectiveness or lack of relevance today. Much of the magical memory of today, however, has been preserved from the medieval period and is therefore quite dark and rather on the unethical side. Curses, love potions, and the conjuring of detrimental spirits have no place in a world where we have access to ethical principles from many traditions and therefore know the difference between right and wrong. The world has changed, human consciousness has evolved, and the astral realms have therefore become different places from what they were five hundred years ago. Magic has also evolved, yet natural magic was, is, and always has been.

Cause and effect or interdependent origination in the Buddhist tradition is the basic principle of manifestation and of the existence of all phenomena, whether seen or unseen. I emphasize the word *basic* here because manifestation is a complex process taking in many causes, conditions, and states of consciousness. All substantial things are the result of its causes and conditions, for example, a beautiful waterlily results when a seed of the plant lands in the right type and stillness of water and is heated by the right seasonal temperature. The waterlily itself then provides the conditions for insects to lay their eggs, and so the cycle of life continues in multiple directions. This pattern of existence, of every phenomenal thing being reliant upon everything else in its environment, replicates to subtle levels imperceivable to our human external senses. It is the great tapestry of life, Indra's net or the endless knot. Everything has the seed of everything else contained within it; all is entangled within the Great Mother's web. Nothing ever truly dies; its energies and elements dissolve or transmute into another to be recycled for life to continue.

One of the fundamental aspects of the human mind is that while it might be habitual, it can also change. We can change our mind at many levels, both in the short and long term. The mind can be trained into working for us rather than against us, producing coherence rather than dissonance. We are therefore cocreators of life if we can actively change the way something works. So applying the framework of interconnectedness to our own awakening and healing processes has beneficial effect. By contemplating personal disturbing emotions or elemental imbalances back along the thread of their existence to their origin, one finds the seed of their opposite or their rebalance. Within the emotion of anger is the seed to inner peace. Within the effect of too much inner water element is the seed to a perfectly balanced water element. The yin-yang symbol demonstrates this paradox beautifully, with the seed of white encircled by its opposite and the seed of black encircled by the white. Everything is intrinsically connected to its counterpart. To apply the antidote to our imbalances, we therefore apply its sympathetic remedy. Applying its opposite can create conflict and energies at loggerheads, yet sympathetic remedy draws on qualities inherent in the imbalance itself to support harmony. If we are experiencing too much anger, for example, we would work with a fiery plant such as nettle to calm the anger and help us get in touch with its cause, therefore healing the mind of blinding emotion and supporting awakening to a hidden aspect of the self. We might also then be guided to the next level of healing that needs to take place: the underlying cause of the anger, which may be a childhood trauma that the anger is protecting. This trauma might require a different sympathetic remedy. By working with the cause and effect relationship between subjects and objects, we produce a life-affirming effect. We are replicating the natural law of emergence and existence within our own part of the web. This is called *sympathetic magic,* an expression coined by anthropologist Sir James George Frazer (1854–1941), author of the famous work on magical philosophy, *The Golden Bough.*[2]

We can now turn to the doctrine of correspondences to assist us in our sympathetic and magical healing processes. Recognizing and working with the corresponding attributes and qualities of groups of objects, such as plants, planets, animals, deities, and numbers, involves engaging with the interconnecting web of life to manifest change on the inner and outer planes. In our part of the web, we will be working with the correspondences among the elements, plants, trees, emotions, chakras, and spiritual conditions to bring psychospiritual healing into our life. In chapter 6 we will place all of our work within the container of the medicine wheel—itself a comprehensive system of correspondences among the elements, the directions, and the spiritual realms—to bring cohesion and amplify our processes. Through bringing realignment on the outer, we effect realignment on the inner—as above, so below. Emotional and spiritual rebalancing precipitates physical balance out of disease. As our inner world becomes less erratic, our outer life becomes calmer and in alignment. The medicine wheel will be our conduit and the plants our gateways between the realms to effect holistic healing. Thus, we are cleaning and illuminating our part of the web.

Natural magic for healing works with the three overarching

principles of most types of magic: creating, energizing, and releasing. We create within our mind and/or upon the medicine wheel the effect that we wish to actualize, we enliven and power it with emotion and/or corresponding action such as prayer, and we release it by naming it, blowing out a candle or asking that it be done now. When working with the plant spirits for healing, the same principles apply. It is the transmutation of energy from one form or realm to another by way of intention. Self-belief is imperative in this process. This is how we communicate with plant spirits for direct healing on an energetic level. We connect through our unique handle that we have nurtured: a handle is the feeling or sensation the plant gives us when we take its medicine or meditate with it. We empower the plant spirit to do the healing through precise and heartfelt prayer (and perhaps a corresponding object in the correct direction on the medicine wheel); and we release the prayer by asking that it be done *now*. We then let the prayer and intention go, as our plant ally goes about its work. Trusting that the work is being done is paramount to it actually being done. Your own magic only works if you believe it does. Adding the word *now* into your prayers ensures that the prayer or request is not answered in ten years' time but within the present moment.

This type of magic is of the air element, working with the power of the creative mind and connections on the inner planes to manifest energetic change. As previously mentioned, ethics and gratitude play an important part, as does the focused belief in yourself. This process works through the quantum field and forms the basis of remote shamanic healing. Applying these principles in cocreation with your plant spirit allies empowers and enlivens the healing process.

Being with Plants

To know a plant on both its physical and metaphysical levels we need to put time and effort into the relationship. We would not expect a friend to come to our party if we did not send a pleasant invitation, and so it is with the plants. They are conscious beings that command respect and love. They are not to be controlled or appropriated. It is a sad situation, but our Western mind-set is very much driven by wanting to own and control things and to be seen as the best or the most knowledgeable. Our colonial past has embedded these notions deep into our psyche so that even some "spiritual" people often only see the plants as something to learn about, tell others how much they know, and profit from.

There is a difference between conceptually being spiritual and a spiritual practice that is integrated into every waking thought and action. Very few people actually put the time in to get to know the spirits of the plants and trees, and even fewer work with them cocreatively because it takes time. The phrase *plant ally* has been diluted down to the meaning of "a plant that helps me recover from illness or that lifts my mood." The true meaning of a plant ally is an active member of your spirit team, with whom you are in direct communication, whose magic and healing abilities you know on all levels and can bring through you at any given moment. This depth of relationship means together you can also heal on all levels of existence, physical, emotional, and spiritual, yet accomplishment evolves over time. The plant spirits live with us and within us. As we do our inner work, cleanse our energy field, and become more aligned with our intuition, we become a clear channel for the plant spirits to bring the impulse of their medicine through us from the spirit to the human realm. Knowing a spirit ally energetically is to know it magically.

When we approach plants and trees with humility, honor, and respect, we are permitted through the guarded gates into their own inner kingdom or queendom. Some of these dimensions are more challenging than others, and many are filled with wonder and awe. As we allow these creative and Gaian forces to rewild our own interiority, our lives change and evolve in ways we cannot imagine. The Great Spirit has a much more expansive dream for us if we recognize and release the limits we place upon our lives through our own small human perspective. It is wise to have a stable mind to be in these inner dimensions; hence, my emphasis on meditation, so that we can familiarize ourselves with these nonpolarized and thought-responsive environments. We become accustomed to the way these other planes of existence work and start to understand the states of consciousness required for human evolution and transcendence. These plant spirit dimensions teach us how to be human to our fullest potential and remind us of our innate goodness and innocence. Perhaps these two qualities might not resonate with mass humankind who are on a path toward self-destruction following the illusions of society and culture, yet by aligning ourselves to the cosmic pattern of our inner divinity we become empowered, wise, and fulfilled. From a Buddhist perspective, when we live by a firm foundation of ethics and cosmic law, we transcend the cyclical existence of birth, death, and rebirth, reaching a level of awareness that allows personal choice of location and conditions for our next incarnation, if we choose to return at all. To become fully conscious in all states of awareness (birth, sleep, waking, other dimensions, and death), we need to balance our inner elements through working to balance our emotions against the backdrop of the understanding of the true nature of the mind.

To attain this depth of the path, we must immerse ourselves in the dream of the plants. Dive into their interiority and invite their life-affirming forces into our life. Most importantly, we must spend time with them. Through plant diets and protocols, meditation and dream work, growing plants and making medicine, we are attuning ourselves to the language of the nature kingdom. It took you a good few years to learn human language so don't be surprised if it takes a while for you to adjust your communications to the plant spirit world. It takes practice, but the good news is that the practice itself is so enjoyable. You get to be with plants and in nature as much as you want, and we all know how good we feel when we've sat under a tree or in our favorite nature spot. To begin with, the message of the plants may be subtle, but the strength and depth of their communications grows over time.

So as mentioned, a rudimentary knowledge of herbalism is required on this path, especially for part 1 of the book, where the meditations and journeys presented can be used for any plant or tree. If you are making any medicines, which I strongly recommend you do, then please use a good reference book to keep you safe. *Hedgerow Medicine* by master herbalist Julie Bruton-Seal and Matthew Seal along with their *Wayside Medicine* are sound and insightful guides to making herbal remedies from your own backyard and environs. Julie keeps her medicines simple, which is always the best, yet her breadth of knowledge is invaluable. Being out in nature and identifying the plants that grow in your area is also a fundamental practice on this path. There is ultimately no separation between you and your environment so allow it in and spend as much time as you can with the trees and plants. Some plants will call you to work with them, and others will remain elusive until the time is right for you. Just go with what you are drawn to and notice the ones that you are avoiding, as very often they hold the most potent medicine for you. Spend time with the plants and trees you wish to work with; look at where and how they grow, what is in their environment, and what they look like. Start to get to know a plant on its physical basis. Observing a plant and paying attention to where it sits on the land is the first step on the path.

Working with others is always a process of mutuality, and again the same principle applies to plant spirits. Whatever teachings and healings we take from them, we must give back in whatever way we can and is appropriate; otherwise, we will drain their energy and willingness to work with us. Ideally, we ask the plant spirit directly what it is it requires in return within the partnership. Common responses are to be honored and listened to so that their guidance doesn't fall on deaf ears or on selective ones. Some plant spirits may require food offerings, and others want their name sung to them to request their presence. Many may need their name said in a particular way or their wisdom and healing gifts honored by being shared with others. Each plant spirit will have its own way of working with you. Taking time to establish this common ground is essential to the flourishing of the healing work.

Once you have chosen a plant or tree to work with or it has chosen you, there are many ways to get to know its spirit, and one of the first that I learned and one that is fundamental to all of the following protocols and practices is finding your own unique connection to the plant, which Pam Montgomery calls the handle. As noted earlier, a handle is the feeling the plant gives you when you take its medicine or meditate with it. Everyone perceives and connects to plant spirits in a different way. Some people connect to their body awareness; their inner pendulum is strong and so they perceive through feeling. They can perceive the change in energies in any space and are finely attuned to varying frequencies themselves. Other people are clairsentient, perceiving through sound and vibration. Whatever activity you perform with your plant ally will have varying effects; however, there will be a consistency in your body sense, such as a particular vibration, movement, or image that runs through the experience.

As someone whose inner landscape is very much alive, my inner vision is clear, and so I often see the spirits of the plants and from there can feel into their energies and teachings. In my early days of working with mugwort, I would feel a wavelike energy moving over my chest. The feeling of oak comes from my core, expands outward, and then moves downward, rooting me to Earth. Once trust is established I merge with them and bring their medicine through me in a cocreative and relational way. There is no coercion or controlling happening but a mutual agreement held with mutual respect.

The sensation that your plant ally makes you feel is unique to you. It may be similar to someone else's connection, but we are all unique individuals having unique experiences within the unlimited cosmic mind, so don't be concerned if your experience is very different from everyone else's. The most important thing is that you repeat the experience and get to know how the plant feels in your body, notice what emotions are connected to your handle or any imagery that arises within your mind as you sense it. This will form the basis of your relationship with your new plant ally; it will be your reference point for working with that plant spirit for healing and for recognizing your ally in any other of its forms that it presents to you during your relationship. Your handle can change over time; it can evolve within your deepening relationship with the plant spirit. Your unique connection to a plant spirit becomes your speed dial, a quick and direct connection to your plant ally.

It is advisable to get to know a plant directly without reading up about it first; this way you will avoid perceiving the plant through a particular cultural or fact-checked filter and will have a more direct experience with it. Obviously, ensure any plant is edible and safe to consume before you embark on your journey, but read up about its folklore and medicinal qualities *after* you have meditated with it or met its spirit and seen how it moves through and interacts with your world. Retrospective validation strengthens our intuition and helps us progress.

Over time, you will find that you connect to some plant spirits more than others. If a plant spirit has a long history of working with humans, such as mugwort and elder, you will find that they are much more accessible and visceral for you. More obscure and rare plants might be difficult to connect with, depending on your capacity for cross-species and spirit communication. You will also find that you have an affinity for certain plants and trees just because you love those particular ones or your energy and your own spirit team are compatible with them.

Setting Intentions

Setting intentions when working with plants, trees, meditations, and medicine wheels is paramount to the cocreative relationship that you are forming. Even if you simply wish to learn what the plant spirit has to teach you, it is imperative that you set this as an intention, asking the plant spirit to reveal the most appropriate teachings or insights for you right now. Any spiritual practice should have an intention in order to direct spirit to align with your will. We live on a free will planet, and while on the mundane level it does not seem that way, when it comes to working with metaphysics it is law. In this regard, if we are too specific in our intentions, then we limit how spirit can work and move. Also, what we have in mind for our greater good is very often limited compared to what spirit can achieve. It is therefore best to be direct with your intentions but open enough for the unexpected. Using the phrase *most appropriate* offers the plant spirits and the greater mind of creative source to manifest change and healing in a way that our smaller, conceptual minds could not comprehend or imagine. This keeps us humble and prevents the ego from asserting too much of our free will: everything must be kept in balance. For example: *My intention for working with mugwort is to bring the most appropriate healing and insights for my life right now.* We want clarity and alignment in our life but the source of that realignment might not be where we thought it was and so we place our trust in our plant allies to know on the spirit level where the imbalance lies and to apply the necessary healing. We are being conscious participants in the work yet allowing our plant allies to work without constraints.

Remember that no matter how isolated or individuated you feel in your suffering right now, we are all intrinsically interlinked within the great tapestry of life. Every thought, action, or intention will create a ripple outward from you to some effect. Intention works at the subtle level to start with, and even the smallest seed can produce the largest tree, the smallest decision can alter the course of an entire life. We have to be responsible and respectful of this as we form our intentions and not get carried away with unrealistic or ungrounded hopes.

Inner Sensation Meditation

This meditation is inspired by my teacher, Pam Montgomery, who taught me the fundamental way of establishing inner connection with the plant spirits. It can be performed indoors with a plant medicine, such as essences, or outdoors with a live plant or tree. Another option is drinking herbal teas (made from loose organic herbs not from tea bags). Although it's preferable to work with living plants for exploring the inner realms of nature, that may not always be possible, for example, during the winter months or if you live in a city. I would recommend, if possible, performing both indoors and outdoors repeatedly to establish a clear sensation of how your plant feels inside you, how it interacts with your specific energetic system.

Sit cross-legged on the ground or on a chair with your feet flat on the floor and your back straight. Take three deep breaths, and on each exhalation, release any tension

held in your body, paying more attention to the jaw, shoulders, and stomach.

Use the dropping the mind into the heart meditation as outlined in chapter 1 to allow your awareness to be grounded in open awareness.

Notice how your body is feeling right now, such as any aches or tiredness. Notice where you are emotionally and how those emotions feel in your body.

Take a few drops of your plant essence at this point, if you are working with a medicine, or bring the plant or tree to mind that you are working with.

Notice how your physical body feels in connection with your plant. Is there a frequency or vibration that is evoked when you connect with your plant? Does a part of your body tingle, or can you detect a new and unusual sensation?

Notice your emotions. How have they changed since the last time you sat under the tree or took the plant essence?

If your mind wanders, what is grabbing its attention? Is it a memory, a person, or a place? Why do you think you suddenly started thinking of this? Notice the movements of the mind in relation to your plant.

Once you feel your experience and meditation is coming to an end, note in your journal any experiences, insights, feelings, or memories that the plant evoked in you.

Repeat the experience to establish similarities and congruencies connecting your experiences. Your handle for that particular plant or tree will start to become apparent.

Plant Diets

One of the most effective ways to build a relationship with plants and to receive their healing gifts is to go on a plant diet. This is where we set aside a period of time to consume that plant or tree and perform meditations and journeys to witness how the plant spirit works within us and learn how it also influences and works within our external world. It is during these plant diets that we often meet the spirit of the plant or tree and receive direct teachings from it for our healing, for insights into how we live, or for our own spiritual development. During any plant diet, we view everything that happens in our life at that time through the lens of the plant we are in a container with. When viewed from this perspective, our eyes and minds are opened within the dream of the plant, and the magic of life and nature becomes more apparent. This is not some fanciful dreaming but a tuning in to the inner realms of nature and the level of consciousness that the plant spirits exist on. This dimension of understanding overlaps and is reflected in normal life; we can therefore observe the plant spirits working through the occurrences and situations that arise.

We owe the tradition of dieting with plants to the South American shamans and to medical herbalists and plant spirit healers, Carole Guyett and Pam Montgomery for bringing it to the West in these modern times, to work and commune with our own common native plants. We can actually find evidence of plant diets in our ancient past when we consider Taliesin's magical spell in the medieval Welsh poem called the "Cad Goddeu" (Battle of the Trees). In this poem from the *Book of Taliesin,* the magician Gwydion calls many species of tree spirits to fight alongside him in his army. This level of cocreation with the trees could only have been performed through deep connection to their spirits, and this would most likely have required some kind of diet or period of deep communion with them.

In the Amazon plant diets are viewed as initiations, thresholds leading into the magical world of the plant spirit. They can take a slightly different form in that the shaman or maestro passes the energy of his plant spirit and other spirit allies to the apprentice, either energetically through the crown of the head or physically via a special phlegm that he has cultivated as part of his own inner storehouse of magic. The plant diet is then the period of time that the apprentice takes to integrate that gift from his maestro.[3] The context of plant diets in the Amazon is one of survival; it is imperative that a shaman gathers spirit allies and types of magic to defend and heal his tribe or to attack others if deemed necessary.

Clearly, tribal warfare is not required in our society; however, once we begin to work on the unseen planes with our plant allies, we can perceive a similar level of energetic battle taking place among people who are not in control of their emotions. People consciously and unconsciously project their own insecurities onto others through jealousy, paranoia, and other toxic thoughtforms or by draining the emotional energy of others. Our plant allies teach us how to cleanse and protect our energy field against these kinds of toxicities without having to retaliate or cause any harm in return. Our directive is toward harmony and balance in all areas of life, and through dieting with the plants, we can open ourselves up to this level of teaching.

Once you have decided on the length of time that you have to dedicate to your plant spirit, we open this sacred container through a ceremony to invite the plant spirit into communication with us. This ceremony can be in the form of a dedicated meditation, it can involve the layout of a medicine wheel altar (see chapter 6) with your plant in the center, and it can involve making offerings to that plant or tree in the wild or in your garden. Whichever way you choose to begin your plant diet, ensure that your intentions for the diet are decided in advance and you can relay them to your plant spirit ally during the ceremony.

Your container could be for three days right up to a few months; the time you can dedicate to this process is your choice. It is recommended to do a lunar cycle with your plant ally, to give it enough time to complete the healing process and for you to work through the energy cycles of the moon and within yourself. This gives you maximum opportunity to understand how the plant works through your unique energy system and for the messages of the plant to come through to you. During this time, it is recommended to reduce contact with your normal life as much as possible and to turn inward. Eating foods that are as natural and plain as possible and avoiding stimulants such as coffee and sugar or heavier foods such as dairy and red meat will help you tune in to the subtle energies of the plant that you will be working with. Some people also avoid sexual intercourse simply to prevent the mixing of energies, which can confuse the process of understanding the plant spirit. The more committed you are to the process, the more profound the experience.

Meditations, journeying, dream work, journaling, singing, dancing, drawing, and walking in nature are some of the activities that you can do on a plant diet with the intention of meeting and getting to know your plant. All of the meditations and journeys in the first part of this book can be used during your plant diet and as a guide to getting to know your ally.

A plant diet is a shamanic process: you are undertaking a shamanic journey into yourself and into the inner realms of nature. You will experience shifts in consciousness and physical and emotional healing. The shape of the journey will come to a crescendo toward the end of your time with the plant. The plant spirits, you will notice, time things to perfection. It may well seem as if not much is happening for the first two weeks; however, all of the new energies, the healing, and the insights will arrive toward the culmination of the process. It does not have to follow this pattern, however, and I often receive the majority of my insights in the first day of the process and then the following time with the plant is the integration. There are no set rules to the contour of your shamanic plant diet journey.

Just as the shamans of the Amazon cultivate a living presence of their plant allies in their magical phlegm, so too can we invite the plant spirit to live inside us within the microbiome of our gut when we ingest the physical plant. To get the plant into you during a plant diet you can work with the following medicines:

- Essence
- Tincture
- Tea
- Hydrosol or spirituous water
- Oxymel
- Essential oil

You can also make a ceremonial elixir out of all of the above by blending infusions, tinctures, and essences into one drink, which is ceremonially consumed throughout your diet. I imbibe teas and tinctures of the plant and put them in a bath, in my water filter, and in oil that I use as a scrub in the shower. I immerse myself in the plant by inviting it into, on, and around me during the course of the plant diet. I then end the plant diet with another ceremony. Ritual helps to both manifest into the earthly plane and to communicate our intentions to the spirit realm.

Essence Protocols

Working with flower and plant essences is another form of plant diet. An essence is the imprint of a plant's bioresonance; it holds the conscious intelligence of the plant or tree within the crystalline molecular structure of water, fixed with alcohol. The structure of water can be programmed or attuned to hold information, memories, and frequencies. In this way, the unique vibratory resonance and spirit of a plant or tree can be held within water to make the essence. Essences should not be confused with tinctures, which contain the actual chemical compounds of the plant.

This bioresonance is a gateway to the plant's consciousness. Taking an essence of a particular plant or tree every day for a certain period of time (and again, I recommend a lunar cycle) allows the vibration of that essence to be incorporated into your own energetic system, repatterning your energy field back to a natural resonance of nature. Our energy fields get clogged by environmental toxicities, knocked out of alignment by anxiety, or depleted through depression and stress. Many factors of our modern lifestyle contribute to most people living with a compromised energy field. Inviting the natural resonance of the plants and trees can reattune us back to our original harmony with Earth, back to the 432-Hz frequency that we are meant to be. This is the natural, uncompromised frequency of life.

Each plant carries its unique medicine, although most plants have a broad range of panaceas and gifts to assist us in this process. Hawthorn carries the resonance of a fully connected and integrated heart, helping us deal with and move through grief, a lack of love, or a broken heart and reestablishes our connection to the heart of Mother Earth. Larch helps us have self-belief and aligns us with the vibration of encouragement and motivation toward our goals. St. John's wort holds the vibrancy of the sun and lifts our mood so that we can feel the inspiration of life again if our inner fire has been depleted.

It is always best to make your own medicines; essences are very easy to make. However, sometimes that is not possible, so we have to purchase them. There are superb essence makers all over the globe, and it is advised to get them from producers who know how to connect with the spirit of the plant; otherwise, the essence can be quite flat and one dimensional. Essence producers who work with the spirits of the plants have a cocreative relationship with the animating and healing forces of the plant and the land in which the plant lives. These essences are more potent, and we can achieve much better results for both our healing and our plant communication practice. Without this connection between essence producer and the plant spirit the essence can work on one level but does not contain the multidimensional and wild frequencies that a plant spirit essence holds when the producer of the essence has a deeper relationship to the plant. My husband, Davyd, makes most of our essences for our Plant Consciousness Apothecary. He spends at least a year getting to know the plant—growing it, communicating with it, and watching it transform through the seasons—and then he asks the spirit if it would like to make medicine with him. He forms a relationship with the spirit before stepping into partnership and cocreation. It is only through the willingness of the spirit of the plant that a potent and vivacious remedy can be made.

Generally, the essence is taken every day, and everyone's dosage will differ depending on intention and our own unique bioresonance. The best way to find your dosage is to dowse for it using a pendulum. Muscle testing achieves the same results. You are looking for the number of drops for the number of times per day, for example, three drops three times per day at morning, noon, and night. If you do not wish to use a pendulum or muscle testing, you can simply tune in to your body wisdom, which is what the pendulum and muscle testing are doing anyway, and ask your body for the dosage required and see which number pops into your head. Our body knows far more than we give it credit for and has a consciousness that understands us better than we understand ourselves. The cleaner your energy field gets through working with the plants and trees, the more your body wisdom will come online, and the stronger your intuition will become.

Once you have your dosage, start your essence protocol in much the same way as the plant diets. Choose your dates, set your container, start by asking the plant to work with you, and perhaps work with the directions and a medicine wheel altar to ground and direct your intentions. It is a good idea to journal your experiences, your mood, what happens in your life during this time, and so on. Include relevant correspondences, such as planetary alignments, the weather, and any environmental factors that you notice. This will help you look back over your time with the plant with the gift of hindsight and draw deeper meaning to your process. This in turn helps you connect more deeply to the plant spirit and helps you to understand its medicine as it works through and within you.

An essence protocol is a simple yet powerful type of plant diet.

The Nature of Healing

Plant diets, meditations with plants, and essence protocols are all methodologies to assist and evoke the healing process within the context of plant spirit healing. Just like us, each plant reflects the whole; by connecting to the plants we can see ourselves reflected in the mirrors of their interiority. If we pay attention, this gives us invaluable insight into the origins of our emotional and physical imbalances. The plants make us aware of how our mind works in relation to the natural world and how our soul can be nourished by the life-affirming qualities of the plant spirits.

When we talk about healing, we are not just talking about relieving the physical aspects of illnesses. The symptoms of any disease in the body are the final stages of a deeper process that has taken place in the unseen realms of our existence over a long period of time. For anything to manifest or incarnate or be brought into the physical, there is a process of involution that starts out as nonphysical—an energy, group of frequencies, thought, or level of consciousness. As cell biologist

Bruce Lipton notes, our consciousness directly affects our biology: "The chemistry that determines our biology, genetics, behavior, and life characteristics is chemistry derived from the brain which, in turn, is derived from the brain interpreting an image in our mind. As we change our mind, we change our biology."[4]

In the context of healing, these forces over time move toward form as they sink deeper and deeper through our energy bodies into an ever-denser manifestation until they arrive in our physical body as sickness. The origin of these forces can be karmic; it can be generated by our subconscious programs, by our conditionings from this life, or from traumas from childhood or past lives. The symptoms of any disease are not the disease itself; they are the result of our experiences in life. Treating only symptoms is bypassing the true origin of our issues and misunderstanding the holistic and emotional human. Underneath the physical symptom is an unhelpful emotion, underneath this emotion is a trauma or conditioning, and underneath that is often either a soul or ancestral trauma. By working with the soul forces of a plant we can work and heal at a soul level within ourselves.

Disease itself is a form of active energy misaligned with the rest of the harmonic energies and forces that keep us functioning healthily. The energies of disease are working against the plan of the whole, but we don't need to demonize them or view them as just something to get rid of: disease can teach us so much. There are many teachings and insights into our true nature to be learned from the pains and wounds that we experience along the trajectory of our lives. Through this process of inner awakening, we are not only moving toward full health but toward spiritual illumination and connection with our own divine nature.

Understanding the forces behind our illnesses allows us to heal on both an emotional and spiritual level as well as the physical. When we address the root cause of an illness, an unhelpful thought pattern or even a small frustration, we start to cure ourselves properly. We can start to clear away the karmic baggage we incarnated with, our energy bodies become lighter, and we start to become more open minded, emotionally balanced, and overall healthier.

Most people, however, don't understand how deep they need to go with their healing, how much their blockages are holding them back, or how detrimental their negative emotions are for themselves and others. This preventive and holistic approach is the normal healing practice outside the Western world and has been the preserve of spiritual traditions and cultures all over the globe, but it is here in the West where it is needed most. Yet quite often we have to hit rock bottom and life has to become unbearable for us to be moved into action and to start looking for a path out of the darkness.

Be careful, though, because the word *path* in the context of a healing path or a spiritual path can be misleading as there is nowhere to go outside of ourselves; it simply indicates an inner change or a process of inner changes. The word *path* keeps us locked in a linear way of thinking and believing that something outside ourselves can fix us or is the key to our spiritual development. The healing process is in no way linear; there is no beginning, no middle, and no end. We only have to look at the cycles of nature to see that everything in our world is circular, spiral, and cyclical. I often see websites listing the stages of healing as if it were a linear process, and once you reach the last stage, you're enlightened! While these types of lists can be helpful to see where you are in one particular issue, they are not holistic and lock us into the dualistic illusion. If we really want to take responsibility for our physical health, our mental health, our soul, our own self-mastery, or our purpose for being alive, then accepting that the process is a lifetime's work helps bring some humility back to what has become an industry of quick fixes. There is no final destination, only the journey, but it does not mean that our health, mental well-being, and life in general will not improve and realign dramatically if we follow the plant path.

To understand healing, we need to understand energy—how it works, how it moves, how it is transmuted—and the main thing to understand is that healing is spiral in nature. We move through layers and layers of our issues, and as the conditions are in place for the deeper layer to be dealt with, then what we thought we had dealt with raises its head again to be addressed. It can be disheartening to realize that the months or years of processing we went through to reach a place of acceptance and transcendence with a particular issue has not been fully healing. But to reach the deeper layer means that we have progressed; we have attained a level of consciousness able to understand this deeper layer of the issue, and so we are experiencing more and more profound levels of self-awareness, emotional freedom, and unconditional joy.

In my personal experience healing happens in a spiral fashion because nothing exists in isolation. No trauma or unhelpful emotion exists separate from the rest of our traumas and emotions. Many moons ago, by chance (or fate) I attended a talk in Ireland about birth trauma. The therapist giving the talk had had the same birth trauma as I had, and the effect of having been born jaundiced and kept blindfolded under an ultraviolet light in an incubator for the first two months of her life had affected her in many ways. The proverbial lightbulb went on, and I started my own investigative journey into my own similar birth trauma. To cut a very long story short, the effect of this trauma was so widespread throughout my whole personality, psyche, and behavior that I didn't know how I was going to heal the effects of it. Abandonment was compounded by fear of the unknown, which was compounded by my third eye being shut down, compounded by a sense of feeling lost in the world, resulting in projections of anger toward others, anxiety, depression—you get the picture. There are many contributing factors to one trauma, but over a period of years I went deeper and deeper into the healing process, peeling away the layers, until finally I was ready for a teacher plant to take me back to the incubator to relive the experience and change the outcome.

We are never alone in our healing process; there is a whole kingdom of plants and trees willing to assist and guide us on our journey. All plants are teacher plants in that they show us how to live in harmony with ourselves and with the world. They support our transitions to greater levels of awareness, they bring the light during our darkest moments, and they seem to know much more about us than we do! But ultimately, we can only truly heal ourselves, and we have to realize we need to step onto the spiral if we want to live a more healthy and joyous life. If we have not dealt with our own inner conflicts, then we will not be in a stable position to effectively manage any societal or familial changes that arise in our lives. As within, so without—the more inner work we do, the more in alignment our external world becomes.

By directing our healing toward the origin of illness, toward the subtler levels of our existence, the healing frequencies then filter down into the physical body. Removing the original trauma or intrusion causing disharmony and illness removes the issue at the root, leaving the physical illness rootless. Only then can the physical illness work its way out of the body; it is no longer trapped and held in place by strong emotions or wounds in the energetic bodies. The symptoms caused by our traumas and imbalances restore themselves as we are supported by the plants. This type of depth healing needs to be understood within the spiritual context in which it resides: that we will only heal once the karmic lessons of the disease have been learned and the origin of the trauma integrated; that we can only become whole by accepting our shadow as well as our light; that our eternal spirit can only become conscious when we have cleared our obscurations of the body and mind.

When we start to go inward and dive into the deep mystery of our own being, it can be rather unnerving. It can feel as if we are descending into a void, an unknowing within which we will lose ourselves. In one sense, this is correct in that when we explore our psyche and discover or unearth an aspect of ourselves long forgotten or previously unknown, it can mean the death of an aspect of our known self. Perhaps a part of us knows that this change has the potential to be painful. Sometimes we grieve for those aspects of ourselves that we are letting go. They have been with us a long time, and they need acknowledging for all they have done for us thus far and so this is a natural process. Perhaps not knowing what is on the other side of the process can also be scary. It is therefore wise to be gentle and kind to yourself at these times. There is no benefit to forcing the process of inner change. We are conditioned to strive for the end result, but this will not serve us well in this circumstance. Once the ball has started rolling, it will gather its own pace, so we need to hold a sacred space for ourselves with tenderness and care, with the understanding that everything changes, with the conviction that one day we will wake up in the morning with the sunlight streaming through the bedroom window heralding a renewed sense of aliveness and natural joy.

The mantra of plant spirit healing is to know thyself—in all aspects and dimensions, in every moment of every day—to live a full and deeply meaningful life. Knowing yourself means having the awareness of both your ancestral lineage, where your genes come from, and your spiritual lineage, the trajectory that your eternal self has taken to arrive to this present moment. When we refer to healing, we are referring to the making whole of both our ancestral or genealogical lineage and our spiritual lineage. However, we must never forget that everything heals and restores due to balance. In this regard, we must also respect and accept mystery, the opposite of knowing. We have to accept that perhaps we cannot know ourselves fully in this lifetime. Yet would we want to live a life without mystery? It is the mystery within things that make them beautiful. It is the liminal space between the trees that gives the forest its magic. Mystery is what lies at the depth of the human soul. Without mystery we would not be driven to uncover the truths that lie beneath the layers of dust in the attic of our mind. But we have to be prepared to leave the cover over the mirror if it is not meant to be removed yet and to accept that revealing and cleaning everything within an inch of its life is tilting the scales in the other direction and creating more imbalance.

When observing a plant or tree, we can feel the mystery of its inner life, and rather than having to know everything, sometimes it is just as soul nourishing to sit in the void of mystery with your plant ally and just be. There is a coherence that occurs as your heart entrains with the vibratory resonance of your plant ally, and simply resting in natural awareness is a pleasure and a joy. We need balance between knowledge and mystery, between being and becoming. Incessant doing distracts us from our inner mystery. Glorifying busyness and always reaching for external stimuli and entertainment is an avoidance of looking into the mystery of the self. The soul is constantly calling us home, but we are too preoccupied to listen.

6

Becoming the
Plant Medicine Wheel

WORKING WITH THE MEDICINE WHEEL is an ancient practice that is just as relevant today as it was to our ancestors. The medicine wheel provides a place where all your hard work can cohere, builds a framework for becoming yourself, and holds a safe space for you as you work through this book. It is a symbol of the nature of reality that sits within most cosmological frameworks and is a true tradition in that it has no beginning; it has just always been. The medicine wheel in its two-dimensional state, as shown in figure 6.1, page 92, depicts the four cardinal directions, a symbol of our existence here on Earth on the horizontal plane. In shamanic reality the medicine wheel is a sphere incorporating the three worlds (Upper, Middle, and Lower), and therefore includes the vertical plane, which is also part of the energetic framework of our reality within third-dimensional consciousness. The equilateral cross, which sits within a circle or sphere, forms the basic structure around and within which our story of creation, death, and rebirth can be told and retold from many perspectives and upon many themes. On a basic level this device highlights the cycles of nature through the seasons of spring, summer, autumn, and winter and their associated energies. On a metaphysical level this cyclical process is the biography of our becoming: we die to the old and are reborn anew through cycles within the great cycle of life and death. Every day we revolve through the wheel of our circadian rhythms, through the wheel of emotions, and through the wheel of sleeping and waking. Through our life we revolve and evolve through our healing processes and through our spiritual unfoldment. Any cycle can be tracked through the form of the medicine wheel. It is the fractal cycle of life from the time of mythos to the present day, allowing us connection to the deepest aspects of ourselves and our ancestors to integrate them with our experience today. It is a map to help guide our way.

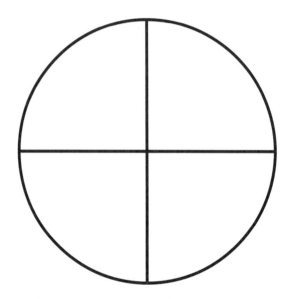

Fig. 6.1. The structure and layout of the Celtic medicine wheel

The medicine wheel lays the foundation for sacredness. We have forgotten the true meaning of this in the Western world as our conditioning, whether we like it or not, has moved us toward colonialism, appropriation, exploitation, and competition. Sacredness is that which brings us closer to realizing the truth of who we are at a fundamental level. It fosters connection, respect, and integrity. It reminds us of interconnectedness and nonseparation from nature, from one another, and from the Divine. This is why plants are sacred: they bring the medicine wheel alive within us and therefore our own sacred self.

Our focus in plant spirit healing is to understand the energetic structure of the plants and how they then interact and transform our own energetic makeup. The medicine wheel brings together the fundamental energies that are the building blocks of everything in our awareness, including the plants. Fundamentally, the cross represents the four directions and their associated energies. The circle represents the realm that we live in, presided over by the feminine power of Earth within universal consciousness. From here we can work with the wheel in many ways as it becomes a primordial symbol for life. It can become a tool to help you clean up your energy field, get yourself in balance, and look after yourself in a world very much out of balance. As your work with the plant spirits and the medicine wheel progresses and is integrated, you become the medicine wheel: your energies become cohesive, your astral body becomes stable furthering your spiritual development, and your life falls into alignment. It is an axis about which we can turn toward balance and cohesion.

In the British Isles the tradition of the medicine wheel differs slightly to those of the East and the Americas. The topography of the isles is unique, and so we associate the qualities of the directions in the following way: north is earth, east is air, south is fire, and west is water, each being one of the four arms of the cross. At center is the great void of creation, the quintessence of the elements, space (or ether), from which all directions and elements are born. Within the ancient faery healing tradition of the British Isles, perhaps the oldest spiritual modality known today, this symbolic device is also known as the faery crossroads. It was a portal through which our ancestors entered the Otherworld, a living symbol that evoked the liminality required to access the inner planes.

Throughout the ages the combination of all of the qualities of the directions produces the most powerful magical spells and the strongest sacred spaces within which deep healing work can happen. Yet there is a tendency within shamanic practice to want to skip the fundamentals and head straight to the juicy bits, such as in part two of this book; however, if we fail to familiarize ourselves with the basics, we have nothing within which to ground our experiences with the plant spirits. Our understanding of the healing process is fragmented, and progress is slower. There is no container for the energy produced from our work, so it leaks and dissipates over time. Without a firm foundation a house will soon crumble and fall.

The Celtic medicine wheel gives you the structure and framework for shorter processes such as a plant diet, medium processes such as your journey through the year, right up to the long cycle of your life. If you view all your journeys through the lens of the wheel, stood at the center of it, you will be tuned back in to the cycles of life, of nature, and of Earth so that we can become one with our eternal self within the collective unity of our species. This is therefore the perfect method to move us out of polarity and reestablish our connection to our wise and balanced self, to our eternal spirit, and to the consciousness of Earth, the ultimate goals within plant spirit healing. Each turn of the wheel that you take can be for different reasons and intentions; it is crucial to have intentions not only for working with the individual plant spirits themselves but the medicine wheel also. This focuses creative consciousness and helps achieve tangible results.

To understand reality it is useful to know and be familiar with its source, from which it is created. The map that we are working with here will guide your way. It is not the actual meaning of your experiences but a framework within which you can navigate your inner world and through which it can organically flourish. Like the words in this book, which provide a framework or vehicle for delivering information, the elements and directions are pointers and signposts on the path to understanding both your inner and outer experiences. We use language to understand and communicate concepts; to understand something we break it down into digestible parts and identify or label each part with words to help us see how the parts fit together to form the thing we are trying to know. But the word itself is not the thing we're trying to know; it is a container within which the meaning of the thing sits. Likewise, with the elements and directions, they do not exist separately; they are all aspects of the whole nature of reality, but it is useful for us to break down the whole in order to gain orientation and a conceptual understanding of their correspondences in relation to ourselves and the plants. As we do our inner work with the plants, we impute meaning and feeling to our concepts. Our understanding supports our transformational process, and our map is brought to life by our direct experiences. Our liberation is catalyzed by our wisdom.

To understand the elements, the building blocks of all life, is fundamental to our well-being. Not only are pure external elements important for our health, such as clean water, healthy soil to grow our food, and fresh air to breathe, but the balance and purity of our inner, subtle elements are vital to our health too. The quality of our life is directly affected by the quality of our emotions, and our emotions are a direct result of the balance or imbalance of our inner elements. To understand the elements therefore is to give ourselves the tools to understand ourselves. To balance our elements is to free ourselves from the dramas, the conflicts, and the stresses of situations and relationships. Knowing how our elements become unbalanced in the first place assists the process of transformation. This is the key to self-mastery.

Working with the Plant Medicine Wheel

Creating an altar in the form of the medicine wheel is an important aspect when working shamanically with plants. It is not essential, but it serves several purposes and can concentrate the energies of your work. During our plant ceremonies and diets, the altar holds the axis of our space, focusing and balancing the energy of the ceremony and teachings. The layout is the Celtic medicine wheel as shown in the figure 6.1, page 92, where items representing the elements are placed on a cloth in the associated location on the layout: for example, a hawk wing in the east, a candle in the south, a bowl of stream water in the west, and a ceramic mushroom in the north. Make sure you know which direction is north within the room or space where you are creating your altar. Ensure the items you choose to place on the altar to represent the elements and directions are oriented toward your actual directions. Crystals, incense, bowls of seeds, pictures, and plants are a few more examples of what can be used to build your medicine wheel altar. Whatever you choose to place on the altar should be related to the ceremony taking place in some way. Any personal objects should be directly associated with the deepest aspect of yourself. The objective of the ceremony is to connect your human self with your divine self; therefore, everything brought into the ceremony should be infused with this intention.

In the center of the medicine wheel or the direction you intend to work within, place the plant with which you are working. Only place live plants on your altar, ones in pots. If we place cut flowers or plants on the altar, we are only working with their dying form. Alternatively, use a representation of the plant, such as a framed picture; however, the plant will be less able to hold your sacred space. Ideally, work with a live plant. By placing the plant or tree in the center of the wheel and then calling in the directions and elements, we are working with the forces already present within the plant, the energies that work through it every day and throughout the year.

Creating an altar or medicine wheel is the earth element of our ceremony and inner work as it becomes ritual; it strengthens our understanding of the sacred and our inner connection to Earth. It links the inner with the outer, reflects the micro in the macro, and vice versa. Once the altar is complete, we open the sacred space for our work by calling to the elements and powers from each of the directions, opening a portal of energy through the altar to purify, transmute what is misaligned, and to call in that which is needed for rebalance. The layout of the spherical Celtic cross contains all the platonic solids. We are thus working with the building blocks of our physical plane, along with the elemental building blocks, all directed by our cocreator consciousness in alignment with our plant spirit team. You can work with the basic prayers below at the start of each element to open your sacred space and develop it to incorporate your own spirit and plant allies of each direction. As you call in the elements to each direction of your work space, you will feel the energies amplify. You are calling in all that is through the lens of your particular plant. Everything that you experience during the session should be viewed through the perspective of the plant in the center of the wheel. This way of working is not entirely necessary; however, it can serve to make your prayers, intentions, and inner work much more powerful and effective. As you open your sacred work space, you become the medicine wheel: do not feel separate from this process. We are nature. We are already the body of Earth; her directions and elements are also our own.

To build and manifest our sacred and healing space, we invoke the energies and associated spirit allies from each of the directions. This is done through prayer and intention. The energies, beings, and plants that we call in from each direction should be the ones that we know, that we have relationships with, and that we trust. As you work through this book, the plants contained in part 2 can become your plant spirit allies with whom you can work in any of the directions you feel are appropriate for your working relationship with them. You can even draw a medicine wheel on paper and draw in your plant allies in their respective directions on the wheel, uniting your inner plant medicine wheel with your outer experience. This wheel of plants becomes our spirit team that we carry within us on our inner plane, and over time as our relationship to them deepens, their numbers will grow and our space will become stronger. Our healing work is able to go deeper, and our space can withstand more powerful opposing forces that may seek to thwart our work. There is no shortcut to this process; relationships with our spirit team take time to nurture but the rewards are life changing.

Once your directions have all been evoked, you can begin your meditation or journey with your plant. Creating space like this for yourself and for your ally gives clear indication to spirit that you are dedicated and sincere, which will increase the effectiveness of your inner work.

When you have completed your inner work and any other ritual aspects you wish to incorporate, bring the sacred space to a close by thanking all the spirits who have held you safe and release them should they wish to be released (some spirits may have more work to do after your ceremony has finished). As you open sacred space you will notice as outlined below that you will start in the east, the place of the rising sun, and finish with below, the direction of earth. When you close sacred space it is advisable to wind backward through each direction starting with the below and ending in the east. We are thus reversing the casting of our sacred space spell. If you are meditating outdoors, you may feel that opening a sacred space is not necessary; however, as we are the medicine wheel, that natural orientation to our place on Earth can still be invoked to ensure you are grounded and protected.

Plants in Their Element

We have all experienced the raw elements in their full expression. I grew up in Cornwall with my bedroom facing the Atlantic Ocean, where wild winter storms would whip up the waves until they crashed over the houses on the shore. The seas would churn huge boulders onto the beaches and move vast amounts of sand, creating dunes within a matter of hours, but in the summer these same beaches would be full of tourists slowly turning red like lobsters in the fiery heat of the sun. The light that the elements created in my hometown of St. Ives was so unique that it has attracted many artists since the late nineteenth century until eventually the Tate Gallery moved in to capitalize on the natural qualities of the town, thus transforming a sleepy and picturesque fishing town into the most expensive tourist destination in the UK. I grew up appreciating the creative and destructive power of the elements.

Everything you see about you and within you, in both the physical and nonphysical worlds, is made of the five elements in varying degrees and expressions. From a physical perspective this book is made from the earth body of a tree, which grew thanks to the raw fire of the sun, the water of the rain, and the carbon dioxide of the air. This book and the tree are located in the space of this physical realm, as well as the etheric realm; everything has an etheric version of itself, an even subtler form of the elements. The elements express themselves in more and more subtle ways and on finer dimensions until, as described in Tibetan Buddhism, they become the five colored lights, the origin of the elements and therefore the origin of our entire existence. Entropy and the death process work in this direction, from Earth to space. The opposite, that of creation and manifestation, starts in the fine, subtle, nonphysical dimensions and filters down into more and more gross levels of existence. Our own birth process works in this way as does disease in the body and anything we imagine and create with our hands. The elements become more and more dense as they descend or move into manifestation in this world of form.

The elements exist on all levels of density: for example, fire exists on the spiritual, mental, emotional, and physical dimensions. We carry the subtle elements within us that behave in the same way as they do in the external world. You are reading this book by the power of the inner air of your mind, made flexible and moveable by your subtle inner water. The words are perceived through the earth body of your eyes and brain, able to be understood by the eternal space of the soul. Even your dreams, visions, and emotions are made from the elements. Have you ever wondered where the light in your dreams was coming from with no discernible light source? How is it possible to picture the face of your beloved when the sun that provides your light is external to you? It is the inner fire element working through the air element that moves and illuminates your inner vision. Yet without a firm earth element to manifest and ground them, dreams and clairvoyant visions are vague and forgettable. All the elements work in unison within every aspect of both physical and nonphysical phenomena.

The underlying creation process of our known universe is fractal; therefore, every aspect and element can also be broken down into the five elements over and over again, ad infinitum. The blood of our body is one of the physical expressions of our water element, and upon closer inspection, blood, itself, is made from the five elements: its flowing quality and plasma is its subtle water, its ability to coagulate is its subtle earth, the hemoglobin is its fire, the ability to change (purification, color, density, etc.) is its subtle air, and its ability to reach into the far reaches of our capillaries is its space element. Each one of these qualities of the blood can be broken down again into subtler forms of the five elements.

In the transformational practice of Tibetan tantra, the five inner elements correspond to the five main pranas or life-force energies that power and animate the body and mind, and the five main negative emotions also correlate to the elements. Tenzin Wangyal Rinpoche states that through visualization, mantra, and certain meditations, these emotions are transformed into their opposite: "anger into love, greed into generosity, jealousy into openness, pride into peace and ignorance into wisdom. The suffering being is transformed into the enlightened buddha."[1] The elements and their imbalances show us how we relate and respond to the world.

We all carry imbalances within our inner elements; if we were born completely balanced, we would already be enlightened. Our karma manifests as these imbalances, so perhaps we will never achieve complete equilibrium in this lifetime, if indeed an end point such as enlightenment or complete equilibrium even exists, but we can reduce how much the scale is tipped in one direction or another and therefore reduce our suffering and that which we inflict upon others.

In just the same way that we are built from physical and nonphysical elements, so are the plants. Understanding how the elements are expressed in their own unique way through each plant or tree goes partway to understanding the particular plant with which you are working and how it interacts with you personally. Every plant or tree is made of every element, and this can initially be seen to correspond to a different physical part of the plant. The roots are the earth element, the stem the water element that carries the sap to the leaves, which are the air element. The shape and contour that the plant takes, the blueprint of which is also contained within the seed, is its space element, and the fire is the flower and its medicine. On the subtler planes we find that each plant or tree has an affinity or a stronger correspondence with one or two of the elements, providing us with much information and indications as to its medicine and to the nature of its spirit. Dandelion, for example, expresses both the earth and air elements in powerful ways. Its deep tap root and its affinity with the liver demonstrate its earth element. The way it quickly transforms from flower to seed clock overnight demonstrates its air element. From this we can already deduce that the spirit of Dandelion will be a powerful ally for manifesting precise and powerful changes within our body and the psyche. Lady's mantle expresses the water element in its affinity with the sacral chakra and to the feminine through association with the planet Venus, demonstrating the quality of its spirit as a guide through the transformation of the emotional realm. The elements help us start to remember and learn the language of the plants.

The healing qualities of the plants exist within all the elements, and we cultivate and deepen our relationship with the plant spirits by working with the elements of their medicine. By growing plants or sitting and meditating with the plants, we are connecting to their earth element, the element most easy for us to connect to and therefore the one on which we must build a firm foundation for our cocreative relationship. It is tempting to bypass this part of the process and want to move to the transcendental air experience, yet without manifest earth our experiences become abstract and are not embodied. Ritual is the grounding of the plant spirits into our earth body so that we feel their presence as we physically draw sacredness through ceremony, offerings, and the medicine wheel.

Once we have spent time with the physical plants, we can move into their water element. These are the medicines that each plant carries and the medicines that we can make with them. The medicines themselves can also be categorized into their own elements; however, as an overarching theme, the tinctures, essences, teas, and hydrosols of the plants offer us the healing and cleansing that the water element brings. These medicines also act as mediator between the physical and the emotional bodies as we move into the transformational fire element. Recognizing the changes in the waters of the body as the medicines heal us is highlighted in the emotional changes that also occur. The fire is burning away the negativity in our energy system and igniting motivation to change and move toward emotional balance. We often spend a lot of time in this place with our plant allies as we are complex beings and it takes time to reveal the true light of the soul, encased in the solidity of the ego. It is only through conscious engagement with the plant spirits and how they heal us that we can understand their own soul force as it moves through our own. After a period of time (and every person and every plant is different), we emerge into the air element where communication with the plant ally is through direct perception and so swift that its physical medicines are no longer required and a working partnership through the direct communication of soul forces creates the causes and conditions for natural magic for transformation and healing.

As we cultivate our inner garden by creating our team of plant spirit allies and our inner landscape expands, working with the elements helps us to relate inner to outer so that we don't lose ourselves in the magical world that is opening up to us but remain grounded in the physical and the self.

As we are all unique in our capabilities, it is best to learn directly from the plants about how to effectively hold sacred space. While the basics are outlined in this chapter, these skills emerge as part of the unfolding of the inward journey. The plants and trees teach us about our own energetic capacities (or lack thereof) and the refinement of our inner senses takes place. Working through the structure of the medicine wheel as a container for all sacred work with the plant and tree spirits strengthens the inner sacred space and therefore the sacred space that we hold. One reflects the other. If you are not balanced within your inner elements, your sacred space holding for others will have doorways through which unhelpful energies can enter to cause disruption.

The Seven Directions of the Sacred Medicine Wheel

The objective of the following exercises is to learn the qualities of each direction and element, to recognize them within yourself, and to see where and how your imbalances exist for each one and how you can build your plant medicine wheel. Generally, most people have one or two main elements that are out of balance, either carrying too much or too little. Relating to the elements within ourselves, we look at the emotions, our general state of mind, our personality, and the types of experience we have in meditation. By familiarizing ourselves with each of the elements, we can easily discern our imbalances and work toward equilibrium through the plants, which strengthens our energy field and allows our senses to sharpen, our intuition to align with every moment, and our unique gifts to awaken and evolve.

The seven directions consist of the five elements plus the directions of above and below. Please use this system with the honor and respect it deserves; it is an ancient practice with a lineage of ancestors whose energies still work through it. It should not be used lightly or without careful consideration to ensure the integrity of its practice is not diminished.

East, Air

> *I call to the east*
> *To the rising sun, to the springtime and to new*
> *beginnings*
> *Home of the sylphs and the great birds of the skies*
> *Place of the visionary plants and trees*
> *I call on you now to bless and hold my sacred space*
> *today*
> *Blessed be*

East is associated with the element of air as both share the same qualities and correspondences. The freshness of spring and of Earth bursting into life and into a new cycle of creation is the ideal metaphor for this direction. East offers us the chance to plant the seeds of new creations with the far-reaching vision of birds of prey who glide high in the sky on currents of air. Spring is the perfect time to launch new projects after having dreamed them in through the dark night of winter. Ever-moving air is a vital element in our quest for transformation as it supports change and flexibility.

Air is associated with the conscious mind, sound, and communication. Master herbalist Sajah Popham states that "it's common in many plants for communication to occur with neighbouring botanicals, insects, and animals through the volatile compounds from the leaves into the Air, carrying chemical messages to the rest of the ecosystem. In this way leaves are a highly important aspect of plant-to-plant communication."[2] Plants associated with the air element tend to be tall and fine, gentle and spacious in their structure, which is reflected in the characteristics of the spirits of the plants who tend to be more elusive and more ethereal than those with stronger earth or fire elements.

Air plants usually have affinities with the respiratory and nervous systems; some calm and some stimulate, depending on requirement. Plants of the air realm tend to support the throat chakra and the expression of our truth as well as the crown chakra and our connection to the Upper World. They are connected to the workings of the mind and therefore the energy field, cleansing and purifying to assist in our clear seeing. Lemon balm (*Melissa officinalis*) is an example of this type of plant whose spirit is purifying and protective in this regard. Some healers carry a sprig of lemon balm when they venture into cities as it collects the unhelpful energies and toxic psychic debris that are ubiquitous there, helping to keep their own energy field clean. Lemon balm is a calmative and can assist with an inner air imbalance after shock, releasing the unhelpful energies in the field to move you out of what can feel like being stuck and paralyzed in that state. Its air element produces the flexibility for change.

A balanced inner air element allows us to stay out of polarization, to remain centered and recognize both sides of any given situation without being pulled into good or bad, better or worse, light or dark. A strong air element supports a flexible and quick mind so we can understand things from many angles and relate to others through an appreciation of their perspective. The qualities of air can sometimes be confused with water where both in their balanced states offer flow and ease. The difference being that water is very much associated with emotions and air with the mind. Too little air means we can easily become stuck in our problems unable to transform or think from a new perspective. We feel trapped and cornered by life situations; our ability to relate to others is compromised. Too much air means we float around, never getting things finished nor committing to anything. A dominant air element allows space for worries and concerns to come in because we're ungrounded and disconnected from the stability of our inner earth element.

The air element supports expanded awareness and consciousness as we experience smells, sensations, and messages carried on the winds. My most enlivening experience of the air element is the smell of damp air first thing on a spring morning. This sensation evokes nostalgia for the innocent days of life as it carries the purity of nature into us. I can smell the wood of the trees in the forest, the sweetness of the spring flowers, the excitedness of the hidden mushrooms, the freshness of the stream close to the house. The air element brings awareness of all of our environment from the horizon into our center. Sometimes I can step out of the car on arrival to a new place and immediately smell the sea on the wind, even if I am thirty minutes inland. The spirits of nature carried in the air are translated through sensation by the light of the soul, and their meaning is revealed.

Embodying the Air Element Meditation

Any meditation that involves the breath or breath work supports the balance and purification of the inner air element; however, as the most refined element after space, it can be for some the most difficult to relate to. For this reason, it is helpful to work with the raw element of air outside. You might think you already know what air feels from likely feeling the wind or a breeze many times during your lifetime, but I encourage you to be more consciously present in and aware of the air element the next time you are outside when it is windy: concentrate on the wind itself and invite it into yourself. This is a very different experience and supports shifts in consciousness. Without the air element we could not develop on our path as the mind would be rigid. My husband spends hours in the forest listening to the wind as it brings news from far-off places and informs him of energies coming our way. Wind listening deepens our connection to the subtle realms of the elements as well as to the great web.

On a day when it is windy, find a place where you can quietly sit outside without being disturbed, perhaps a hilltop or your back garden.

Bring your attention to the breath for a few minutes as you settle into your space. Feel the powerful air element all around you and invite it into you. Let your mind wander over the qualities and aspects of the air as you feel it in, upon, and around you. Feel the freedom that air brings, the lightness that pervades your body and mind when you merge with it. Do not get lost in the air. Always keep a sense of yourself during any practice but allow the air to cleanse the conditionings of the mind and bring flexibility to your thoughts. Expand your awareness out to the horizon and allow the smells, sensations, memories, and thoughts to arise within you as you allow the air element into your center. Simply watch and observe. After at least ten minutes, bring yourself back by opening your eyes gently.

Prayer and Clearing Practice with Air

A simple and effective method to send prayers to the Great Spirit or the Divine—or whatever construct you use to conceptualize all that is or to release a particular energy from yourself that has served its purpose—is to take some dried plant leaves, state your prayer or intention into them, and blow them into the wind, requesting the wind to carry them to all four corners of Earth. Any plants are fine; however, air plants such as elecampane, lavender, maple, or hazel are more suitable. The head of a dandelion that has gone to seed is fun to use and reminds us of the magic that we believed in as children. Make sure your prayers are clear and concise like arrows, as that is how you need them to be recognized and returned. Lengthy, rambling prayers send distorted and often contradictory messages to the universe and therefore having them answered is less likely.

South, Fire

> *I call to the south*
> *Home of the salamanders, the midday sun, of the*
> *   summertime and the goddess of fire*
> *You give us the creativity and passion that ignites our*
> *   hearts and minds*

I call on you now to bless and hold my sacred space
    today
  Blessed be

South brings the heat of the summer and the warmth of the fire that keeps us warm at night. It is the energy and vitality, brightness and creativity that we bring to our work and our projects. The power of the south is strong and forthright. It keeps us safe and confident, allowing spontaneity to flow and our sense of self to be expressed.

We are born of fire and water: the spark of spirit catalyzes the main fire organ, the heart, to develop as the first functioning organ within the amniotic fluid of our mother's womb. Fire needs a container and a counterbalance to keep it in check. Earth is its opposite, holding and grounding the fire, preventing a volcano from forming. Water pacifies and prevents fire from going out of control. The solar plexus chakra holds the inner fire element and feeds all the other chakras, the energy field and the mind with light and vitality. Fire is seen as a life force in itself, a process rather than an actual thing, an adjective rather than a noun. It constantly consumes in order to reproduce itself, both being born and dying in every moment. It is the symbol of life itself.

Fire is one of the most misunderstood elements and evokes polarity in us. Meditating on this element can bring up fear of its destructive and painful quality yet we know we could not survive without its warmth and light to cook our food and heat and illuminate our houses; we are blessed to have the sun manifest here on Earth with us. Feared by its association with destruction, we have forgotten the true nature of fire as a creator and teacher of purification and transformation. Without fire our inner water cannot be transformed into visions. The alchemical transmutation of the inner fire into spiritual fire is the objective of the great work and relates to the spiritual body of our energy field being reborn into conscious awareness. Learning to sit in the middle of these two extremes with peace is key to balancing our inner fire and therefore our acceptance of the changing aspects of our lives. Inner fire is not only the power of the digestive system and the warmth of the blood but the passion and creativity that fuel our life and the light that illuminates the mind. Fire is the only element that has heat, and without it we would be cold, lifeless, and spiritless. Some of the ancient mystery schools considered fire to be the archetypal substance of all things. Rudolf Steiner stated that "the force which is physically active in fire lives on a higher plane in the human soul, which melts in its crucible mere sense-knowledge, so that out of this contemplation the eternal may arise."[3]

Fire plants tend to be strong and transformational. They may sting our skin and mouths and have thorns; they are powerful medicine. In herbalism they are generally used to bring warmth and movement to cold, damp, and stagnant tissue. They detoxify us on the physical, energetic mental levels. Wormwood, for example, is a powerful cleansing fire plant that shifts physical, etheric, and astral parasites from the body and energy field. Ginger is a general cleanser for the body; by stimulating the digestive and circulatory systems, it helps to rid the organs of toxins. On an energetic level ginger removes heavy energy and toxic psychic phenomenon from the energy field. This then purifies the mind and brings clarity of inner vision. Tinctures are considered fire medicines because alcohol is used to extract the active chemicals from the plants. It is therefore not advisable to use tinctures if you carry too much inner fire element.

The inner fire element is stored in the solar plexus chakra, which provides fuel for the heart with the passion and love that it requires to nurture the soul and live a life of balance between our true nature and the external world around us. Balanced inner fire means we are content with joining others in team work and are naturally joyous for no reason. Enthusiasm infuses our action, and we experience the bliss of simply being alive. The inner fire element in the Tibetan Buddhist tradition is mastered through a practice called *tummo*, which means "inner fire." Monks who practice this technique can, by meditating on their third chakra, raise their body's temperature, enabling them to survive freezing nighttime temperatures on top of a mountain while wearing only a thin robe. We do not have to go to this extreme to understand fire; we need only acknowledge and welcome it through our spirit as it transforms everything into harmony.

Too much fire in the energy system makes us quick tempered, unstable, and irritable. It creates too much yang energy, which causes us to push our energy onto others. It precludes us from being a good listener or allowing others the space to express themselves as we hog the limelight. An overactive fire mind makes sleep and meditation difficult. Full of ideas with no way to ground them, excessive fire people can become trapped in loops of unfinished projects. They quickly tire of a project and become annoyed and stressed because, in their impatience for a quick result, they feel they are wasting time. They soon move on to the next thing, hoping for a different outcome.

Deficient inner fire results in a lack of inspiration for anything, including the spiritual path. A marked lack of inspiration means life can devolve into soul-destroying routines with no creativity.

Embodying the Fire Element Meditation

There are two ways that you can perform the following meditation, either working with an actual fire or with the father of fire, the sun. Either way is fine, although sensible precautions must be taken with both.

Find a quiet spot on a sunny day or next to a fire and feel the warmth of the fire on your skin; allow it to relax you and bring you into the present moment. Invite the fire element into your body and mind, feel it penetrate through the skin, the bones, the marrow, the veins, the muscles, and the organs. Feel the fire moving throughout your body, circulating with the blood and burning away any blockages and negativities held in the body. Feel how alive and pleasurable the fire is, how it fills you with light and bliss. If you are meditating with an actual fire, gaze into the fire for a few minutes (not into the sun) and watch how it shape-shifts, how it color shifts and interacts with the air yet how it relies on the earth for its manifestation.

Prayer and Clearing Practice with Fire

All the elements are purifying in some way. Fire is a powerful cleanser; it can transmute unhelpful energies. Take some dried plant leaves and infuse them with anything you wish to let go of. This could be an unhelpful thought pattern, situation, or problem. Cast the leaves into a fire, asking the spirit of the fire to take your troublesome issue directly to the Great Spirit for transformation. Over time, the issue will either dissipate, or you will be presented with the means to overcome it. You just have to be receptive enough to recognize what has been offered. Fire plants that are more suited to this practice include sacred tobacco, angelica, oak, and cedar.

West, Water

> *I call to the west*
> *Land of the setting sun, of harvest time and the fishes*
>   *of the great rivers and seas*
> *Place of the undines and the ocean-going mammals*
> *I call on you now to bless and hold my sacred space*
>   *today*
> *Blessed be*

Water is associated with the direction of west. They both share the qualities of the autumn, the moon, and the feminine yin energies that draw us inward at the end of the day. The west invites us to start to turn inward and be thankful for the spring and summer where our energies have been spent. What are the results of all of our efforts through the yang time of the year? How can we hold the newly learned or acquired energies as we prepare for our descent into the composting earth of winter? This quality of drawing in can be directly experienced when we immerse ourselves in water and are instantaneously taken into a dream-like space or into a reverie. Water is the most magical and mysterious of the elements as it can embody other elements: as ice it becomes solid like earth, as steam it becomes like air. Within a molecule of water, the oxygen atom favors a negative charge while the hydrogen atom holds a positive charge, which attract each other to create an interconnected crystalline molecular structure. The inner architecture of water therefore attracts and holds influencing energies from its surroundings, such as memories, emotions, and even thoughts. Water favors integration and repatterning of our inner world. It is magical in that we can manifest our becoming through it and be reborn while still alive in this life because water flows through our bodies: we are mainly made from water and the air we breathe contains it. The seas and rivers around and through our lands are the lifeblood of Earth. We, ourselves, are approximately 60 percent water. We are effectively water beings.

Ocean waves are the only means of visually experiencing the movement of earth energy (unless you have witnessed a volcano exploding or been in an earthquake), and we flock to the beach to soak up this revitalizing energy that surges through the sands. The waters of the world are the emotional body of Gaia. They express her innermost thoughts; they capture her grief in raindrops and her joy in the rivers and streams. Water allows our bodies to move and our senses and organs to function; without it we would be rigid. Our world is illuminated by the light of the sun refracted through the water contained within the air. Similarly, our consciousness is illuminated through the water contained within our body and senses. Water is both a carrier and an enabler of consciousness.

Associated with the sacral chakra and therefore with fertility, germination, and new life, we are born out of the amniotic waters of the womb. The divine spark of life carried within the fire element is translated into matter through water. Our emotions are held and sometimes trapped within the waters of the body, yet they can be cleansed and released through working with the same inner element.

As an expression of consciousness, our inner water element helps us to flow through life with ease and be comfortable in the company of others as we can accommodate and accept all that they bring. A balanced inner water element supports freedom from stress, worry, and constriction, allowing better and unobstructed connection to our intuition. The subtle inner elements are a great framework through which to understand our inner experiences as we relate to the outer world, where the inner imbalances exist, helping us identify what needs to be addressed to establish balance once again. Through this process we can support physical vitality, emotional freedom, and self-mastery.

In the Celtic tradition water holds a special place as a symbol of the veil between this world and the Otherworld, an opaque division through which we can glimpse the distant shores of other realms. Wells and springs are portals of healing and wisdom, each manifesting its own devic spirit or guardian. The merfolk and the undines are beings from the watery realms of this tradition. The great sea god Manannan Mac Lir is known to have pulled the veil down between our world and the Otherworld and stands as a guardian between the two worlds, as well as of the seas around the British Isles. Water guardians are usually feminine in nature, such as the well maidens and the goddess protectors of lakes; perhaps this indicates an older maternal aspect of our ancient sea god Manannan from the time before the patriarchal system in which we now live.

Experiencing the Water Element Meditation

Conscious immersion in water is the most effective way for embodying the water element. Wild swimming is ideal, but if this is not possible then a bath will also be effective. Float in the water, notice how the water feels against the skin, and invite that feeling inside, onto the inner planes and into the realm of the imagination. Feel the gentle movement externally and internally at the same time. Feel your subtle inner water element along with your blood and the waters of your body all blend into one. Alternatively sit next to a stream or waterfall and lose yourself in the sounds of its flow.

Prayer and Clearing Practice with Water

Any unhelpful energy or issue that you feel you are ready to let go after learning the lessons it has brought for you or anything that you wish to transform in your life can be blessed by the power of the element of water. Speak your truth into the dried leaves of water plants, although any plant can work, and cast the leaves into moving water, such as a stream or river. Ask the devic spirit of water or the undines as well as your plants to carry your prayers to the four directions and transform them into the most appropriate form. Mallow, elm, seaweeds, and black-berry would work well.

North, Earth

> I call to the north
> Place of the darkness of winter, of midnight and of the
>   dream time
> Place of our ancestors who love, honor and respect us
> Place of the Otherworld and our plant spirit allies
> I call on you now to bless and hold my sacred space
>   today
> Blessed be

After an exhilarating journey around the wheel, we take our last step into the north, which turns us inward. The medicine of the north is a pilgrimage into the darkness of our interiority, into the depths of our physical body at the stroke of midnight. Within the blood and bones are the memories of our ancestors; between the sinews and the muscles we find our past dreams and inherited gifts and traumas. Breathing in the wind of the north infuses us with the energy of the Otherworld and the wisdom of our plant allies. The north encompasses both the physical and nonphysical realms; it overlaps our physical world just as we exist in both physical and nonphysical bodies (the auric field can be subdivided into layers and bodies of existence). The words *matter* and *mother* have the same Latin root *matr,* showing us clearly that Earth is our mother who offers us nourishment, support, rest, and recuperation. The north also corresponds with the deepest part of winter when our energy levels drop from the expressiveness of the summer, and we retreat like the hibernating animals, to drift into the dreamworld and incubate plans for the following year.

The earth of north is solid, holding, stable, and reliable. Like a mother with her baby, Earth protects and envelops us with a loving embrace. Our physical body is the expression of our inner earth element and is a gift bestowed upon our spirit from Mother Earth herself. Illness is expressed through our earth body, the symptoms of disease notifying us that something is out of balance within our energetic body. The earth element is the last stop on the road to manifestation. Therefore, symptoms are the results of imbalances within the unmanifest dimensions; they are not the disease itself. Symptoms provide the evidence of the inner elemental imbalance, for example, a rash or inflammation denotes too much inner fire and potentially a lack of earth.

Plants of the north direction have affinities with our bodily earth organs, such as the liver, skeleton, blood, and stomach. They are highly nourishing and often bitter as they stimulate and purge the digestive and cleansing systems of the body, such as the lymphatic system. Earth plants ground us and align us back to our center; they encourage sympathy and compassion for others and for oneself.

Too much inner earth can make us lethargic, unmotivated, and uninspired. We can be compelled to drag our feet or kick the can down the road and avoid responsibilities. Depression and being stuck in a rut can be results of too much heavy earth. As earth acts as a container for the other elements, too little earth can knock all the other elements out of balance. The results of this imbalance will be unique to yourself; however, the root chakra will often exhibit compromised functionality, so this is a good place to start to restore balance. An inability to finish what has been started, a lack of concentration, unclear inner vision, and a lack of self-confidence are all consequences of a lack of inner earth element. We can also become ungrounded both energetically and spiritually with a deficiency of this essential element.

Embodying the Earth Element Meditation

Sit on the floor or in a chair and face north. Imagine a circle around you. Feel the weight of your body in your seat; feel where all the parts of your body touch one another, such as your arms against your waist or your feet against your legs. Now bring to mind that your body is of the earth element, just as the chair you are sitting on and the ground beneath your feet are of the earth element: they are all the same. You are no different from the land on which you sit. Feel how you are not separate from the ground or the chair. Feel at one with everything physical that touches you. Then bring that feeling inward, into the center of your being.

Prayer and Clearing Practice with Earth

Despacho is a South American tradition during which beautiful mandalas are created from seeds, plant products, foods, and crystals, each representing an element and infused with a strong prayer for Mother Earth. The mandala is then buried or burned. Having participated in many despacho ceremonies, I can testify to their power, with prayers sometimes manifesting within twenty-four hours. In much the same way, we can bury our prayers and intentions in plant matter, asking Mother Earth to receive and transform that which no longer serves us. Connect deeply to the holy heart of the Great Mother: she will hear our prayers and help where appropriate.

Space (Ether), Center
> *I call to the inner void, the space of my own truth and*
> *   inner knowing*
> *The place of deep calm and wisdom*
> *I call on you now to be present and to hold my healing*
> *   space today*
> *Blessed be*

The point in the center of the medicine wheel where the vertical and horizontal axes cross creates a portal for the emergence of the space element, containing the potential for all the other elements. The magical place from which everything manifests into this realm is the creatrix or womb of life. The space element as emptiness or the void can be a challenging aspect to wrap our logical minds around because of its contradictory and paradoxical nature. No-thing-ness exists at the center of everything and yet doesn't exist at all. It provides pure potentiality for existence. We therefore can only point toward it; we cannot directly point it out. In other words, we cannot put into conceptual words that which is nonconceptual. The only way that the Tibetan Buddhists could explain this aspect of reality was through negation: it is what it is not, emptiness as the absence of form. In the native wisdom of the British Isles, this liminal space is where magic is born: it is the space between everything, the Great Mother who births everything into being. It guarantees our continuity as the great web is constantly born and reborn at every moment. The center of the galaxy is the great Cosmic Mother, and the center of Earth is the womb of Gaia.

As you would expect, space is unbounded and free, vast and nonlocal. The true nature of the mind is therefore related to the space element, it being awareness itself. Within the chakra system the throat chakra is associated with this element, the place of our psychic perceptions into all known and unknown space. The throat chakra is also the expression of thought into manifest sound, thus transforming space into form, awareness into communication with the other.

We relate to our inner space element through the direct perception of our own consciousness. The awareness of awareness meditation in chapter 4 is therefore the most powerful way to balance our inner space. Inner space will always be in balance if the rest of the elements are in balance, so another way to master this element is to work with the plants to balance all your other elements by working through your issues and blockages. Balanced inner space means a balanced outer space where we are able to manage our life without stress. Too much inner space results in being ungrounded and spaced out, unable to connect to others or to our daily experiences in a constructive or direct way. On the other hand, too little space leaves us vulnerable to being overwhelmed: small issues seem insurmountable, and we have no time for our children or our meditation practice. When a problem arises the mind becomes constricted, and we feel that we cannot break free of the perceived limitations.

Plants with a dominant space element are often ones that affect and alter consciousness in a very tangible way. Commonly known as psychoactive plants, these plants reflect consciousness and its blockages or *samskaras* in a distinct and observable way through visions. Of course, all plants affect the mind to some degree; some are simply more dramatic in their effect. The space aspect of the plant itself is the seed, containing the potential and pattern of the whole plant or tree.

Embodying the Space Element Meditation

In the ancient tradition of Dzogchen, the practice of sky gazing is recommended to balance the inner space element.[4] Find a place where you have an expansive view of the sky such as a hilltop on a clear day. Clouds are OK but not complete cloud coverage; otherwise you will not experience the vastness of the sky. In a relaxed state simply gaze into the open sky and feel into the freedom and experience of infinity that this evokes. There is space before you and also within you. Allow the dissolution of anything you are holding tightly to, including the ideas you have about yourself. Negativity and stress can be released within minutes, assisting the embodiment of inner subtle space. Whenever I practice sky gazing, I feel as if I am staring into the depths of my own mind, the sky as a reflection of the vastness of my own consciousness. Both outer space and inner space feel the same, and this is incredibly liberating.

The Sixth and Seventh Directions

The sixth and seventh directions within the medicine wheel are above and below. The wheel is in reality spherical not flat, and so all aspects need to be acknowledged and evoked to establish and maintain strong and safe sacred space. The Upper World is the home of the celestial beings, the high elves, the sun, the Buddhas, the bodhisattvas, and the cosmic star families. Below is Pachamama, Gaia, and rock and crystal beings. We are honored to share existence with these amazing beings, and we invite them into our healing space to support our inner work.

Integrating the Medicine Wheel with the Plants

To effectively work with the plants for inner transformation and ultimately self-mastery, we need to understand the inner energy imbalances that we are dealing with and how this relates to the plants. Inner is a reflection of outer, so we can work with outer correspondences to effect change on the inner planes through the medium of the medicine wheel. You do not have to take the medicine wheel route; you could simply work with any plant and do the protocols and meditations in this book to get to know it and yourself better. The meditations and plant workings are effective within and of themselves, but the addition of the medicine wheel into your processes increases the effectiveness of your work by aligning you to the cyclical nature of reality and helps you understand and integrate changes in your life on many dimensions and levels. This is stepping into natural magic, and your life will expand both inward and outward in unexpected and unimaginable ways. There are many ways to work with and integrate the medicine wheel into your life; however, they all are based on an understanding of the elements and their associated energies. How we integrate the wheel into our meditations, projects, and life intentions is our choice. We can concentrate on one element, or if we are working through the year or on a long-term project, we can move our intention around the wheel, depending on where we are within the process and where we want to go next.

See the table on pages 120–21 relating the plants in this book with outer correspondences and inner elemental states. This gives you a starting point for your work and guidance on where to place items on the medicine wheel, which plants to assist with your inner transformation, and the direction within the psyche that the inner work will go.

Symbols of Nature

Symbolism is the language of nature, of the astral realm and the subconscious mind. Energies, impulses, insights, and messages come to us through this nonlinguistic medium. In the healing world of plants and within the alchemical system of self-liberation, the doctrine of correspondences and the doctrine of signatures can assist with the translation of symbology and their interconnections. First compiled by the great Paracelsus, there have been many useful doctrines of correspondences written over the centuries, and we can even create our own. This magical system of reading the web of life is not set in stone and can evolve over time, as well as through the evolving consciousness of humans themselves. It proves a useful tool for relating the esoteric with the exoteric, the inner with the outer for clarification and manifestation. For what use are our inner experiences if they cannot be brought into our Middle World life for our and others' benefit? As Rudolf Steiner notes: "Things are clothed in pictures of form and colour, and through imagination we must ourselves 'unriddle' the beings who are showing themselves to us in symbols."[5]

The doctrine of correspondences lays out the energetic framework of aspects of our world, such as the planets, the gods and goddesses, the elements, the animals, and the days of the week in correlation to one another. Objects are analyzed for their attributable energies that connect or associate them with something else in the cosmos, each carrying a resonance of the other. As a basic example, Venus carries the love vibration, so if we wanted to feel more love in our life or heal a broken heart, we would turn to Venus and perhaps her associated plants such as hawthorn or rose. If we want to find more inner peace and pacify inner turmoil, we might think of the deep yin energies of water and the peaceful feminine moon to guide us toward a plant such as lemon balm and the inner soothing that she offers. We find the plant that can help stimulate the natural healing response of the body and energy field to bring it back to homeostasis, through complementary means. This methodology of working is fundamental to working with nature and to understanding natural and sympathetic magic.

Chakra	Element	Attributes	Too much of the element	Too little of the element	Spiritual	Plants/Trees	Planet
Root / Muladhara	Earth	Birth / Nourishment / Abundance / Acceptance / Balance / Comfort / Smell & Touch / Sensuality / Manifestation / Support / Ordinary Life / Confidence / Mother	Overindulgence / Laziness / Depression / Stuck in a rut/ Resignation / Lack of dreams / Ignorance	Disconnection from others / Non-commitment / Anxiety / Agitation / Ungrounded / Dissatisfaction	Nature spirits / Wisdom / Death / The Otherworld / Dragons / Silence	Oak / Rosemary / Burdock/ Mugwort / Mullein / Sage / Vervaine / Elder / Holly / Rowan / Juniper	Earth Saturn Venus
Sacral / Svadhisthana	Water	The unconscious / Emotions / Empathy / Creativity / Ease of being / Adaptability / Inspiration / Joy / Innate contentment / Sexuality/ Taste/ Fertility	Over emotional / Floating along/ Lack of responsibility/ Lack of productivity	Loss of appetite / Lack of joy / Lack of spiritual commitment	Mystery / Magic / Life / Undines / Merfolk / Divination / Dreams / Memory	Lady's Mantle / Alder / Beech / Willow / Yew / Lotus / Meadowsweet / Skullcap	Moon Mercury Neptune Pluto
Solar Plexus / Manipura	Fire	Yellow/ Willpower / Self-esteem / Action / Achievement / Presence / Enthusiasm / Excitement / Inspiration / Bliss / Discernment / Focus	Agitation / Anger / Impulsivity / Lashing out/ Restlessness / Lack of tolerance / Lack of grounding / Sleep issues / Erratic mind	Lack of energy & enthusiasm / Lack of vitality / Lifeless routine / Uncreative	Universal life-force / Intuition / Visions / Clairvoyance / Blessings/ Purification / Transformation	Fireweed / Dandelion/ Angelica / Holy Basil / Primrose / St John's Wort/ Hawthorn / Elder / Oak/ Cedar / Walnut	Sun Jupiter Mars

Chakra	Element	Attributes	Too much of the element	Too little of the element	Spiritual	Plants/Trees	Planet
Heart / Anahata	Air	Harmony / Love / Compassion / Connection / Green / Change / Curiosity / Intellect / Smell / Father / Fresh / Light / Communicative / Flexibility of mind	Lack of stability / Lack of focus / Worry / Uncertainty / Uncentered	Lack of focus or progress / Inability to transform /	True center / Interconnectedness / Soul / Connection to the divine / Rebirth / Wisdom / Unconditional love / Sylphs / Elves / Fae / Astral realm	Dandelion / Mugwort / Lavender / Mistletoe / Pine / Plantain / Hazel	Jupiter Mercury Uranus
Throat / Vishuddha	Space / Ether	Sound / Blue / Truth / Expression / Balanced mundane life / Tolerance / Emotional balance / Openness / Unity	Spacey / lack of connection to other elements / Superficiality / Lack of presence	Overwhelm / Other elements dominate	Spirit / Eternal spirit / Bridge between realms / Prayer / Song / Mantra / Spells	Angelica / Holy Basil / Yarrow / Elder / Thyme / Chamomile	Saturn
Third Eye / Ajna	Spiritual Fire	Conscience / Clarity / Gnosis / Connection / Balance / Strong imagination		Separateness / Doubt / Lack of trust in spirit / Sleep issues / Loneliness	Duality & nonduality/ Unconscious & conscious / Paradox / Oneness / Psychic ability / Intuition / Visions	Wormwood / Mugwort / Helichrysum / Violet	Venus Uranus Mercury
Crown / Sahasrara	Spiritual Space / The Void	All senses / All colors / Bliss / Boundless	Lack of boundaries in negative sense	Delusion	OM/ Pure consciousness / Divine connection / Enlightenment / Wisdom / Blessings	Angelica / Rose / Lavender / Chestnut	Neptune Saturn Uranus

Pythagoras taught that everything is vibration. "Each celestial body, in fact each and every atom, produces a particular sound on account of its movement, its rhythm or vibration. All these sounds and vibrations form a universal harmony in which each element, while having its own function and character, contributes to the whole."[6] All vibrations therefore arise within the entire universe because of and in sympathetic harmony to other vibrations. When working from the basis that everything is interconnected, that nothing can exist in isolation without interdependence on other causes and conditions for its existence, we can apply a system of correspondences to dive deeper into the meaning of situations, symbols, and actions. We can work with correspondences to understand our physical world around us, our inner experiences, and how to blend them into a coherent narrative for our spiritual development. With a basic understanding of the qualitative forces of the elements, the directions, the planets of our solar system, and our emotions, we can start to unlock hidden and deeper meaning within our dreams, visions, and life occurrences. We can then expand these correspondences out to include the attributes of archetypes, crystals, colors, animals, or whatever works for you. For example, when getting to know a plant spirit, it is useful to know its ruling planet, its predominant element, its associated chakras, and its organ affinities to better understand its physical, emotional, and spiritual medicine. Through these correspondences we can then interpret the impulses we receive in our meditations and better understand their relevance to us. Each chapter in part 2 explores the energetic framework of a particular plant or tree and translates that energy into a medicine that you can use for your own healing and awakening. This approach can be applied to all plants and trees.

For three years I suffered from eczema from head to toe, and it was only by working with the plants and meditation and through a series of correspondences that I managed to cure it. Within a week of naïvely attending my first ayahuasca ceremony with an unscrupulous shaman who had made a plant medicine so strong the grief of hundreds of lifetimes came rushing through me in a matter of hours, I broke out in chronic eczema. As an adult I had occasionally suffered with psoriasis on the back of my head, and as a child small patches of eczema would appear on my arms and behind my knees in the summer, so the signs of required healing were there, but the symptoms had not fully manifested. Following this plant medicine ceremony where my psychic channels were blown wide open, I hardly stopped crying for the following six months. It was the first three months of the eczema that were the worst as I woke up each night screaming with the pain of my body burning up from the inside and the overwhelming intensity of the itching skin. Nothing would relieve the fierce patches of weeping red skin down both arms and legs and across my chest. Allopathic creams only made it worse, and I became very aware that doctors simply do not understand the root causes of autoimmune issues or that applying chemical-based drugs to weeping skin does not bring relief!

The only thing that kept me sane at that time was meditation. I was studying for my master's degree in Italy at the time, and contemplation was part of the course. I discovered that all of the itching and burning sensations ceased when I reached a deeper level of meditational stillness, which also gave me the space I needed to analyze my situation and understand through a series of correspondences how I would find my cure.

I knew that the skin is known as the second lungs as it breathes and detoxifies in a similar way to the lungs. Through a rudimentary knowledge at that time of Traditional Chinese Medicine, I also knew that the lungs are associated with the emotion of grief and sorrow: according to TCM, unresolved or inherited emotions collect and are stored in the lungs. Because of all the crying I was experiencing, I suspected that unresolved trauma related to grief had manifested through my skin for healing. As someone with strong aspects of Virgo in my astrological birth chart, I process all my experiences through the body as my predominant element is earth. With such a severe case of eczema, I knew I was dealing with something potentially very transformational, but because the root cause or origin of this autoimmune issue was buried deep in my psyche, it would be very difficult to locate.

The next correspondent clue on my path to healing came through the plants. Hawthorn essence supports the heart, sorrow, inner freedom, and challenging situations. I began taking this essence, and through Hawthorn's inner guidance, I received insights into the nature and depth of my grief, helping me move toward the origin and key to the cure. I became aware of the sadness that my mother carried throughout her life, and through my strong bond with her, I had soaked up much of her sorrow as a child, which resulted in asthma. My absorption of her grief was facilitated by the existing condition of grief from my previous lives, which I started to understand as it bubbled to the surface through the hawthorn medicine. This soul trauma was the doorway for sorrow to be accepted into the depths of my psyche and then manifest in my body.

On a physical level, nettle was the only plant that could help me. I would sting my eczema with the nettles to alleviate the itching. The buzzing of the nettle sting replaced the itching (much more preferable!) by injecting antihistamine straight into the skin. Nettle is a fire plant and brings balance whether there is too much fire or too little. It calms the emotions and is associated with Scorpio, the zodiac sign known to brave the depths of the darkness in order to bring the light of clarity. Nettle was the perfect plant spirit ally on my quest. I needed to dive into the murky depths of my grief to find the hidden key to my predicament, and I prayed to the plant spirits to help me in my quest so that I could bring harmony and peace back into my life.

For three years I meditated, worked with plant spirits, and practiced qigong, trying to get to the root of my grief, but I continued to suffer from eczema. One day I decided to take a spoonful of cannabis butter, a beautiful psychoactive medicine that opens a healing space within. After just half an hour, I started to have what felt like a panic attack. I was being pulled out of my body and could not get back in as waves of intense energy coursed throughout my system. I shook my rattle, took grounding plants, and danced around the room, as my husband smudged me with mugwort. I was trying to stay focused on being here in my body and not losing consciousness. After an hour of trying to get a handle on what was going on, I became aware of the spirit of Cannabis through my inner vision. It said to me, "You have a choice.

You can either choose to be alive despite all the grief and heartache that life brings, or you can leave right now." In that moment I realized that deep down and all my life I had never really wanted to be here, incarnated into a world rife with pain and suffering. I realized in that instant that no matter where I was, no matter how joyous my present moment was, I had always wanted to be somewhere else, even if I didn't know where that place was. During all the best moments of my life, I had not been fully present, part of me was somewhere else. The spirit of Cannabis was giving me a choice between living life fully present or leaving this earthly realm and heading off to where I thought I wanted to be. I thought quickly but deeply about this. I was married to the love of my life, I had wonderful parents, and I felt that I had not fulfilled my purpose yet. I could not leave. I had found my core existential question that I had not yet answered. I made the decision to stay, the kind of decision called a *sangkulpa* in Sanskrit, which means "100 percent commitment with all the cells of the body." In that instant all the intense energies left my body, and my heart chakra burst open with love for life, with love for everything around me, and with love for the plants that had revealed to me the web of correspondences required to heal my mind, body, and soul. I felt a sense of presence like I had never felt before, and within a week, all traces of eczema left my body. It has never returned.

This is perhaps an extreme example, but one that emphasizes the power of the plants and the importance of meditation as a tool to access the origins of our issues and the usefulness of correspondences to work out a pathway to liberation. Gaining an understanding of our unresolved issues and emotions is paramount to spiritual development and self-liberation from illness. Unresolved traumas create blockages to the development of our inner world; only through their processing does our inner landscape become revealed. We are cultivating our inner garden. In the great work of the alchemists, we are revealing the inner kingdom.

By thinking and acting from a spacious, loving, free-flowing perspective, we can bring so much release to our spiritual, emotional, and therefore physical bodies. By expanding our consciousness into states that exist outside time and space and by reading the symbols presented to us there, we can free ourselves of so many conditionings of this and past lives. When we do this our lives start to align to a higher purpose, higher in the sense of conscious service to the world. Of course, there are ultimately no such things as higher and lower levels of consciousness, but for our conceptual minds to understand something nonconceptual, we need to apply some kind of structure and so higher and lower denote states rather than hierarchy.

The compassion we are giving to ourselves therefore supports and catalyzes an inner transformation that takes us to more expanded states of awareness. We are able to directly perceive energy and the nonphysical beings that exist on planes of existence that overlap ours. We start to understand from a nonpolarized perspective, unswayed by perceptions of good and bad, spiritual and nonspiritual. We find an inner flow within timelessness as we observe everything that arises in front of us as equal. There is quite a lot of shadow integration and inner work that needs to be done to get to this place; however, it is the plants and trees that can guide us and show us the way. They are our lamps on the path, our gateways to higher levels of consciousness and to the magical inner kingdom.

Receiving a Symbol from a Plant Meditation

In this next meditation we will journey into the depths of our inner world to receive a symbol from a plant or tree that will give us insight and meaning to a particular issue, problem, or situation in our life. This journey works through the power of intention and can be performed with any plant or tree that you are getting to know. If you have your own drum, you can drum yourself through this meditation. Alternatively, there are recorded drum beats that can be downloaded from the internet.

Start by settling down next to your plant or tree or in your meditation spot after taking an essence or tea.

During this time set your intention for the journey: What is it that you need assistance or clarity with? Is there an aspect of yourself that you want to better understand?

Make sure you are comfortable. Take three deep breaths down into the belly and exhale any tension or stress from any part of the body.

Work with the dropping down into the heart technique as outlined in chapter 1 and feel the warm glow of your heart.

Imagine yourself standing in front of a beautiful old tree, towering above you and spreading far below you. In the base of the trunk you notice a hollow just wide enough for you to fit into.

As you squeeze in you can see light emanating from the bottom of a spiral staircase circling down through the roots of the tree.

You find the handrail and start to take the steps down and round, down and round, down and round.

As you leave the last step behind, you arrive in the womb of the tree, a large space dimly lit by candles in recesses in the walls.

As your eyes adjust to the twilight, you can perceive the spirit of your plant standing in the center of the space. It greets you and asks you to come forward as it has something to show you.

Stepping to one side your plant ally reveals a small well in the floor, full to the brim with crystal-clear water bubbling up from its depths. You are invited to peer into the ancestral waters of Earth to see that which you seek.

At first you may not see anything, but patience and the wish for clarity will slowly reveal a symbol for you. Don't worry if you feel you are creating it yourself: in one way you are. The symbol could be a reminder of something you already know. Etch it into your mind for later contemplation. Withdraw from the well and thank your plant spirit for the gift.

Find your way back to the spiral stairway and climb up and round, up and round, up and round until you reach the hole in the trunk and emerge into the sunlight.

The meaning of your symbol may not be immediately apparent. Record it in your journal for later contemplation or for when more light has been illuminated on your issue or intention. Draw it and stick it on the wall to see it often and allow the deeper teachings of the symbol to percolate through into your conceptual awareness over time.

PART 2

Thirteen Plants and Tree Spirits

The second half of this book builds upon the foundations of the first half and introduces you to specific plants and tree spirits with whom you can perform meditations, journeys, and healing techniques. Now that you have become familiar with the fundamentals of healing with the plant spirits and this methodology of spiritual unfoldment, you can take your practice into more specialized places. Each of the following chapters introduces the energetic landscape of thirteen plants and tree spirits native to the British Isles, with an inner work technique for each. It is important that you have grasped the methodology of communication with the plant spirits as outlined in part 1 before applying them to the following plants and undertaking the specific meditations provided. You are not limited to these particular meditations for these plants and trees, but they will open the doorway to deeper self-investigation with them. Your journey is your own, but the chapters in part 2 provide the gateway into deeper aspects of the inner worlds and the realms of healing. As you progress through the plants and the meditations in this section, they will take you deeper and deeper through the layers of yourself to uncover the truth of your existence.

Fig. 7.1. *Artemisia vulgaris*

7

Developing Inner Vision
with the Spirit of Mugwort

IF THERE IS ONE PLANT to start your journey with the plant spirits, it should be Mugwort, the stunningly beautiful and beneficent *Artemisia vulgaris*. For beginners to this work, Mugwort is one of the most visceral plant spirits who weaves her spirit through all aspects of our life to bring alignment. She is therefore the perfect guide to teach the external reality of the plant spirits, that they work in our external world as well as our internal. I could write an entire book dedicated to this most bounteous and gifted healer, but here I want to present some of her most powerful metaphysical qualities to galvanize this part of the journey with a plant spirit that could easily become a lifetime friend.

We covered the importance of psychic hygiene in chapter 3, and Mugwort is one of our key allies in working with us to achieve this energetic integrity. A master cleanser and tantric genius, Mugwort can transmute many types of toxic energies and release all manner of entities and intrusions from the energy field and body. Over time, as Mugwort does this on a deeper and deeper level, she helps to unfurl our shamanic and psychic senses from their hibernation place. Through cycles of time within spirals of healing, she realigns us back to our original human blueprint. Instantaneous healing is not uncommon with the witch queen, but don't underestimate your complexity; other realignments are not overnight processes.

Known as the queen of herbs or the witches' first herb, the physical healing capabilities of Mugwort are expansive. From curing indigestion to realigning a potential breech birth, Mugwort offers powerful physical remedies. But beyond the phenomenal world, where she is not bound by the mundane, her metaphysical prowess and mastery of the spirit world becomes powerfully evident. The spirit force that moves through Mugwort is a powerful witch within her own right who works with her inner air, fire, and water elements with virtuoso skill. Her objective, like all good shamans and witches, is to bring balance and harmony, to address the misaligned energies and blockages that prevent flow and creativity. Many of these blockages occur in the cavities of the body and in the emotional layer of the energetic field, these locations being the most affected by toxic psychic energies. You will notice a thread running through all of Mugwort's healing gifts and that is the power of realignment: she pushes energy or chi. She is a disruptor, an agitator, and is known to bring chaos for a new state of balance to emerge.

Ideally, one should work with Mugwort in her natural habitat. She is wild at heart and is associated with Artemis, the goddess of the hunt: she can only be her true self when she is unbounded. She will grow in a pot and easily transplants from the wild into the garden, but the most magnificent specimens of this plant can be found on the edges of woodland and the banks of rivers. She is powerfully connected to the moon, and it is advisable to collect her leaves for tea or tincture at dawn on the full moon. If you can wait until summer solstice, this is her power day: any medicine harvested on this day will be especially potent and full of her dynamic spirit. If you do not have a wild plant, then a plant spirit essence can be tremendously effective. I personally like to bathe with her, and adding her to magic baths will facilitate deep cleansing and a clearing of unhelpful energies from your auric field (see chapter 3 for psychic hygiene).

The spirit of Mugwort first appeared to me as a female wizard in a long multicolored robe, standing on top of a hill and surveying the surrounding forests. It was summer solstice, and I had been up since before dawn to get down to the river to make offerings to the mother plant before the sun arrived. The mother plant is the one plant among the many that feels like it has the most power. We do not harvest from this plant but from others surrounding it. You can sense the mother plant by simply opening your awareness to it. The moments before dawn hold a special liminal power, which facilitates prayer and intention. Mugwort heard my prayer of becoming her student, and the following night during a ceremony dedicated to her, she gave me her first teachings. For two hours this elemental master and wisdom-bearing spirit showed me areas of blockage within various chakras, guiding me to aspects within myself that needed clearing and healing, ones that prevented me from living my full potential and from expressing myself from my heart.

The fire within Mugwort facilitates creativity as she aligns us back to our own soul force and its expression. Her earthy grounding quality assists in the pulling of the etheric into the visible, allowing unstructured feeling to be organized into expression. Very similar to cannabis, Mugwort opens our channels and brings an expansive quality to the mind, free of the usual boundaries and barriers. *Artemisia vulgaris* is also known as sailor's tobacco, and I find smoking dried mugwort leaves encourages me to relax into inner space. To allow creativity to flow, we need to drop out of the linear monkey mind that jumps from past to future and step into the infinite present to give space for concentration and the expression of the soul, of natural unfoldment. Through open presence and focus of the mind, we can become channels for divine inspiration and expression. Our general state of being is one of compulsive and discursive thoughts, an avoidance of presence when we don't know and recognize our true self. Wisdom teachings outline methods of taming the mind, such as single-focus meditation, which calms the conceptual mind, moves us from survival mode, and opens the door to new levels of conscious awareness and eventually to a cocreative partnership with the living cosmos. Mugwort guides us into alignment with our inner axis connected to both the cosmic divine and the soul of Mother Earth so that inspiration can flow. It is our connection to this inner axis, which is both centrifugal and centripetal in its force, that ultimately determines our energetic sovereignty.

Mugwort is the British equivalent of sacred tobacco. The tobacco plant in its unadulterated form is a master healing plant of the Americas but was unfortunately appropriated by the Europeans, bastardized through production, and turned into a potentially life-threatening and addictive substance. When we force unnatural change on the spirit of a plant, when we stretch it out of its natural expression and desecrate the sacredness of its soul, it can be disastrous for us. We alter the harmonic resonance of a plant, causing it to fragment, and by doing this, we receive a dissonant energy from the plant, which creates internal conflict to whoever invites it in. The result is addiction and lung disease and cancers caused by smoking. But if you head into any part of the Amazon, you will find the original tobacco plant at the heart of community. In its natural form it has seemingly unlimited healing capabilities and connections to the spirit realms. I have an Amazonian Kichwa friend who is a master *tobaquera*. She can heal almost anything with tobacco, just as the moxibustion masters of Japan and China claim to heal any disease or malaise of spirit with *Artemisia vulgaris* or *àicǎo* (艾, 艾草) in Chinese.

Just like sacred tobacco, Mugwort cleanses by stimulating stagnant energy into warm and moving circulation. The more we clear the energy field and body with her medicines, the deeper the layers of karmic baggage and heavy toxic energies that can be transformed. The energy field can be seen as having layers relating to various aspects of our holistic existence. Close to and running through the physical body is the etheric body, without which our material body would fall apart. It is the animating soul force that binds our spiritual force to the phenomenal world. About two to fifteen inches from the body, yet still running through the physical body, is the emotional layer where we find the majority of attachments, imprints of trauma, and intrusions. Our negative emotions create weaknesses in our field, which become doorways for unhelpful energies and toxic entities to enter and build layer upon layer of toxicity, also known as obscurations in Buddhist philosophy. These blockages create blind spots in the mind and illusion in our perspective. They also drain our life force and therefore our vitality. The next layer of the aura, further out from the body, is the mental layer, pertaining to our belief systems, thoughts, and the structure of our life through which we operate. After that are the spiritual layers, the more refined aspects of self.

We separate the layers for ease of understanding, but in reality, they exist as one whole within the unified field of Earth. The physical body itself emerges from the densification of the types of energies present within the field, as an expression of the soul, and our mind operates from both the subconscious and from the energy field that surrounds our physical body. Through working with Mugwort externally and internally, we can start to clean the dirt from the window so that we can see the view clearly again.

When it comes to working and journeying in the spirit and imaginal realms, it helps to have clear inner vision, and this can be achieved through a combination of techniques and methods. If you are not a particularly visual person, do not be dismayed: these techniques can be applied to any form of inner perception, whether it is through feelings, hearing, or vision. Whichever way you perceive on the inner planes, however you tune in to the unseen, is perfectly fine. We are all unique, and even the levels and strength of visioning can vary widely between people.

The first and most important aspect of clear seeing or clear perceptions is having a clean energy field. We experience everything through the field of energy that surrounds and moves through us. Whatever is in our energy field directly affects the mind, so if your auric field is full of toxicity and unhelpful energies, then these will obstruct and interfere with your perceptions, creating a false mind or false thoughts. Work with Mugwort and the techniques suggested in chapter 3 for psychic hygiene to cleanse and purify your energy field. She is an amazing smudging plant for your energy field and your sacred space. If you don't feel like cleansing yourself, it means you really need to! Whatever is in your energy field has a nice source of food: it likes being there, so it will not want you to remove it.

Being aware of our emotions and motivations helps us find our way forward. Our chakras are connected to the various levels or dimensions of existence within the energy field (there is a range of frequencies of energy within the energy field), and so if toxicity is held within our chakras, this also affects the mind and emotions and therefore our thoughts and beliefs. We communicate with and experience the world through our chakras and energy field; it is vital therefore that they are cleansed so that we align ourselves to truth rather than delusion, and we can move from illness to health. The causes of blockages in the energy field can be found in trauma, in our own toxic emotions and projections, in our toxic environment, and as an inheritance from others. To work on release of the imprints of trauma, it is advisable to also work with fireweed (see chapter 15). Combining the plant spirits to work on various levels of our healing is vital.

The cleansing capabilities of Mugwort go hand in hand with her ability to ground us, to root us into the earth and stabilize our energies. As Mugwort grounds she centers, pulling our scattered thoughts and energies into the central channel, aligning us to presence and clarity. This not only has a direct influence on our quality of life but also on the quality of our perceptions, our dreams, and our inner visions. To strengthen clairvoyance abilities it is important to be grounded and have strong earth energy to hold the potent inner fire. It is essential for healers to have good inner vision, to be able to perceive the energy with which they are working; otherwise, they are essentially working blind.

Yet let's not forget that inner vision comes in many forms. Dieting and undertaking protocols with Mugwort specifically for this reason can bring such depth of inner knowing. There are myriad reasons why the third eye becomes restricted and therefore many ways in which Mugwort can teach how to release the blockages, bonds, and denials that keep us from its clarity. Perhaps you inherited short-sightedness of the physical eyes, and so there is an ancestral wound of not wanting to see the truth of a distressing situation, of not wanting to acknowledge the world as it truly is. Perhaps your birth into the world was so traumatic that your spirit retreated far into itself, not wanting to look out into this new world. We are complex creatures, so these, along with many other stressful and life-denying situations, can have a detrimental effect on the inner eyes.

When we step onto the healing spiral, we are never healing for ourselves alone; we commit to facing and releasing the traumas of our forebears, our descendants, our genealogical family, our soul family, and ultimately the collective of humanity. It is best not to get carried away with the latter. It should be acknowledged, but I have seen ego take hold and overshadow real healing that needs to take place when the individual gets caught up in the thought of releasing birth pain for all women who have ever given birth or for all the men who have ever been emasculated. Noble thoughts, perhaps, but getting caught in the head with these thoughts undermines the work that the individual needs to do within him- or herself. Elevating our ego to new heights within and creating a god complex, especially when working with psychoactive plants, can be very dangerous.

Inner vision along with a strong sense of presence and alertness, which Mugwort encourages, are also essential in the practice of lucid dreaming. Mugwort is known as the dreaming herb for her capacity to assist us with this ancient human ability, and lucid dreaming further activates our seership abilities. Mugwort sits on the edge of our psychoactive group of plants as she contains small amounts of thujone. This chemical helps her be the dream shaman who guides us into the astral through sleep. To become consciously awake within the dream state is a practice of the highest yoga tantra in Tibetan Buddhism, but it is also a phenomenon available to us all. We can train the mind through repetition and affirmation to recognize when it is dreaming. Many people have had dreams where they know to some degree that what they are experiencing is a dream, but that is as far as their lucidity goes. By applying techniques and working with Mugwort, we not only recognize that we are dreaming but we can also make choices and actively change or leave the dream. A high level of lucidity often makes the dream seem more real than the waking state even though we may be flying, swimming beneath the ocean, or visiting other planets. A reminder that this state is natural for us: it is not abnormal. It is possible to do almost anything you want to in this lucid state; however, it can be a balancing act to remain lucid as the dream always wants to pull you back into unconsciousness through habit, so it is a good idea to use this time wisely.

Through the fire and earth elements of Mugwort, she ignites the lucid process and can shift our dreaming practices into new realms of expansion. Dreaming is an important aspect in shamanic practice as it reveals the concerns of the subconscious mind and the shape of our shadows through symbolism and metaphor, both valuable insights on the path to self-liberation. Mugwort, therefore, helps cleanse the dream space and the subconscious. By ensuring you have a plan for your lucid adventure—such as meditating in the dream, flying, or facing an inner shadow—you make the most of your time in this altered state of consciousness.

The objective to practicing this type of dreaming for the Buddhists is to learn to die consciously, to be able to remain awake and move through the *bardo* realms consciously rather than being swept unconsciously on the winds of karma. In this way they are able to consciously choose their next rebirth, one that is conducive to their path of enlightenment or to their selfless path of achieving *bodhicitta*, a Sanskrit word that means "enlightenment mind," a mind that wishes to attain awakening, motivated by empathy and compassion for all beings. If you do not have such aspirations or belief in enlightenment, there are a multitude of other benefits to learning how to lucid dream, such as the expansion of consciousness beyond the limits of mundane life and the phenomenal world. All shamans of old have worked within this state to be the walker between worlds, and it is a very similar state to the gateway experience of psychoactive plants. The main lesson I have taken from my lucid dreaming practice was the direct experience of nondual awareness. I felt the inner peace of experiencing that I was both the dreamer and dream. I saw how my thought would manifest in front of me in the dream and how I was creating my external reality from my imagination or internal power. Inner and outer perceptions are one and the same.

What lucid dreaming teaches us through direct experience is what quantum scientists are trying to prove as we speak, that the quantum potential of the universe is nonlocal, meaning that everything is interconnected at a fundamental level, everything is an expression of one whole. Each moment is an unfolding and enfolding from one state to the next, including our thoughts. By becoming lucid in the dream, this theory becomes directly experienced, as we recognize that we are (a) completely conscious outside the physical body yet not located in any particular place, and (b) we are inextricably linked to everything that happens in our external world. We can have a direct experience of the paradox of life, that everything exists yet is an illusion at the same time, that things exist in a different way from what we thought. This is paradigm-shifting and spiritual-development-enhancing territory. As our physical bodies are a part of nature, so are our dreams, illuminated by the light of the dream realm of Earth herself.

Wholeness can be experienced by leaving the dream and experiencing the luminous void. This is the level of existence, according to quantum theory, that is the underlying pool of potential information from which the universe emerges. In spiritual terms this is the womb of the Great Mother. In Buddhist terminology it is emptiness. As humans we are channels of this creative potential if we allow the soul of the world to express itself through our individual soul. We are participants in the emergence of our world; we are cocreators and therefore have more influence over the direction of our life than we think. Mugwort works with the fire and light of the mind to ignite creative processes, to awaken us to our own thoughts and dreams. She assists us in our reconnection back to this fundamental level of the planet. We can overcome our fragmentation and disconnection, reestablish our inner wholeness, and recognize our unique place in the world. This changes how we interact with the world and with each other, and this is a continuous part of our evolvement as humans.

The spirit of Mugwort is so diverse in her healing gifts I have decided to offer two ways of working with her to assist your journey around the medicine wheel. You could place Mugwort almost anywhere in the wheel, depending on what aspect of yourself you wish to work on. If it is your inner vision or cognition that you wish to develop, then placing her in the direction of air for the awakened mind would be beneficial, or if you would like to concentrate on inner transformation and realignment, then the southern direction of fire would work.

In part 1 we worked on orienting the mind toward our interiority, bringing more focused awareness on the inner planes, allowing ourselves to become more familiar with our inner landscape and whether we are operating from the conceptual mind or from the heart and deeper awareness. Mugwort then takes us a step further and shows us how the inner and the outer are one and the same. She is a visceral plant spirit, exhibiting her powers in our waking world around us, demonstrating that inner spirit is also outer spirit: they are two aspects of the same reality. We are thus able to tune in to the great web of life with more ease.

Precaution: Mugwort is not recommended for pregnant women or people who are allergic to celery, fennel, or wild carrot.

Nonlocality Meditation

The following meditation is one used by both modern-day meditators as well as practitioners of the old ways of the British Isles to break the mind out of habitual ways of focus and to orient it toward a deeper inner wisdom. The great meditator and philosopher Alan Watts would say that this is how we get into the true state of meditation. The witches of the British Isles would say that this is how we develop our second sight.[1]

Find a quiet spot next to some mugwort in the wild or take some mugwort tea or essence and sit in your safe space indoors. I find smoking mugwort to be the most powerful way of ingesting the plant for this particular meditation.

Relax into your space, exhaling any tension and thoughts of the day.

Begin by bringing your awareness to all the sensations in your body taking place right now. Feel yourself sitting on your seat, notice any feelings of tension or discomfort. Notice the sensation of the clothes on your skin or any feelings of joy of peace that are present. Without labeling or naming any of what you experience, just notice them.

Then turn your attention to everything that you can hear. Without actively listening just allow any sounds around you to wash through you without labeling them. Allow all sound to just be; allow all sound to simply be happening while you just observe.

Now turn your attention to any thoughts that are arising in your mind. Notice them come from nothing and return to nothing without interaction from you. Don't try to stop these thoughts: just watch them as they happen. Things are happening both within and without you, and there is no difference to the happening.

Allow all sensory input to blend into one happening and simply observe it without following or labeling.

Practice this for as long as you are comfortably able but do not push yourself. Even if you can only manage five minutes, return to it tomorrow and the next day until it becomes easier for longer lengths of time.

Cleansing Meditation with the Spirit of Mugwort

The more time you spend with Mugwort, the quicker and more effective this cleansing technique becomes. It is recommended to also spend time getting to know your personal inner resonance or your handle with Mugwort, as this will not only assist you with the following meditation but will also instantly deepen your connection to her spirit and open a doorway of healing on the inner planes.

Find a quiet spot next to some mugwort in the wild or take some mugwort tea or essence and sit in your safe space indoors.

Relax into your space, exhaling any tension and thoughts of the day. Use the dropping the mind into the heart meditation, which you learned in chapter 1, to bring yourself into calm in the inner space.

Through intention, connect to the spirit of Mugwort, asking her to be with you now. It is at this point that it is advisable to know what Mugwort feels like to be sure that the spirit you are connecting to is indeed Lady Artemisia.

Ask her to send her beautiful spirit through your energy field to cleanse, purify, and transform anything dead, toxic, or dying. Grant that it is done now. (Similar instructions can be used if you need grounding or cleansing of a particular unhelpful energy you feel you have picked up.)

Then sit quietly and observe any movement, changes, or insights that arrive. Do not doubt your own magic; otherwise it will not take place.

As soon as you feel you need to sigh or you simply feel the inner knowing of completion, thank Mugwort and enjoy your clearer state of being.

Fig. 8.1. *Quercus robur* (English oak),
Quercus petraea (durmast or sessile oak)

8

Inner Wisdom with the Spirit of Oak

UNIVERSAL TO HUMANITY'S philosophy of life is the tree. It is one of the oldest symbols in history and is a visible expression of the hermetic axiom "as above, so below" or as "as within, so without," which underpins many of the ancient mystery schools and wisdom traditions. The visible part of the tree, its trunk and branches, is reflected beneath the surface of the earth through the lower half of the trunk and the tree's root structure. A tree represents strength and power, abundance and change, none more so than the mighty oak, and our ancient ancestors, the Druids, drew their power from this powerhouse of a tree. Trees were totems and allies for many other ancient British tribes, such as the Silurians who revered the yew. More than just a symbol of the gifts of the sun, the oak stands at the center of all druidic life, lore, and magic. It is the Druids' gateway to the three worlds of Upper, Middle, and Lower, a tree of life connecting beings of all realms, allowing them to interact with all dimensions: spiritual, physical, and astral. In the Norse concept of the world tree, which the Norse called Yggdrasil, it is the Y axis about which all three worlds turn—or, in Norse mythology, nine worlds. Even though the true world tree is often thought to be the ash and is most likely the yew, we can imagine a great oak reaching its leaves up to the heavens to soak up cosmic forces, its trunk standing solid in the Middle World and its roots reaching down into the belly of Mother Earth and the Lower World. Its branches surround the sphere of this universe and hold space for all, which are contained within the safety and goodness of its energy field. Oak is a masculine protector working in harmony with the feminine goddess of Earth. It is associated with the three elements of air, earth, and fire, another reflection of its interworld existence and balance. Oak would therefore be an excellent ally to stand in the center of your medicine wheel.

In British mythology the Oak King rules summer and holds the dream of so much in the British Isles. The oak has been with us—clothing us, sheltering us, and protecting us—for thousands of years. It has remained a firm ally despite the war of exploitation we have raged against it for hundreds of years. It has seen the consciousness of humanity evolve throughout our entire time here on Earth. As far as evidence shows, the first *Homo sapiens* appeared only two hundred thousand years ago,[1] yet oaks have been standing on the British Isles for approximately fourteen million years with perhaps a short break during the ice ages.[2] This benevolent and noble tree has witnessed the passing of epochs, seen human kings and queens come and go and humankind rise from humble beginnings to a treacherous god-like status through fame and infamy. Oak carries the energies of tenacity, endurance, and wisdom, abiding in love and grace despite everything it has experienced and witnessed. It also carries and preserves the true meaning of royalty and nobility, that of being the guardian and protector of the sovereignty of the goddess of the land, something that is part of our own ancient past before authoritarian powers devolved into a greed and narcissism. A true king holds his power only for guardianship and protectorship of others. Anyone who is corrupted by his power and uses it for his own gain is not an authentic king.

Kingship is the archetypal highest achievement of man, the culmination of all good qualities such as a strong and benevolent heart and concern for all life whether incarnate or discarnate. Yet no man exists alone or without his complementary opposite. Within every male human exists his anima, the feminine aspect that balances and guides his soul. The feminine greatness within.

It is the same for a woman. To achieve queenship she needs to have a relationship to her inner king, her animus. The feminine needs the masculine structure and protection to step into her power as the creatrix of life. A man needs to be in touch with his inner feminine qualities if he is to establish his power. This is a balanced relationship between the inner masculine and feminine energies. In every man there is a feminine aspect and within every female is a masculine aspect. This dynamic allows us to be in balance with all of nature, whether seemingly masculine in archetype or feminine. By recognizing the sacredness and interconnectedness of both genders, we transcend the polarity that leads us away from the soul. The human qualities of the past that are no longer so appreciated today, such as nobility, truth, and honor, are still available if we choose to rediscover them. They have not been eradicated. Nothing truly is. We can integrate the essential gifts that both the masculine and feminine offers. In this way, while the soul force of Oak is masculine in its grandeur, it cannot stand in its power without the grace of the Goddess.

The Oak King presides over the year alongside the Holly King, who rules winter. Together, they work in unison to hold the wisdom of the ever-increasing and decreasing light of the life-giving sun. Holly steps forward at the summer solstice to oversee the descent into winter as its strength can be found in the darkness. The spikes of the holly leaves are not there to attack but to exhibit strength during challenging times; it is a tree not easily harmed. Holly hands the baton of guardianship over to Oak at the winter solstice because this solar being heralds the return of the light as the daylight begins to grow again. Tuning in to this particular cycle of nature through Oak emboldens the heart and strengthens connection to the land.

During my time in the Amazon, we were convening with our teacher's mother and sister on the edge of the jungle before our two-day dugout canoe journey down to the Peruvian border. There was electricity at the place we were staying, and so after ceremony one evening during a conversation about the sacred trees of the Kichwa, we played a track by Dartmoor musician Nigel Shaw. Nigel makes beautiful, ethereal-sounding flutes from the wood of trees native to the British Isles and plays their sacred song through them. Truly sublime. Without disclosing the name of the tree so as not to influence our new friends (I'm not sure they would have known it anyway), we all sat and listened to the evocative calls of the English oak resonating through the jungle. Afterward, I asked my teacher's sister what she thought of the music, and she said she didn't like it at all, that all she could see were battleships and bloodshed. She had tuned in to the energetic frequency of all of the European armies who had used oak wood in their shields, ships, and spears during conflict. With senses highly attuned to the resonance of plants and trees, shamans can journey into the frequencies and allow their spirit to speak to them, allow them to reveal their inner life and their ancient stories. Through the morphic field, the past is still alive within the present moment. Past, present, and future can all be accessed through what is present right now. Wounds and experiences from past lives can still influence our current state of mind and our health. Trees teach us about timelessness.

Working with the conscious intelligence of Oak is a delightful and empowering experience. The chief spirit of Oak appears as a tall bright column of light, emitting the most noble, honest, and powerful energies. Oak is an elder of our society and a highly realized being. Sitting within the branches of an oak is like a hug from a loving grandfather and provides instant grounding during times of upheaval and uncertainty. This feeling of being pulled down into the earth is my energetic handle for oak, so whenever I am in need of grounding, I simply evoke this feeling within and ask Oak for the assistance I need. Go and sit under or in an oak and pay attention to how you feel—what images come into your mind and what memories arise for you. In this way, you make a connection and cultivate a friendship with the spirit of this magnanimous guardian.

It is important now as ever to find and nurture the qualities of Oak within as humanity goes through huge transition and is in desperate need of inner strength, self-belief, and leaders who stand in the light of their integrity. All solar plants and trees bring illumination; they make us feel good, joyous, and celebratory. Plants such as St. John's wort and juniper all lift us up through their inner fire to a higher state of mind and radiance. This lightness of being is necessary to hold space for ourselves and others. Oak teaches us how to maintain our own sovereign space and how to maintain that space with equality, compassion, and strength, as it does for the thousands of creatures and other forms of life that live in, upon, and around it. When we hold space for others, we are not only listening to them and sharing with them; we are also holding them within an energetic field of protection in full awareness and management of everything taking place in the seen and unseen realms of that space. The level of consciousness required to manage the unseen is what working with the plants and particularly Oak can teach us.

Oak stands in full awareness of everything that lives in, upon, or around it. Its light shines so brightly through its noble qualities that disruptive or toxic energies cannot stay long and are transmuted. Dried spring oak leaves therefore make a great smudging smoke for your sacred space.

During a plant diet retreat with Oak, many attendees reported that they felt they already knew Oak, that drinking the elixir we provided was like meeting an old friend who took them by the hand and showed them the abundance on all levels already present within their lives. When we have the wisdom to see that everything we need is right here, we don't need to be searching outside ourselves for that elusive key to all our problems or that final bit of information that will make everything all right. We are enough. This wise perspective allowed participants to look at their lives with new eyes, to see their path with a renewed sense of confidence in a world that is constantly telling us we should be aspiring to something different from ourselves. This self-assuredness is grounding and confidence boosting and allows other leadership and motivating qualities to emerge. If our leaders truly had these qualities, we would not be experiencing the devastating depth of corruption that is endemic in the world. It is time for a new paradigm of leadership, one that has the humility to learn from the elders in our society, the trees.

In this time of great transition in the world and in the development of human consciousness, many of us are starting to remember our past lives, the trajectory that our soul has come through to get us where we are today. Many are starting to remember their origins, why they are here and what their mission in this lifetime is. Many feel they are called as guardians of Earth, as healers to hold space for others, and as leaders who can help guide us into the new paradigm, a new way of living in cocreation with Earth. It is useful to understand the energies that run through you, such as your family lineage working alongside your spiritual lineage. What does your surname mean? Where were your ancestors from? Perhaps you are mixed race. How does that combination of cultural and national energies work through you? Understanding our genealogical inheritance is beneficial to understanding our true self. There are many issues surrounding DNA testing, which was popular for a while. Ideally, it is best to do your own research rather than rely on someone else working with a limited number of DNA samples against which yours is tested and a likelihood of DNA origins is given. These tests are not 100 percent accurate.

Many people today have been initiated by indigenous cultures (including that of the British Isles), by spiritual leaders, or by the plants and trees, or they have maintained a practice such as kundalini yoga or meditation, which has taken them into expanded awareness and spiritual maturity. All these spiritual lineages belong to humanity and must be honored if we are to work with them to access energy channels and skills to which they are the gateway. The spirit of Oak reminds us of these lineages and the profundity of them; it grounds them into us so that we can feel them as aspects of our deepest being and facilitates their flourishing. If we do not integrate the energies handed to us through initiation, they will dissipate over time. But by working with the spirit of Oak and consciously accepting these energies as part of our existence, our soul force is enlivened and strengthened and our inner world and spiritual and healing practices are empowered.

Guidance and Insight Journey

This shamanic journey is best performed while sitting under an oak, but journeying in your house with some oak essence or after an oak leaf smudge also works well. Make sure you have read and understood the process of the shamanic journey as outlined in chapter 3. We will be drawing upon the ancient wisdom and techniques of the Druids and journeying into the spirit of Oak to receive wisdom, insight, or guidance on a particular issue. You might also simply receive a blessing of some kind. Perhaps you would like to explore your own ancestral or spiritual lineage and don't know where to start. Perhaps you would like to be made aware of what is in your energy field and to clear it. Perhaps you would like to better understand your own triggers and doorways that prevent you from maintaining balanced space for yourself. Alternatively, you could simply ask Oak to reveal whatever it is you need to know and is appropriate for you right now. As always, it is important to have an intention for the journey to guide the spirit of Oak and to open the door to cocreative partnership.

If you are indoors, you may want to put on some gentle meditation music or a recording of a drum to journey with. With shamanic journeys it is imperative that you return the way you entered, so ensure that you exit from Oak.

With intention set, relax into your space through your exhalation and feel the solid earth beneath your body, holding you firmly in the Middle World.

Close your eyes and imagine you are standing in a beautiful meadow. The sun is shining overhead, the birds are swooping and chirping around you, and you can hear the bees gathering nectar from the sweet-smelling wildflowers among the tall grasses. A gentle breeze runs over your skin. Breathe in the beauty of the place.

You see before you an incline in the meadow and on top stands a beautiful noble oak, majestic branches reaching up to the cosmos. You decide to head toward it.

As you walk you feel the warm earth beneath your bare feet and the long grasses brushing past your legs.

You approach the oak and see it is hollow, the gap being wide enough for you to climb in. A guardian of the tree stands at the entrance; acknowledge him and ask permission to enter.

Having been granted entry (if you receive a no then you must listen to this and return another time), you step inside the hollow trunk, and the spirit of Oak decides whether to take you to the Upper World, keep you in the Middle World, or take you to the Lower World.

Surrender to this process and allow the spirit of Oak to take you to the most appropriate place for your own guidance, to show you the most appropriate symbology, or give you the most appropriate information and blessing.

You will instinctively know when you have finished your journey and it is time to leave. Do not linger once you feel this; return to the hollow trunk of the oak and look for the light to emerge back at the top of the hill in the meadow.

Descend back down the hill, noticing the sunlight once again and the sounds and smells of the beautiful day.

Fig. 9.1. *Crataegus oxyacantha*

9

Awakening Mythos with the Spirit of Hawthorn

THE HEART IS SADLY MISUNDERSTOOD, particularly on a spiritual level where its capacity to understand infinity and its role in translating the language of spirit has largely been forgotten. There are many references in modern culture to the role the heart plays in our life when it comes to love, such as a broken heart or a passionate heart, but we don't often learn the science behind emotions. Every time we feel love or empathy toward someone, the brain secretes a fabulous neuropeptide hormone called oxytocin, or more commonly known as the love hormone. This powerful hormone plays a large role in what makes us human, helping us to bond with our loved ones and with Mother Earth. The period just after childbirth is critical for the development of the oxytocin receptors within the baby. The more love and loving touch the baby receives, the stronger the receptors become, and the more empathic or loving the individual will be, making it easier for him or her to connect to the plant and nature kingdoms. However, even if we have not received the level of love required for full capacity receptors, their receptivity can still be developed later in life through the repeated exposure to the vibration of love, and that's where Hawthorn comes in.

It is well known and accepted that the heart as the primary organ of perception is intrinsic to our spiritual unfoldment. The heart holds the key to forgiveness, gratitude, nonjudgment, service, and compassion, all necessary attributes on the path to awakening. We can cultivate both oxytocin release and all of these beneficial qualities by offering positive impulses to the heart to generate heart rhythm coherence. According to the research of the HeartMath Institute, this coherent pattern produces balance and harmony throughout the mind and body. Both, therefore, operate more efficiently, and our electromagnetic field is also in coherence within and without. It is at this point that oxytocin is released from the posterior pituitary via signals from the heart. This process is restorative, regenerative, and perception enhancing and can be catalyzed by the medicine of the spirit of Hawthorn. It is only through the heart that we connect with the spirits of the plants and trees; it is not a mental process.

Hawthorn is a small and easily recognizable tree that will bring its vibrant love to almost any soil, even scrubland. It can be found in woodland, hedgerows, mountains, and valleys up and down the length and breadth of the British Isles. It is our heart medicine, a powerful healer on the physical, emotional, and spiritual levels. Known in herbalism as a powerful heart tonic, hawthorn regulates blood pressure, dilates arteries, and helps to repair tissue damage especially to blood vessels. It is a relaxant and therefore relieves anxiety.

One of my favorite medicines to produce is hawthorn berry tincture. Not only is it very simple to make, but it is a beautiful reddish-pink color, smells divine, and tastes great. Taking medicine should be a pleasant experience, as master herbalist Julie Bruton-Seal once told me, and I heartily agree. When we accept something into our body with openness because it tastes great, then it will be assimilated into our bodily systems much easier. To make your own hawthorn berry tincture, simply collect a jar of fresh hawthorn berries, cover with 40 percent proof brandy, and leave for two months at least. In most herbalist books it says that the medicine will be ready in five to six weeks, but leaving the medicine to brew longer makes it sweeter and more delicious. Waiting to collect your berries after the first frost also helps develop the sugar content in them and therefore makes them tastier. Once ready, remove the berries through draining and keep the liquid bottled in a dark cool place. I like to nibble on the spring leaves when I am out on my nature walks and collect the blossoms for tea also. Hawthorn is a safe plant to consume; however, it may interfere with certain allopathic cardiac medications such as beta blockers.

Hawthorn is associated with Beltane, the Gaelic May Day festival, halfway between the spring equinox and the summer solstice, when the hawthorn tree flowers. The Beltane tree expresses the atypical aspects of fire through its physical structure, its medicinal affinities, and its spiritual attributes. Fire plants generally have sharp thorns or stings, such as nettle and holly. Hawthorn has strong thorns, particularly the young trees.

The flower of any plant is its outward expression of the yang energy of fire, revealing the depths of its interiority through the color and structure of its reproductive organ. We can peer into the mind of the plant spirit through its flower. Hawthorn blossoms are white, reflecting the purity of Hawthorn's own heart; she is only concerned with truth, clarity, and higher wisdom. The blossom has five petals, the number associated with the Mother Goddess who dwells in the land. The fire of Hawthorn purifies and transforms the emotions held within the hidden heart wall, the barrier of protection we build around the organ of emotion to protect it from life's pain and sadness. Continued work with this transformational tree will help to reveal the deepest truth of the heart. What really is our passion in life? What truly motivates us and makes us feel alive? Not what we think is acceptable to society, what we can monetize, or what our family thinks we should be doing. What is it that makes the heart sing? That is what the soul wants to express, and coupled with our unique gifts and skills (we all have them), our purpose in this lifetime can be revealed. Hawthorn then inspires you to act on this newfound inner wisdom, which also explains her association with the enthusiastic planet of Mars.

From a place of compassion toward ourselves, our true nature can be perceived more easily. The truth of who we are can unfold through direct experience of our essential goodness, our Buddha nature, that divine spark that we all carry within. We can perceive beyond the self-imposed barriers and blockages we have created around ourselves out of self-defense and preservation. "A loving heart is the truest wisdom," stated Charles Dickens, and Hawthorn helps us to see the beauty in all things and the interconnectedness of life.

When we are suffering from a broken heart of any kind, Hawthorn holds us in a state of peace so that the mending process can take place from the level of the soul. When we heal from this level of existence, we are not only healing manifest issues but preventing future ones from arising by healing them at their source. The heart is the seat of the soul. If we leave a broken heart unattended, or simply believe time alone will heal it and make no effort to engage with the pain, we neglect the trauma experienced by the soul. This deepest aspect of ourselves needs attention and healing too. By working with plants at a soul level, we can address those existential questions within ourselves: the meaning of our life, who we truly are, and our purpose for being here. Healing at the dimension of soul offers a completely different and lasting effect than healing at the symptomatic level.

When we work with and connect to Hawthorn through meditation and/or medicine, we are drawn down into a deep place of stillness, the busy chattering mind dissolves and our consciousness is expanded into a deep inner awareness. We are drawn into a timelessness that holds us safe in the infinite awareness of the heart. Hawthorn is the perfect ally for meditation and inner work. My first plant diet was with Hawthorn, and I was so surprised that after the first glass of the hawthorn elixir an immense peace that I had not experienced for a long time came over me. My perception shifted as I lay outside under a hawthorn tree, and I perceived multicolored energy emitting from the tree to create a stunning aura of what I could only describe as its magic. All of the busyness of my life fell away so that my soul could speak and I could listen.

Running underneath and throughout all hawthorn medicine is unconditional love and compassion. Two qualities of love without conditions are openness and peace. There is no fear when we allow ourselves to love in this expansive way, yet it takes the warrior heart to do this. Remaining transparent in our heart can bring feelings of vulnerability if we have not cleared the pains and traumas of the past. Hawthorn teaches us how to think and operate from the heart by opening it and allowing us to feel in an embodied way. At this level of awareness problems are solved for the greater good, judgment evolves into understanding, and anxiety makes way for inner peace. A deep sense of gratitude for life and everything we already have bubbles to the surface.

Sometimes when a sense of anxiety rises in me and I'm not sure where it has come from or something has upset me during the day and I have pushed it to the back of my mind while I am busy, I find it useful to run a hot salt bath to purify my emotions and take some hawthorn essence when I get in. This combination of water, salt, and hawthorn essence can bring emotions to the surface so we can understand them and accept them, and then the salt and our open heart can release them, often through laughter or tears. In days gone by, before any family disputes were discussed, everyone would be served a cup of hawthorn tea so that matters could be resolved openly and from the heart rather than from wounds and hurts. Hawthorn is a mediator and moderator for many life situations.

With the heart as Hawthorn's primary concern, it is not surprising that there are myriad folk stories and mythical beings associated with this wondrous tree. Hawthorn allows us to open ourselves to the myths within once again. Myth brings meaning to our lives. The race of beings that Hawthorn concerns herself with are the fae. She is known as one of the most magical trees in the British Isles and a portal to the faery realm. She is the guardian of the gateway into this dimension through which we can only enter with her permission. The spirit of Hawthorn is the faery queen, the sovereign soul of that beautiful realm.

The inner landscape of Hawthorn is silvery with luminescent colors emanating from within structures and organic forms. The flora are of the red spectrum rather than the green due to the twilight quality of light there. Magic runs through everything in her world, and she feels more elven to me than faery, but nonetheless she is the queen of her land. She has conquered herself and lives completely from the heart. It is not all fluffy love and rainbows in this place, however. Hawthorn has a very witchy side too, and this regal being will show you what is lying hidden deep within the recesses of your heart, and this can be challenging. Radical honesty with yourself is required if you wish to learn and understand your experience here. Whatever we carry in our hearts will be reflected back to us in her watery realm. If we hold selfish or deceptive perspectives, then we will meet grasping and possessive energies there, but venture into that space with humility and grace, and the majesty of your own heart will be revealed.

The spirit of Hawthorn is as old as the hills yet vivacious and full of youthful exuberance, hence she is also known as the May Queen, the herald of life in its full expression of summer. She appears to me as a youthful maiden with the swiftness of a light spirit and the tenderness of a young mother. The hawthorn tree itself looks old and twisted yet its medicine promotes a vibrant life full of vitality, an indication of the higher wisdom teaching of paradox that the spirit of Hawthorn holds.

By calming the mind, Hawthorn can more clearly show us the deeper meaning of our connections to people and places as she reveals the shape of our particular part of the web. She offers insight into the emotions trapped in the barriers we build around the heart as we travel through painful life experiences. Releasing these trapped emotions can happen simply by bringing a deeper conscious awareness to them as quite often they have been buried there for a long time. The light of awareness can be healing within itself, but teamed with the panacea of Hawthorn, we can truly be set free. Hawthorn connects the dots for us, entraining our emotions to truth. Not only does Hawthorn nurture our heart and soul on all levels, but she connects us to the inner heart of nature, the beating life force and mythos of the land, and the holy heart of Mother Earth. We live in the domain of Gaia; she gives us the energy to live and the body to live within.

When we heal the connection to our own heart, we are healing our connection to the heart of Earth.

Precaution: Hawthorn may interfere with medications such as beta blockers. Please consult with a health care provider before consuming this plant if you are taking any prescription drugs.

Freedom within Meditation

Ensure you have plenty of time for this meditation and that you will not be disturbed. Take your time with each step, and do not rush yourself or jump to the next stage without full integration. Be kind to yourself and allow hawthorn to bring you the gift of freedom that this meditation can offer.

Sit under a hawthorn tree or take a few drops of a hawthorn essence and create your safe and sacred space within and without. When you're comfortable take a few deep breaths in through your nose and let them out through your mouth.

Take yourself into the state of grace as detailed in the heart meditation in chapter 1.

From the stillness, silence, and expansiveness of the mind, drop the same awareness down into your heart. Feel the expansive and light-filled quality of the energetic field of the heart reaching out from your chest in all directions. Ask hawthorn to hold you in peace and truth as you explore your interiority.

Now bring to mind something with which you would like to feel more love, something or someone that you would like to experience more love with—perhaps a person, an animal, a plant, nature in general, your meditation practice, or your hobby. It can even be an aspect of yourself.

With your awareness resting on your heart space (or the rear heart space if it is too intense with your front heart chakra), ask yourself why there is a blockage to love toward this thing, person, or aspect of self. There should be no judgment here; accept whatever arises and every aspect of yourself through loving-kindness and try to see the blockage to love that lives in your heart.

Welcome this blockage into your awareness and feel into it. Is there more than one emotion wrapped into it? How does this blockage make you feel in the rest of your body? What does this blockage want to express? Every sensation is accepted and shown gratitude as a valid part of you. Take your time here and allow the nurturing qualities of hawthorn to help you feel safe in this place.

From this place of safety and gentleness, allow yourself to imagine what it might feel like without this blockage. Peer underneath the layer of protection. How does this thing, person, or aspect of self feel without this blockage there? How could life be without it there? Allow the intensity of the blockage to be slowly dialed down as you flow into this new place, knowing that the protections of both the blockage and Hawthorn are there should you choose to engage with it again. You have freedom of choice.

Be patient and kind with yourself; do not push yourself too hard in this process. We have created our inner boundaries for good reason, and we need to deconstruct them carefully without force.

To finish, thank Hawthorn for her kindness and bring your awareness back to your body and the space you are sitting in.

Fig. 10.1. *Urtica dioica*

10

Balancing and Healing with the Spirit of Nettle

THE HUMBLE STINGING NETTLE is one of the most overlooked plants in the garden and hedgerows. Often viewed as a problematic weed, this powerful plant not only nourishes the soil with high levels of nitrogen, therefore supporting other life to flourish, but it can also do the same for us. Nettle is packed with protein, minerals, and vitamins that our body desperately needs when we are sick, recovering from illness, or trying to cope with the stresses of modern life. In fact, this plant is our most powerful adaptogen, a natural substance that restores the body back to balance, allowing it to adapt to difficult situations and to support the recuperation process. Nettle tea is therefore a great support for this and is easy to make by nipping the top two leaf layers of nettles in the spring and drying the leaves on newspaper for a few days or in a dehydrator for a few hours. These dried nettle leaves will keep throughout the winter for when they are needed most.

Nettles provide potent food and survival for many insects. One of the most magical experiences I have had with the nettle is standing in a nettle patch in the evening sunset with fifty red admiral butterflies in their mating dance, swooping and whirling about me. A precious moment to bear witness to. With nettles supporting so many species of insects, it is advisable to keep a patch of them in a corner of your garden for the insects, as well as for your nettle tea.

The leaves of nettle are arranged in pairs, sitting at 90-degree angles around the stem, creating the four directions of the medicine wheel when viewed from above, physically demonstrating the rebalancing quality of the plant. On an emotional level nettle offers the same gift: it harmonizes, brings us back into alignment with our emotions, allows us to see where our imbalances exist, and guides us naturally to that state of stability.

One of the basic principles of meditation practice in the Tibetan tradition is equanimity, adopting techniques to bring the mind into equipoise and therefore the emotions and subsequently the bodily systems. We are looking for the still points between the movements of the mind, the middle path between attachment and aversion, and the equanimous state that sees every physical and nonphysical sentient being as equal. It is difficult for the mind to attain this level of balance, however, because karma can take us on a roller coaster of emotion during the course of a single day. While we don't want to deny or negate the existence of emotions that make us human, the objective is not to be ruled by them but to give ourselves the space to change our response to them rather than responding from habit, wounding, or ego. If I am feeling anxious, I can recognize that something within me needs addressing rather than externalizing the cause of the emotion and blaming others for making me feel that way.

Nettle can help us attain emotional balance and emotional maturity, taking responsibility for our feelings rather than believing they are dependent on whatever or whoever is associated them. Western society does not encourage looking within but teaches us to outsource all responsibility of health and well-being to a narrow health system and reductionist scientists. Remembering our own power and ability to heal ourselves brings an instant level of inner peace. This calmness that Nettle also offers seems contradictory to the energizing power of its medicine. Nettle seed tincture is one of the most powerful medicines to provide energy and sustenance to tired-out adrenal glands. If plants did not operate within this dichotomy at some level, they would not be of Earth and would not be the life-affirming beings that they are. We need to shift out of our linear and conditioned mind-set if we are to understand plants at their most profound.

Nettle also has a very disciplined nature to it, pulling us into a state of self-care and self-awareness that is required to get through difficult situations. The famous Tibetan yogi Milarepa was said to have existed solely on nettles during his many years of meditation retreat up in the Himalayan mountains. Consequently, in many of the paintings on the walls of Buddhist temples, he is often depicted as green in color or with a green halo. Nettles were said to be the only sustenance that Milarepa had and so in effect he was undertaking a plant diet. Nettle calms and balances then delivers insights like bolts of lightning to the psyche during meditation, so I cannot imagine that Milarepa did not meet its spirit during his many years alone with this plant. He became enlightened despite committing terrible crimes, and the Buddhists have chosen to show nettle as part of that transformation, demonstrating the power of this incredible plant.

Probably one of your first memories of Nettle is its fiery sting. Plants that sting and are pungent or hot in taste are often ruled by Mars, and Nettle also falls under this ardent planet. Enthusiasm and high ideals are the lighter side of Mars; tempestuousness and conflict are of its shadow. We need to be careful when dealing with such dynamic energies, which is why the wisdom of Nettle holds us while we integrate them. Nettle creates strong boundaries with its stings to keep predators away and is often seen in centurion-like rows around trees (particularly hawthorn trees) and edges of fields. This speaks to us of our own sovereign space and where we place our own boundaries, the limitations we set according to what is acceptable to us and what is not. Our boundaries exist on many levels: those we implement with our family and friends, those we implement with our spirit allies, and those we set for our safety in our spiritual work. Have we reset our boundaries as we have grown older or wiser? Do we allow others to transgress our boundaries easily? If so, why is this? Working with nettle we can more easily see where the imbalances in our boundaries lie, where more assertion is required or where a softer approach can be applied.

Understanding and maintaining boundaries is a lifelong process and requires constant reassessment if we are to progress on our spiritual path. Weak boundaries are one of the main causes of suffering. Our narcissistic society does not like us saying no, but to maintain sovereignty over our self and our life we need to develop this inner strength within our own truth. Having strong yet flexible boundaries helps reduce drama in our lives and therefore reduces the amount of energy wasted on unnecessary situations, prevents others from projecting their own issues onto us, and allows a healthy sense of self-preservation and self-love to arise within us, assisting us in all areas of life. This is nettle's form of protection. When we read in metaphysical-oriented plant books that a plant is protective, we need to determine exactly how it is protective, as each plant offers different forms of protection. It is thought that keeping nettles on the boundary of the house and garden offers security for the inhabitants. Keeping nettle on your energetic boundaries can do the same thing.

All the qualities that we associate and experience with fire are contained within the nettle at some level. Fire is warmth, inspiration, creativity, transformation, wisdom, passion, and spontaneity. By meditating with either the tea or an essence, we can cultivate those beneficial qualities within us too. By placing nettle in the south of our medicine wheel, we can focus these energies into our intention for the wheel. In modern times we are taught that fire is dangerous; it destroys things and is to be feared. Yet fire has always been regarded as having its own consciousness by indigenous cultures, including that of the British Isles, and for the Tibetans it is an enlightened goddess who brings purification of karma and transformation to those that can learn to work with her. To other cultures it is Grandfather Fire who offers profound wisdom and great bliss. In the mythology of the British Isles, fire is Freya, the goddess of the three worlds who carries the impetus for the Great Web to manifest. In all cultures our subtle, inner fire is the spark of creation, of passion, and of joy; it is enthusiasm and excitement for life. Too much fire, however, creates agitation and irritation and a lack of tolerance of others and fuels the erratic monkey mind. Too little fire on the spiritual path results in a lack of enthusiasm to maintain principles and ethics, no enthusiasm for meditation, and therefore slower progress. Whether you have too much fire or too little inner fire, nettle can rebalance you back to equilibrium and therefore is a great support to your inner work and your meditation practice. Balanced inner fire brings illumination and powerful visions.

The spirit of Nettle is a strong teacher. Students in our classes report the feeling of being chastised by Nettle and that it is the strictest of teachers. It takes a lot to hold the human monkey mind in balance, and Nettle needs his own firm boundaries in order to do his work. For me, Nettle is one of the more elusive spirits to perceive directly as its adaptogenic nature comes through in its energetic form and I can't seem to grasp it within any one aspect or guise. So for me, Nettle moves through me without form, adapting and changing to circumstance as it does its work.

The most shamanic aspect of Nettle is his appreciation of the dismemberment process. With his serrated leaves and uncompromising fiery nature, he revels in taking people through the death and rebirth process to help us move through illusions. Dismemberment is a surrendering to a spirit ally who will tear your astral body limb from limb, roast it over a fire, or melt it down in a vat of acid to release unhelpful patterns or blockages. There are myriad ways our students report this spiritual death process taking place, some very beautiful and some rather terrifying. Yet always, the enlightened spirit ally will lovingly rebuild and put us back together so that we resonate with a new level of consciousness more in alignment with universal truth and freedom. We also become more in tune with the consciousness of our spirit ally and embody its wisdom on a more profound level. We become liberated. Generally speaking, this shamanic process is best held by an experienced shaman or healer; however, it may also happen spontaneously if Nettle decides you are capable of holding and learning from it.

The following meditation is adapted from an ancient elemental meditation from Bon, the pre-Buddhist shamanic tradition of Tibet.[1] This healing meditation was used for thousands of years to bring harmony to body, mind, and soul. Here we will be working with both the energy of nettle as well as the element of fire.

Healing and Balancing Meditation

Sit quietly in your garden with a nettle plant or take a few drops of its essence or a cup of nettle tea and connect to the conscious intelligence of the plant. Ask it for healing.

Calm your mind by taking a few deep breaths in and thoroughly relaxing the body on the exhalation.

Visualize red fire energy moving toward you from Nettle. Feel the radiating pure red fire element as it envelops you; feel the warmth all around you. Move your awareness to your crown chakra and feel the warm red light enter your body through this chakra. Feel it throughout your body transforming you into fire. Feel the change in your skin, bones, flesh, muscles, and cells; feel that they are all transformed into fire.

Now move your awareness to your liver. This is where the fire element is concentrated in the body. Visualize and feel the red fire element of Nettle in the liver. Ask the consciousness of Nettle to remove any unhelpful energies from your liver so you may cultivate the positive qualities of fire instead, ones of inspiration, creativity, warmth, and willpower.

Bring your awareness to your breath and breathe slowly and deeply into your belly. With each exhalation breathe out the unhelpful energies from your liver as gray smoke. As you inhale breathe in more fire and nettle energy into the liver. Imagine energetic blockages being cleared.

Spend a few minutes with this slow, deep breathing into the liver—exhaling what you don't need and inhaling all the positive qualities that fire and nettle bring you. Feel the breath permeating your body.

Feel the changes in your body, energy, and mind.

Now visualize more red fire element coming down through your crown chakra into your central core, filling it with vibrant fire and nettle.

Feel the energy flowing down through the core or your torso. Feel the fire element flowing up and down, removing obstacles and blockages, allowing yourself to feel increasing bliss and peace.

Feel the pure fire and nettle energy slowly accumulate in the heart center, the seat of the soul, and integrate into your soul consciousness.

Feel the light at the heart center and in the deepest levels of experience and integrate it with your awareness. Feel that whatever needs healing is healed, whatever needs strength is strengthened. Take a few minutes to rest in this state of bliss and peace.

Fig. 11.1. *Taraxacum officinale*

11

Breaking Old Habits with the Spirit of Dandelion

MANY SPRING FLOWERS are yellow in color, calling in and anchoring the healing and creative forces of the sun as it becomes a growing part of our life once again during spring. Dandelions are one of the most abundant of spring flowers and are present on every continent of the planet apart from Antarctica. The power and genius of this plant are evident also in its self-replicating skills and medicine. There are currently an estimated two hundred types of dandelion—and counting. If you collect lots of dandelion leaves and look at them closely, they will all look similar and unmistakably dandelion, but each leaf will have its own unique shape and contour. Our favorite garden weed masterfully demonstrates the cosmic law of sameness and difference in its expression.

The name dandelion most likely comes from a mispronunciation of its French name *dent-de-lion,* meaning "lion's tooth," and it is generally thought that this refers to its leaves, which do indeed look like rows of sharp teeth. Yet there is another aspect of its name embedded within the medicine of this wonderful garden plant. When we work with Dandelion on an emotional level, and again I emphasize that our intentions when taking any plant medicine are key to its effects, the experience can be similar to a lion roaring in your face! This is a loud plant, and you may suddenly find that behavioral patterns that are no longer serving your highest good and life issues, which you have put on the

173

back burner to be dealt with later, become intolerable. When this lion appears in your life, it can be the proverbial kick up the arse that you need, but beware because it will not stop until you address what is out of balance. The lion asks for your active cooperation. He expects you to pull the threads of your life into alignment. If there are old habits that need breaking and working through, if there are patterns that need changing or a forceful shift required, then Dandelion is your plant. In fact, just as medical herbalist Carol Guyett teaches, Dandelion works with the design of energies, and this can be applied to all areas of life.

How do the various aspects of your life blend together? How do you flow from one role in life to another? Where are the imbalances that have regressed into stagnation? Seeing how we can fuse and integrate existing and new influences into our work, family, and spiritual life is a great blessing. On a mundane level, if you are a designer, project manager, or creator of any kind, Dandelion helps to pull the threads of projects together into a cohesive whole. It presents the bigger picture with an eye on the details so we can see exactly what needs to be put into place and when. I work with Dandelion during the winter when I need the sunlight of inspiration to cut through the winter gloom to help me put together the following year's courses and retreats for our students and attendees.

The sacred geometry of the flower of life held within the flower head and seed head of the dandelion demonstrates its association with all levels of human consciousness from the mundane to the cosmic, from the solar to the lunar. This powerful air plant knows how our world functions within the solar system and how that is reflected into the micro of us mere humans. The unification of our polarities into oneness through the integration of our shadow is the ultimate teaching of all of the plants; however, Dandelion offers us visual as well as spiritual aid. The pattern of the flower of life is the key to time, space, and multidimensionality and is why the spirit of Dandelion is known (to me anyway) as the lord of time. During one of my plant diets with this mind-blowing being, I experienced profound coincidences, which taught me about divine timing, that when we listen from our higher self-perspective, we can surrender to the divine plan of life. I used to have a tendency to want to know that something would happen or be successful before it actually took place. I would get anxious before an event, or I would need repeated validation that my intention was going to be fulfilled. It was a lack of trust in the flow of life alongside a lack of trust in myself and my spirit team.

Dandelion shows us through clever circumstance and demonstration that when we make decisions and take actions from the perspective of higher mind—that is, one in alignment with the divine plan, with the cosmic pattern—then everything happens exactly as it should and when it needs to. There is no need to doubt or question your own intention because it is also the intention of spirit. When we expand our mind into the divine plan for Mother Earth, we can be part of the consciousness shift happening right now, a shift that is taking human consciousness into a fifth-dimensional state. This state of mind is non-polarized and comes from unconditional love and from the realm of the eternal spirit. We are becoming more and more ensouled as we evolve and remember our place in the cosmic dance.

Human consciousness is ever evolving but none more so than the last hundred years. To easily see the evolvement of human consciousness taking place on the planet, I look at all the ways that women have found freedom and liberation, even within my own living memory. When I was a child in the late seventies, my mother had to get my father's permission to open her own bank account! While we have still not yet achieved parity within this masculine-dominated world, the societal mind, at least in the West, has changed and allowed women, as well as other marginalized members of society such as homosexuals, to be accepted in a way that was unthinkable forty years ago. These are very welcome changes, indeed, as we remember that biodiversity within the human race is just as important as the environment. We are all members of the same race so let's celebrate our differences and our diverse contributions to society. This growing acceptance of differences is a great advancement for our species, and while we have a long way to go, I have found that Dandelion offers us the chance to take this expansion of consciousness to the next level. This cosmic plant aligns us with the cosmic plan of the planet, and the collective. Dandelion is directly helping the evolvement of humanity!

The air element is the messenger. It can move between the physical world and the spiritual world with ease. We can feel air, but apart from space, it is the only element we cannot see; it is not fully manifest. Air moves between the seen and unseen realms, communicating impulses and information between states of consciousness. The breath is the mediator between our physical and spiritual worlds. When we work with the breath in meditation, many existential questions and realizations arise. What is our relationship to the physical world? How easily do we allow the outside world in? What blockages can the intake of breath reveal in our acceptance of life in the manifest world?

As a medicine woman and spirit worker, it is my job to read the web of life or the web of wyrd, as it is also known. I never consider anything to be mere coincidence; there is always a multilayered understanding to every moment. The universe is ordered; it is not random. The word *cosmos* comes from the Greek word *kosmos,* meaning "order" or "world" because "the cosmos is the product of a single act of generation that has set a signature upon everything."[1] Everything is therefore connected, either through cause and effect, karma, or evolvement. Many of our spiritual traditions have been influenced by the *Hermetica,* philosophical texts attributed to Hermes Trismegistus that outline the universal laws that connect all things, the truths that lie at the heart of all existence. Magicians, witches, and alchemists all work through the doctrine of correspondences to understand the web of life and orient their endeavors through it for their practice, as we do here with plant spirit healing. The clearer your inner vision and intuition become, the easier it is to read the signposts of life. Dandelion helps connect those dots through synchronistic and diachronistic occurrences.

Allowing ourselves to flow with the current of life's river does not, however, mean that we can bypass the things we must take responsibility for. I have seen this often in spiritual communities where "divine timing" has been used as an excuse for simply being disorganized and not holding space well for others. Dandelion is all about taking responsibility for all areas of your life; you are a cocreator and so you are responsible for what happens in your life. This plant is therefore a great ally in the cultivation of that warrior spirit within, the warrior heart and mind.

Our understanding of time, which is drilled into us from a young age, is that it is linear when we only have to look outside our window to see this is not true, that everything is cyclical and spiral. There seems to be a linear progression as we age yet only on the level of cause and effect. Outside space-time there is no linearity of time as we know it. The sacred geometrical patterns within the structure of dandelion flowers deconstruct the frameworks of time that we have built our ivory towers in, collapsing their walls so that only the present moment exists. It is hard to put into words this experience. When this particular penny dropped for me, I was sunbathing in a park in London, surrounded by dandelions, speaking to the spirit of Dandelion, and as the realization of no-time occurred, it felt as if the ground were falling away from me in every direction until I was left on a plinth of rock in no-man's land. It only lasted a minute or so, but in that short time, my whole worldview shifted. Suddenly, my past lives weren't past anymore and my ancestors were (are) still alive within my cells, and therefore at certain levels of my consciousness, every incarnation I had had both within and outside the human race was now accessible and the power lines to my lineages opened up to a vista of new inner space. Time took on a whole new meaning as ancestral and soul healing took on a whole new dynamic within my work, thanks to this cosmic plant spirit.

If we refer to the symbology of continuance presented here, the circle and spiral present deeper insight into the medicine of *Taraxacum*. Dandelion offers completion, renewal, regeneration, and wholeness. Its medicinal offerings are so broad that it provides remedies or relief for fifty-eight known conditions and illnesses (possibly more), from joint pain to yeast infections, from Alzheimer's to eczema: this plant is a powerhouse of a healer and has many spokes to its wheel. The actions of its leaf, flower, stem, and root are incredibly diverse, which is why indigenous peoples and cultures around the globe have prized this plant for its healing gifts. In the West dandelions are most well known and appreciated for their benefits for the liver and gallbladder. Dandelion bitters can purge, clear, and reinvigorate a clogged and tired liver, the organ that gets most abused by our modern lifestyle.

In Traditional Chinese Medicine the liver is where we store our anger, locked up amid all the toxins our liver is protecting us from. It is the master organ as it tirelessly helps us to live more than any other organ, hence its name. The liver is one of the only organs that can regenerate itself if part of it is removed, a reflection of its sympathy with self-regenerating dandelions, which can grow back as a full plant from just a root fragment left in the earth. The liver can even be viewed as having a visceral consciousness of its own. "It prepares ahead when it knows you need extra support, and it's there to clean up the mess after your earthly mistakes. It's a storehouse, a filter, a processing center, a garbage service, and more. It shields you, it protects you, and it defends you from every angle. It's been looking out for you all along—dying out fires, defusing bombs, taking bullets for you, rounding up the bad guys inside of you, and preventing internal disasters. Your liver is the reason, after everything you've been through in life, that you're still alive."[2] Often overlooked because it quietly does its thing in the background with no discernible grumble, our liver needs more support today than ever. We live in a chemical world; the varieties of toxins that we come across in just one day are vast. Even gasoline that gets on your hands while filling up the car will soak through the skin and be processed and stored by the liver to protect you from harmful petrochemical toxins. It is advisable, therefore, to do a regular liver cleanse, and this can be as simple as taking dandelion root tincture every day for a month.

Through the support of a benevolent liver and the purging action of the dandelion, we are free to explore our anger in all its varieties as toxins are released. From frustration to rage, from self-preservation to enthusiasm, all types of anger serve a purpose; we just have to decide whether we need that purpose or not. Is it an energy that is required for our higher good or not? Anger can be a protective force from an underlying depression, and it can also indicate what we have been suppressing. Anger does not only have to be part of our shadow; it can be seen, transformed, and accepted as part of the rebuilding of our sovereign self. Suppressing anger can, however, lead to serious health conditions, and it is with the help of Dandelion that we can release and alchemize our anger, even if we didn't know it was there, giving us the inner freedom to move around our inner landscape without the fear of encountering a prowling lion. The purification of the liver has a direct effect on the mind, and we become clearer with fewer erratic thoughts and are then able to connect the dots of the sacred geometry of our life.

With all of this serious work that Dandelion is involved with and promulgates, it is a relief to discover that the spiritual force that works through this plant is actually very cheerful. During our training courses where we spend the weekend with just one plant, there is always a childlike joviality when we are getting to know Dandelion. We observe a reconnection to the inner child and a lightness of spirit that enables consciousness shifts to take place. Strong in both air and fire elements, the spirit of Dandelion works at a fast pace and encourages us to keep up through making the teachings fun and rewarding. One student even reported that the spirit of Dandelion appeared to her dancing in a silly way and encouraged her to do the same; she admitted she hadn't danced for many years. By inspiring a deeper connection to our sense of self through the solar plexus, dandelion can help us experience freedom on a whole new level. The spirit of Dandelion encourages us to move beyond our self-imposed limitations to rediscover our lion's heart and express ourselves fearlessly. Weaving in and around us as we hold sacred space for our shamanic journeying, the spirit of Dandelion breathes transformation into our dreams and visions.

In the following meditation you will learn how to work with the spirit of Dandelion to start to break old habits and move through patterns of thought or behavior that create obstacles and blockages in your life. The brain is habitual; it likes to use the same familiar neural pathways for its functioning, and so we get stuck in a rut. The great thing about the brain is that it is flexible and can be changed; new neural pathways can be created to orient us toward healthier and more mindful approaches to certain areas of our life.

Be Here Now Meditation

With a monkey mind jumping backward and forward to the past and the future, more concerned with what we are about to do or would like to do rather than appreciating what we're currently doing, it is very challenging to change our unhelpful habits. If the mind is not present, it does not notice the habit in the first place, running on autopilot to maintain a crutch it needs to sustain and appease the grumbling soul forces within. Your habits could be anything from being addicted to a substance, to spacing out when anyone mentions something you don't want to deal with, to eating junk food in front of the TV, to being instantly defensive over minor issues. Patterns that are repeated over and over again end up being performed on autopilot as our mind is most often not present with the habit but is thinking about the emails it still has to send or the disagreement it had with so-and-so last week. The causes of habits are lost in the depths of the psyche as they become more and more autonomous and automatic.

The following meditation is again a traditional and popular Buddhist practice adapted to work with Dandelion. It is popular because it works. Single-focus meditation brings calm to the monkey mind and retrieves the energy of lost thoughts from the past and the future. Each time we retrieve our awareness from thoughts that powerfully catch our attention, we come back to the present moment, and a certain level of awareness is brought to the habitual thought. Being in the present moment helps us identify unhelpful habits and bring them into the light of awareness, making them much easier to deal with.

Find your comfortable place to sit with your feet or legs on the earth and your back nice and straight. Take a few drops of dandelion essence or soak in the energy of a dandelion you may be sitting next to.

Use the dropping the mind into the heart meditation in chapter 1 to calm the mind in advance of the practice, which will make the single-pointed focus practice a little easier.

After you feel you have a new sense of inner peace, take your awareness to your breath; do not grasp too tightly to your breath but just notice one aspect of it, such as the cool feeling as it enters the nostrils or the space between the inhalation and exhalation.

Keep your mind resting in this one place, and if it wanders or gets caught up with a strong thought, simply catch it and bring it back to the breath. Start off with five minutes of this and then build up to twenty-four minutes, if you can. You will find that insights about the habitual thoughts of the mind are illuminated with a recognition of its subtler workings. Habitual thoughts will no longer have as much power over you.

When you feel you have become proficient with resting the awareness on the breath, you can introduce a symbol that you hold within the mind's eye, resting your attention there. Moving from something physical to an object less tangible presents more challenge and variety for the practice.

The symbol received from the plant in chapter 6 could be the perfect option here; alternatively, you could use a sacred symbol such as aum or ah, depending on your preference.

Fig. 12.1. *Alnus glutinosa*

12

Emotional Balance with the Spirit of Alder

CONCEALED WITHIN MYSTERY and the liminal space on the banks of streams and rivers stands the dark queen of the forest, Alder. She resides in the background of the ever-evolving tapestry of the woodland, quietly working with the mycorizhal network, the water element, and the light of the moon to bring elven magic to the twilight. For her own soul purpose in this realm, she needs to be comfortable with the shadow being so close. She can only achieve this by holding her inner light so strong that the darkness becomes her ally, as the seed of her power lies within its realm. Just as the moon reflects the light of the sun while holding its dark side steady, so Alder teaches how to allow the mind to reflect the will of our divine eternal self with full acceptance of all that we are. Without the lessons and the wisdom from our deep feminine interiority, the masculine light cannot shine into the world. Only through learning the lessons of our karma and accepting the fallibility of our humanness can we stand in our power. Alder is the messenger of the transcendence of paradox. Associated with both Mars and Venus, Alder would hold the west of your medicine wheel with power and grace.

Alder's power can clearly be experienced on the fifth full moon of the year, also known as the Wesak moon, when Gautama Buddha achieved enlightenment. This powerful spring moon climbs over the horizon in all its fiery golden splendor and holds the hills in magical suspense, reminding us of the power of inner illumination and the human potential that we all possess. The moon teaches us about our dualistic existence, it being a metaphor for the mind.

In Dzogchen and Buddhist philosophy, the mind is like a crystal: it refracts and reflects. The mind that perceives dualism is the conceptual and therefore finite mind, which we employ to operate and function effectively in the material world. This is the aspect of mind that we use on a daily basis and reflects the exterior world. Behind the conceptual mind is the higher mind, the mind that perceives from the fundamental laws of the universe, that of love without conditions and witness without polarity. This level of consciousness works through the heart and can be said to lie dormant until it also is given the acknowledgment and energy it requires to reflect the inner light of the divine eternal self through us into all dimensions. We experience this state of consciousness through creativity, music, art, poetry, and the flow state. It can also be expressed as no-mind, as it communicates to us through symbology and feeling rather than words. The full expression or awakened state of this part of our consciousness needs acknowledgment, development, and nurturing if we are to live a life in harmony and connection to the cosmic universe around us. Unfortunately, it has been neglected in favor of earning a living and achieving status and power; however, it still remains a part of the unconscious until the subconscious aspects of the conceptual mind are cleansed and purified to allow the light of the eternal mind to shine through. By working from this level, we place our eternal self at the forefront of our existence, and we can start to accept the wonderful guidance and wisdom that comes from this divine aspect of ourselves as it filters and flows through all aspects of our life. Making the eternal spirit conscious in this way is the objective of plant spirit healing, the same as the ancient mystery schools and the true alchemical system.

Alder holds illumination in the shadows and is a guiding light for our inner work. She holds other wonderful healing qualities when we work with her water element in the emotional realm. Alder wood does not degenerate in water; it has mastered this inner element and does not rot. She has conquered her emotions so they do not rule or weaken her in any way but work alongside her, as her own inner rudder on the great ship of life.

When extreme emotional and psychic stress causes our mind to become paralyzed or go blank, we are disconnecting ourselves from the painful experience, blocking it out of our mind and therefore potentially suppressing the resulting emotions and traumatic imprints. When we suppress and repress emotions, we store them in the dissociated part of the body, and they remain there until addressed, causing all manner of imbalances, pain, and illness over time.

In an emergency where we are dissociated from ourselves, such as with shock, grief, or psychic attack, Alder can reconnect us back to ourselves so that we can witness what is happening to us. In such a situation I turn to Alder as my ally. By shining her moonlight of illumination into our darkened inner vision, inspiration is allowed to flow back into the mind and thoughts can start to flow again, providing a route back to our sense of self. She is a lifeline in dark moments. When we remain in the present moment in contact with a sense of self, we allow the emotional and psychic disturbance to take its natural course and move through us. By remaining aware of what is happening to us and facing that which is arising in our experience, we stand in our power.

Doing this also prevents unhelpful energies from taking advantage of a body where the lights are on but nobody is home. This does not mean that we do not express our emotions or that we're not kind to ourselves. It means we accept the situation and don't go into panic mode. We don't give our energy away to something else but remain sovereign.

This process can also work when we suffer from an issue that is eluding us, such as a strange illness or some emotional imbalance that we just can't get to the bottom of. By taking a tea or essence of alder and meditating with her, asking her to shine her lantern into the murky depths of our emotions, bubbles of inspiration and insight can arise, freeing us from the master-slave relationship we have with our emotions and forming the basis of our psychospiritual healing. This queen of a tree spirit teaches us how to conquer ourselves rather than other people, and this means mastery of our emotions until they no longer rule us but work with us as we navigate this energetic world.

We are highly emotional beings, never properly taught how to manage these powerful energies that flow through us and influence our behavior. Yet by getting to know the unhelpful ones, which we experience through watching out for their triggers, we start to bring conscious awareness to our subconscious reactions. I have found this process so enlightening over the years as I witness and realize which are my own emotions and which are ones I have soaked up or learned from someone else. As well as being emotional, we are empathic creatures and can absorb the atmosphere and energies of our environment if we are not careful. We want to experience and be connected to our environment and others but not be consumed by their energies.

To avoid this we need to strengthen our energetic boundaries through meditation, working with plants, psychic hygiene, and a good diet and exercise plus understanding ourselves and our doorways. The axiom from the Oracle of Delphi, know thyself, means self-awareness at all levels, including the emotional and psychic. As adults, if we do not distinguish between our own emotions and those of others, we remain in a quagmire of unknowing. Through this state of unconsciousness, we are rudderless on an ocean of samsara, at the mercy of toxicity that is not even our own. We allow other people's issues and emotions to transgress our boundaries and cause inner disturbance, not realizing that the energy is not even ours. How can we make important decisions when we do not truly know what is influencing them? Through a process of inner inquiry with Alder, we can start to establish healthy boundaries and gnosis of our emotional body, which in turn balances the astral body, creating the causes and conditions for spirituality and life purpose to flourish.

We can build firm foundations for our soul to emerge fully into this world by working with Alder. The beautiful watery city of Venice is built upon strong foundations of alder wood, which I feel also contributes to the magic of the place. I didn't recognize most of the Otherworld beings when I visited this surreal city but did not feel threatened by them; I was more intrigued by their biodiversity. The Otherworld of Venice is quite different from the Underworld of the Amazon, where much more dangerous seemingly malevolent and threatening *supai* (jungle spirits) dwell. Alder carries impulses and medicine from our gentle yet powerful Otherworld, supporting life and enabling it to thrive, just as the merchant city of Venice has done over the centuries.

When I first met the spirit of Alder, it was through the illusion of a hidden tree. Near my house there is a track that runs through the forest and winds alongside a stream that feeds into a larger stream, which flows past my house. Along this track and hidden behind bracken, brambles, and a thicket stands a very old alder. I had initially mistaken it for one of the many hazels that proliferate along the rivers and streams in this part of Wales, but during one particular spring walk, I looked at the newly unfurled leaves on one of the branches that hung closer to the track and realized I was looking at mysterious Alder. She had remained hidden until now, perhaps through her own influence, who knows. I beat a path through the hedge as I wanted to meditate under it immediately. As soon as I sat down, the spirit of Alder rose above me as a beautiful queen in brilliantly colored robes and stood towering over the top of the tree. After checking three times that this was indeed the spirit of Alder (just to be sure!), I asked her who she was in terms of her soul force. She reminded me that in the elven realm I may work with elven allies, but I had never met the elven queen until now. Just like Alder, the elven queen stands in the background; she keeps herself and her powers hidden so that she can work through the element of water and from her deep feminine mystery. She told me she would teach me the magic of the moon and that I was to return at midnight on the next full moon for my teachings. I asked her in the meantime if she would show me her heart so that I might understand her better. I did not expect an immediate response and realized it was now time to leave the meditation. A few days later my husband and I were taking a twilight walk along the same track, one of my favorite times of day to be out in nature. We approached the old alder tree, shrouded in the protective dusk of the surrounding forest, and stopped on the path to pay our respects. As we stood in reverence toward the tree, a buzzard emerged from behind the trunk revealing its resplendent white and brown patterned underside against the gloom of the forest as it turned in the air and flew into the dusk. We were both speechless for a while at this stunning sight until I remembered that I had asked Alder to show me her heart, and she had done so in the most magical of ways.

I later came across a reference to the elf queen in association with Alder in a book called *Under the Witching Tree* by Corinne Boyer.[1] In it she mentions a Norse saga where the spirit of Alder "is a wild looking woman called 'Rough Else.' She enchants a hero who then goes mad and stays for six months in the forest, living on green herbs. Then she takes him to a land where she is Queen and bathes herself in a magical well and transforms into a beautiful woman. It was believed that an Elf Queen or the daughter of the Elf King lived within the alder tree." True initiations such as those endured by the Vikings and outlined in this mythological story push us to our limits, often to the brink of death, to help us break through the self-imposed boundaries of our conditioning and to embody our full potential. The essence of Alder's magic, power, and beauty shines through this story and, as is often the case the Norse mythology, aligns with that of the British Isles. Alder is considered a powerful ally of Manannan Mac Lir, as both share an elven spiritual lineage and affinity with the realms of water and magic.

There is a lot of folklore associating the alder tree with battles, death, and blood; however, I feel these come from a fear-based perspective, and in true alder style, this hides the true origin of her spirit consciousness.

Emotional Balance Meditation

Ideally, this meditation is done at twilight under a live alder tree; however, you may not live close to one or it may be midwinter right now, in which case taking an essence of alder will achieve similar results. You will need a quiet and undisturbed environment for this meditation; if indoors, it is advisable to open a safe and sacred space for your work.

Becoming aware of the origination of our emotions helps us bring clarity to our way of being and offers immediate opportunity for release.

Calm your mind and drop into your heart using the method outlined in chapter 1.

Bring to mind an unhelpful recurring emotion that has a negative influence on your life and one that you would like to bring balance to. Hold that emotion within the space of stillness that you have created within your heart.

Feel the vibration of that emotion in your body. It may be unpleasant, and you may feel you want to just get rid of it, but this will not assist your knowledge of self. Remain centered within the emotion without getting caught in story or scenario.

Try to think back to the first time you ever felt this emotion. Cast your mind back over the years, perhaps to your childhood, when you first encountered this vibration in your body. What was happening at this time in your life? What was the situation that caused this emotion? Look at this first occurrence through wiser adult eyes.

Within the situation try to determine whether the emotion was your own or coming from someone else. Did the emotion arise from within or did you absorb it from another person? Or did you learn this emotion from one of your parents or siblings? Remain here until illumination arises within your understanding of the cause of this emotion within you.

If, after this process, you still feel you have not got to the cause of this emotion, you can repeat this meditation, or it could potentially have its origin in a past life, in which case it is advisable to do a plant diet or protocol with an ally such as yarrow or cedar.

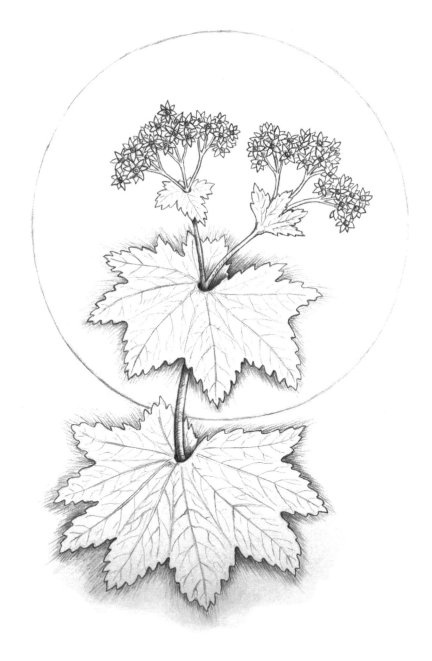

Fig. 13.1. *Alchemilla vulgaris*

13

Alchemical Transformation with the Spirit of Lady's Mantle

THE FINEST SPECIMEN OF a lady's mantle plant that I have ever come across sits patiently on the bank of the stream in the graveyard by my house. The jewel-encrusted crown of hand-sized leaves dripping with dew sits on its own, giving itself the required space to complete its full and unique gesture. The shape of this plant is unusual in our environment, and upon closer inspection, this enigmatic plant holds many other surprising and unique qualities, as we shall discover. Lady's mantle's Latin name is *Alchemilla vulgaris* with *Alchemilla* meaning "alchemy," from the Arabic word *alkemelych,* which refers to both inner and outer transformation of spirit and matter. This is a transformational plant in the truly alchemical sense and offers powerful healing at both a physical and spiritual level.

The droplets of water that form on the leaves of lady's mantle were at one time thought to contain powerful transformative and catalyzing properties, a great addition to any alchemist's work or witch's potion. These droplets of water, which are formed from an excretion of the plant itself and not necessarily from condensation, are also considered the first flower or plant essences, collected in the morning once the water has been potentized in the sun. I feel this vibrational medicine has its roots much deeper in our healing past than is commonly recognized; it has a resonance of elven magic in it. Through an alchemical process that takes place within the composite of all five elements, the crystalline structure of the water is imprinted with all the energetic qualities of the plant, capturing its quintessence. The essence reflects the consciousness of the plant and is an energetic portal through which we can communicate with the plant spirits. This is one of the reasons why lady's mantle is associated with the element of water and indicates flow, an ease of being and balance. The best lady's mantle medicines are all water based, including tea and essence. My favorite is hydrasol distilled by my wonderful plant spirit healer friend Jackie Lewis. Lady's mantle's powerful expression of the water element is also why this graceful plant is associated with the sacral chakra in the Vedic system, which in itself regulates the flow of fluids in the body.

Water like our emotions needs to flow; water that stands still becomes stagnant and rancid.

Suppressed emotions fester and become toxic. Many of our early childhood traumas and, of course, our sexual traumas are held within the sacral chakra and the womb. Healing and rebalance of this chakra is essential for the establishment of emotional maturity, healthy relationships, and spiritual awakening. Another contender for the west direction of your medicine wheel, this feminine plant could also reside in the north if your intention for working with her is physical healing.

This graceful plant is very common in the higher lands of the British Isles and is a long-lived perennial of the rose family. Generally recognized for her ability to heal the female body, Lady's Mantle regulates the menstrual cycle and is a uterine tonic, both contributing to the preparation of the female body for conception, for new life. Antispasmodic, anti-inflammatory, and full of tannins, this plant also helps with painful menstrual cramps and excessive bleeding. In men the same astringent qualities of the plant can assist with impotence and pelvic venous congestion, promoting the flow of bodily fluids and also new life.[1] So despite its name, this plant is not only about the feminine body; every human on the planet carries both male and female aspects.

The energetic and metaphysical healing qualities of Lady's Mantle are beneficial for all, as we shall see.

To understand plants in a truly holistic sense, we need to consider all the frequencies or patterns of energy that run through them. From folklore to ruling planets and from its expression of the elements to archetypes, all aspects and associations of the plant give us an indication of how its spirit works and moves on the metaphysical level. Lady's Mantle is ruled by Venus, the goddess of love, beauty, and attraction in all their guises, including their shadow aspects. She brings the sweet and enjoyable aspects of life but also the overindulgence in these if we do not hold her in balance. Associated with the empress in the tarot deck, with rose quartz and the goddesses Brigid and Danu, Lady's Mantle embodies beauty, creativity, nurture, and pleasure.[2] She has been venerated for millennia as the symbol of feminine power, rebirth, and immortality in many mother cultures around the world.[3] Venus is also associated with the sacral chakra in ayurvedic medicine, and so we see the connections and correspondences resonating through Lady's Mantle and her energetic framework. The symbol of Venus is the same as for the feminine, a circle with an equilateral cross underneath it, very similar to the Egyptian ankh, which is also the symbol of life and immortality. The perfect cross has been ascribed much esoteric meaning throughout the ages; however, in the British Isles, it symbolizes the four directions and the four elements, which arise out of its central space, the center of the medicine wheel, the great void. In the symbol of Venus and the feminine, this is the circle rising above the elements and directions, the spirit emerging and transcending matter not in the sense of a negation of the feminine but as an acknowledgment that both form and spirit are required in unison to awaken the eternal self, to be reborn to a new level of consciousness. The symbol for Venus and the feminine indicates the potential of inner transformation when in human form. The circle is also emblematic of the womb, the sacred portal of creation through which all life emerges. If we look at the well-known symbology of the ouroboros, the snake that eats its own tail, we see a suggestion of not only birth but rebirth emerging from the circle, and this motif is reflected in Lady's Mantle throughout her entire being.

Find a living lady's mantle plant out in the wild or your garden. Sit quietly and allow yourself to drop into deep observation of the plant itself, its structure, its flower and leaf patterns. You will notice how the flowers burst out from the center of a leaf like a cluster of stars bursting forth from a black hole, the birth of a new universe. On a spirit level, when we have worked with lady's mantle medicine for a longer period of time, she can take us through a profound process of inner transformation, being reborn into a new perspective and new state of consciousness in appreciation of the Goddess within us all.

There are many plants and trees ruled by Venus, and each one expresses her beauty in different ways. Birch expresses the youth and rejuvenation of Venusian qualities, elder her abundance and more earthly magic. From deeply nurturing unconditional love to obsessive and controlling misplaced love, Venus reflects back to us our understanding and misunderstanding of the most powerful force in the universe within the energetic architecture of lady's mantle. Venus is the embodiment of the divine feminine and dances the flower of life pattern as she moves through her daily and annual cycle in the sky. The flower of life is a series of overlapping circles creating a sacred geometrical pattern showing the basic formula of all life-forms. It is formed from the golden ratio and can be found in many ancient temples, texts, and even works by Leonardo da Vinci. Venusian plants embody the flower of life pattern within themselves. Plants ruled by Venus face toward her and follow her design as she flows through the heavens, appearing as the evening star that descends below the horizon to be born anew as the morning star. Creation, birth, and rebirth are all held within the conscious spirit of this alchemical plant.

Venus and her expression of the feminine earth and Lady's Mantle, which strongly expresses the water element, work together to manifest healing on the emotional plane, addressing the wounds from past relationships, assisting with the energetic cleansing of sexual trauma, and restoring the spiritual and physical integrity of the sexual organs. Venus is the ruler of relationships and especially relationships with females, whether as friends, lovers, or mothers. Lady's Mantle offers insight into the nature of these relationships in our life and what we offer to the oversoul of each of these partnerships. We come to understand any imbalances and how they are reflections of our own connection to the personal inner divine feminine. Whether male or female we all carry feminine aspects, and how we relate to them is how we ultimately relate to the Great Mother herself, the soul of Earth.

Lady's Mantle took me to Iceland. My diet with her ended on the geothermal mountains of this angelic island, where my husband and I, much to our surprise, discovered five species of lady's mantle. We went to Iceland to look for *Angelica archangelica* in the wild, yet the entire trip was dominated by the teachings and proliferation of Lady's Mantle and her subspecies at the culmination of a six-week diet with her. Working with the mountain spirits and the pristine elements of that land, my husband made the most divine essence of alpine lady's mantle, a much more delicate yet no less powerful subspecies of our own *Alchemilla vulgaris*. We returned from those ten days rejuvenated and changed on levels that would unfold in profound ways over the following year.

We now know all too well that one of the greatest problems facing humanity today is the destruction of the planet. The disconnect that has occurred between us as a species and the one that gives us life is phenomenal, yet at the same time we instinctively know that being in nature is healing, calming, and makes us feel good; hence we all flock to the beach every year and to all of the national parks we are blessed to still have in the United Kingdom. Our indigenous brothers and sisters say that Western people are sick; they have forgotten their spirituality and therefore forgotten their place as guardians of Mother Earth. This next meditation can address the imbalances and disconnection from our own divine feminine, to the deep void within us from which all life springs, from that place of great potentiality, creativity, and wisdom.

Lady's Mantle teaches us how to love again, teaches us how to open our hearts and put our trust and faith in the love that binds everything together. She shows us how we are reflected in nature and so can heal our perceived disconnect from Mother Earth herself.

Precaution: Internal use of this plant is not recommended for pregnant or breastfeeding women.

The Goddess within Meditation

This meditation can also be performed with a specific intention or prayer for healing in a certain area of life. Avoid forcing a response from Lady's Mantle or from Earth; patience and expansion into potentiality are the key. Simply remain open to what occurs over the following days.

This practice can be performed by both men and women alike to assist in the understanding of your own feminine qualities and your own connection to the Great Mother and the source of creation. While we all desire order and structures in our daily life, we must not forget the opposite, the wild emptiness at the foundation of life. Yet how comfortable are we in this place? Let's find out.

It is helpful to take either a few drops of lady's mantle flower essence or have some fresh tea made from the dried leaves of the plant in advance of the meditation.

Sit quietly either in a chair or on the floor. If you are on the floor, cross your legs and sit with your back straight; it is fine to have back support if you require it. If on a chair, also make sure your back is supported upright with your feet flat on the floor.

To start with, bring your awareness to your breathing for a few minutes; just allow your attention to rest on the inward and outward flow of the breath. If your mind wanders, gently bring it back and sink into the present moment.

After a few minutes or when you feel your mind is nice and calm, drop your awareness down to your womb if you are female (if you no longer have the physical womb its energetic counterpart will still be present) and to the sacral chakra (located two finger widths below the navel) if you are male.

This is a potent and creative space within your body. Allow your attention to simply rest here, not expecting to see, feel, or experience anything. Sink into the spaciousness of the womb and sacral chakra. Simply by bringing your awareness to this part of your body, more energy and vitality will naturally follow. Rest here for ten minutes.

Now drop your awareness into the womb of Mother Earth, that great void from which all of her life springs. Where is her source of power located? How does she birth all life within and upon her? Allow your awareness to sink deep into Earth and connect to her source through intention. You may just experience a feeling of this; have no expectation of seeing anything, although images may arise in your mind's eye and insights into how you live alongside Mother Earth may occur. Let go and allow yourself to be held within the watery depths of the Great Mother for as long as you wish.

When you are ready bring your awareness back to your own womb or sacral chakra and then back to the room.

Fig. 14.1. *Rosmarinus officinalis*

14

Uncovering Hidden Memories with the Spirit of Rosemary

WITH ROSEMARY we sink into the realm of the kitchen witch and the surprising healing power that common culinary herbs can have. Yet Rosemary not only warms herself by the stove but plays in the sparkling sunlight, casting her inspiration through the molecules of her pungent volatile oils. Intriguingly, she is also known as elf leaf, perhaps a nod toward her hidden magic and soul-soothing gifts.

Rosemary is a highly aromatic and slightly bitter hardy plant of the Lamiaceae or Labiatae family. It is antibacterial, antifungal, and antioxidant and is also a great nervine. One of the most powerful traits of this plant is that it combats or binds free radicals, toxins that permeate and damage the cells. She is a purificant and cleanses pathogens from the air. Rosemary is a great plant for smudging and can be added to a salt bath as part of a psychic hygiene practice. Used during the winter months to smudge the house, the essential oil of this pungent plant can lift the energies of the home and lighten the spirits. Releasing toxicity from the cells is always a healing objective, so we have chosen the perfect plant ally to assist us with our meditation.

One easily recognizable quality of rosemary is its stimulating effect on the central nervous system, and it is widely used in aromatherapy for this benefit. You can experience this directly by simply taking a good whiff of rosemary when you are tired, and it will wake you up and make you more alert. "It helps a weak memory and quicketh the senses," Nicholas Culpeper noted, and while little scientific study has been done of the memory-enhancing quality of Rosemary, it has held this reputation for centuries with good reason. An old folk remedy states that if you "wish to receive knowledge or the answer to a question, burn rosemary on charcoal and smell its smoke."[1] Through all of these qualities, Rosemary expresses her inner fire and close association with the sun and the root chakra. She expresses the qualities of Mercury through her affinity with the mind, intellect, and communication. She is also associated with the moon, with the hidden and illusory depths, the subconscious, and therefore the source of our sorrows and perhaps our nightmares.

What happens in the body affects the mind, and what happens in the mind affects the body. The body and mind are one; they are not separate. They are in constant communication and are continually influencing each other. Simply thinking about a tragedy increases the heartbeat and elicits the first signs of the stress response. We also know that hormones produced in the body have a powerful influence on mood. The connection between physiology and thought processes behind behavior are the underlying emotions, memories, and traumas, each influencing the other and all influenced by the many factors of our uniqueness, making this area of study highly complex.

We can explore our own body-mind connection and learn the language of our body, also known as body wisdom, through inner investigation and our healing processes. Our body has a natural and innate wisdom that always seeks health, balance, and vitality, a biodynamic force within us that animates us, regulates our bodily responses to the environment, regenerates our cells, and regulates the communication among all the bodily systems that keep us functioning on both a physical and spiritual level. The autonomic nervous system is part of this level of consciousness and regulates involuntary bodily functions such as heartbeat and digestion; however, there is a deeper more profound level of body consciousness that we can tap into that knows how to maintain homeostasis on a spiritual level also.

The body knows more than we do in our normal waking state: it is our pendulum, our inner dowsing mechanism that directs us toward what is positive and healthy for us. We can observe how nature always moves toward balance and how fragile ecosystems can become when imbalance in just one area occurs. As our earth body is not separate from nature but part of it, it too always wants balance and harmony; it always seeks health. Many beneficial and effective healing modalities work with the body-mind wisdom, such as kinesiology and craniosacral therapy, assisting the natural movement back to health through gentle repatterning or nudging of the body wisdom. Rosemary helps awaken this body consciousness within us as she directs us toward the emotions and memories that we are subconsciously still attached to and are therefore influenced by.

It is not only toxins and bacterias that become trapped in the cells of the body. Everything physical has an energetic or etheric version of itself. The toxins that are trapped in our cells have an energetic cause, which is often the destructive and traumatic memories of the past.

Experiences that we view as detrimental and push away are locked into cellular memory as toxic thoughts. Through the science of epigenetics, we also know that transgenerational transmission of traumas can take place across multiple generations. Our issues are not necessarily our own. It is imperative that we save future generations from the sickness of our and our ancestors' traumas and release them today. In Native American wisdom it is said that any healing we do on ourselves we do for seven generations back and seven generations forward. In this meditation we will focus on retrieving our own memories, releasing our own destructive thoughts and behavioral patterns to bring insight into our personal healing process and to discover our own internal equilibrium.

Through our senses we learn the language of the body as we feel into the parts of ourselves that are unhappy and carry disease, as we dive into the inner workings of our psyche. The body is the expression of the soul, and therefore soul traumas can also arise. The most powerful sense in relation to memory is smell. As part of the nervous system, there is a whole section of the temporal lobe of the brain dedicated to the olfactory. The olfactory cortex is also part of the limbic brain, which deals with emotion and feeling. Smell is associated with the root or *muladhara* chakra, the most fundamental and primordial aspects of ourselves related to our survival, safety, and security. According to modern psychology, many of our unhelpful behavioral patterns are the results of experiences and traumas from between the ages of zero and seven, and knowing how vulnerable we are at that age, we start to get a clearer idea about the amount and depth of traumas, imbalances, and imprints stored in the root chakra.

My journey with the spirit of Rosemary took me to the nature of memory itself. She appears to me as a blue moth and works through my dream space where on one particular occasion I saw a white room full of many objects scattered on the floor. There were many different colored and shaped things laid out, but I could not discern any one specifically. Crawling over the objects was a huge spider. I was being shown the web of memories that make me, me. I was seeing how I was a culmination of all of the memories that I have collected within the house of my eternal spirit. Many memories were lost to time, but all were still imprinted in my personal web of lives. I was given the opportunity in the dream to sweep them all down into a large hole—not to deny them, escape from them, or completely forget myself but to detach from them so they remain a part of me but do not hold me back in any way, to free myself from the unhelpful emotional binds preventing me from inner evolvement.

Precaution: Pregnant women or those sensitive to the Lamiaceae family of plants should not undertake this meditation. Those with epilepsy should not take high doses of rosemary.

Following the Threads Meditation

This meditation can be done with either a live rosemary plant, a piece of rosemary that you have taken from the plant, or a bottle of essential oil. I prefer the live plant; however, this is not always possible during the colder months depending where you live.

It is also best to perform this meditation first thing in a morning when your mind is calm and clear and has not engaged with the mundane, the internet, or other people yet. Memories can emerge easier when they are not having to fight their way through surface noise.

Create a nice meditation space where you will not be disturbed.

Take your preferred meditation position, and set your intention for the session. This is the most important aspect of the meditation as this will direct the spirit of Rosemary. What issue do you want to get to the bottom of within yourself? What is the hidden memory underlying your physiological issue?

Take a few deep breaths and sink into your space and then proceed with the dropping your mind into your heart technique. Alternatively, you could use the single focus meditation first for fifteen minutes if your mind is more disturbed or jumpy than usual.

Once you feel calm and centered, take an inhalation of the rosemary. This may involve rubbing the rosemary plant with your hands to release its volatile oils and inhaling the aroma from your hands or inhaling from the essential oil placed on some cotton wool or tissue. Take a few deep breaths of Rosemary.

Ask the spirit of Rosemary to assist you with your issue and to take you to the memory hidden in your body to release it. Then take your awareness to the silvery space of the heart, full of the interwoven and luminous threads of your life.

Ask Rosemary to find the thread that leads to the memory underlying your issue and then follow that thread wherever it takes you. Surrender to whatever lies at the end of the thread. Be open and receptive to whatever arises in your mind's eye or within the experience of your body. You may wish to release any emotional charge associated with the memory, so allow this to come to the surface in whichever way feels appropriate, such as crying or laughing, or it can even release through burping or sighing.

When you feel the experience is over, and only you can decide that, slowly and gently bring yourself back to the room and open your eyes.

Fig. 15.1. *Chamerion angustifolium* syn
Epilobium angustifolium

15

Releasing Trauma with the Spirit of Fireweed

WITH REJUVENATING Fireweed we will stay with the theme of self-liberation from suffering as it is useful to approach our blockages from various angles and perspectives. Rosebay willowherb, commonly known as fireweed, is one of the tallest and most beautiful wildflowers on the British Isles. This striking and elegant perennial likes damp meadows and grows in swathes of abundant deep pink during the summer months. It is also native across Europe and North America, including Canada and right up into Alaska, where it is well known for its many healing qualities. This plant regenerates wherever it grows, often being the first plant to move into burnt or traumatized land. The vitality and soothing renewal that Fireweed offers works in a very similar way for Earth as it does for us.

Every part of the plant can be used for medicine; however, I tend to work with the leaves and flowers. They can be easily harvested and dried during the summer and kept in a dry, cool place for infusions at any time of the year. On a physical level Fireweed helps to keep the digestive system in balance. It is a mild anti-inflammatory that helps various conditions, including stomach and intestinal inflammation and irritable bowel. Within the spring shoots of this soothing plant is a high level of mucilage, a calming agent for irritated tissue that is also helpful for sore throats and lung congestion. Fireweed also has antispasmodic properties, making it useful for asthma, coughs, and intestinal spasms. The essence of fireweed is known for its powerful work with trauma, and it is this aspect of fireweed that I work with most often.

Fireweed exhibits the Saturnian traits of structure of whirling growth patterns and tough stems, which are expressed from its inner energetic architecture. Fireweed is ruled by Saturn, the planet of matter and the material, of both fixing and releasing. It is the bridge between the physical and the spiritual and is the last of the planets in the solar system that can be seen with the naked eye and therefore concerns itself with the final lessons of earthly life. An often-feared planet due to its disruptive effect on our material life, it can create the causes and conditions for old karmas to arise, but we need the awareness to recognize the opportunities that Saturn also brings us and be able to face our inner truths. In spiritual terms this is the perfect opportunity for healing, growth, and renewal, and this is Fireweed territory.

When we experience anything threatening to our body, our life, or our loved ones, the effect that it has on our energy field is one of disruption and distortion. Our perception of what is threatening is key here. Children and adults, for example, see potential threats very differently. What is to an adult a seemingly small and innocuous incident can be to a child traumatic, with the individual experiencing detrimental effects throughout his or her entire life. Likewise, an event that an adult considers traumatic may be seen quite differently from the perspective of a child. It is imperative to remain open minded when dealing with our blockages as the origin or root cause can often be surprisingly innocuous.

Childhood trauma can have pervasive and long-lasting effects, but trauma experienced as an adult can be equally disruptive. Grief, abuse of any kind, neglect, threat, and accidents can all create chaos in our energetic systems on both the emotional and spiritual levels. We can be left feeling powerless and hopeless and with low self-esteem. The physical body experiences a flood of stress hormones, which lowers the immune response. When this immunosuppression is coupled with distortion and fragmentation in the auric field and chakras, we become energetically vulnerable to toxicities and entities, with the result that illnesses manifest. Trauma, born from something perceived as very frightening or painful, knocks our energy field out of alignment. We become ungrounded, knocked off center; our consciousness seems to partially or sometimes fully leave the body, and we disconnect from our sense of self. Depending on the type of trauma, such as physical injury or abuse, various distorted patches or balls of energy get lodged in the etheric body. Complex trauma, which is the repeated exposure to abusive behaviors or situations, can result in very deep cuts or splits in the energy body. Distortions settle into the area either directly affected by the trauma, in and around a chakra associated with the type of trauma, and/or into the cellular memory of the weakened area of the body where we store those particular hurts and pains.

The spirit of Fireweed through its Saturnian energy plunges into the cells of the body to release and repattern the imprints of trauma; it is a master healer in this regard. A protocol or continued use of this plant can dislodge the energies and memories bound up in these imprints and allow them to bubble up to the surface for release. These released energies can be experienced in both visual and kinesthetic form. We may have to revisit old memories and view them with new eyes to allow transformation to happen.

Be gentle and kind to yourself and accept all that arises as a necessary part of your journey; however, it is imperative during this process to avoid the pitfall of victimhood or self-pity. It can be difficult and painful, but we must strengthen the warrior within and take the opportunity to learn something about ourselves and thank the people involved for their part in allowing us to do this. Left unattended these misaligned energies embed themselves deep into our etheric body, and as a result of the fragmentation of the mind, they can eventually cause disease and/or body pain. Fireweed holds a large space for us, clears out the old, and holds us in a warm embrace while we heal and process, leaving a clear space to be filled with love and with new beginnings.

Very often trauma becomes imprinted into the sacral chakra as our memory blocks out the pain and suppresses it into the unconscious. The *svadhisthana* chakra, located two finger-widths below the navel, is associated with the moon, water, and the unseen forces of the subconscious mind. Unprocessed emotions as well as the pleasurable ones find their expression through this vortex, and many of our bodily fluids, such as lymph, blood, and tears, are all influenced by it. This focal point of energy is where our creativity and deeply personal instincts abide, and as many traumas become imprinted and held here, our entire sense of our relationship to the world and to others can be disrupted. Connection to our true self is also obscured as we view everything through the distorted lens of unprocessed trauma. It is in an integral part of the path to self-liberation to address and release these blockages. By doing this we transform ourselves back to the original blueprint of our cellular structures and clear the mind so that we can directly perceive truth. Simply put, if you do not address your issues, you will continue to live in delusion.

The beautiful benefit of working with the plants to assist us on our path to inner freedom means that we can be held within the entire energetic framework of the plant spirit. As plant spirit healer Pam Montgomery teaches, the spirit of Fireweed will hold and nurture the pericardium, the protective membrane that surrounds the heart. As we are taken into unstable and choppy waters with the release of old traumas, we are held within the safety of the heart of this benevolent plant spirit. Trauma release addresses the dissociation within us, and Fireweed at the same time reminds us of our connection to the healing powers of nature. It draws the healing energies to us from many levels and dimensions.

Fireweed can also work as a preventive. When we are going through a particularly challenging period in our life, when our external world is changing rapidly and spirit is asking us to cope with many things simultaneously, taking Fireweed essence or drinking its tea every day for a lunar cycle can help us to move through difficulties with more ease. Any problems that feed into our weaknesses and create tension and stress within us can be processed and let go. With Fireweed, distorted patterns resulting from these challenges, which have the potential to create trauma within us, are instantly moved into harmony and alignment, thereby avoiding any long-lasting effects.

Fireweed can also help us to resolve old destructive patterns of behavior among friends when they arise and need to be addressed. Engrained patterns of communication gradually build up toxicity and eat away at our sense of self. It is a slow form of trauma that needs to be recognized by both parties and resolved. Very often in family situations, the dysfunctional patterns of thought and speech are very difficult to resolve and seem immovable. We have to accept that even if we change, the other person may not want to.

As the world around us goes through seismic transitions and structural changes, a lot of old traumas are being bought to the surface for clearing, and this includes national karmas. The modus operandi of the old British Empire is one of colonialism, and this energy still runs through the land and some of the people in various guises. We carry the trauma of the land and our ancestors within our cellular memory. The ruling classes of the British Isles have not only colonized other countries, they have also used their destructive strategies of divide and conquer on their own people and their neighbors over the centuries. Instances of this continue to this day; for example, the British government wanted to lead the way on vaccinations during the COVID-19 pandemic, threatening to make them mandatory for certain sections of society. This is another form of colonialization, that of the body. Mandates like these take away the freedom to choose the fate of our own bodies and therefore our own minds. Body, mind, and energy field are not separate; they work as a unified whole. Giving away sovereignty over any aspect of ourselves gives away sovereignty of our entire being. As we are the children of Earth, we are therefore handing over the sovereignty of our land at the same time. Our soul forces work through and create our body; if you allow others to dictate what happens to your body, you offer them your soul on a platter.

Colonialization is only ever thought of in a negative way, from its shadow aspect; however, there is a positive side to it that Fireweed can help us with. When we consider that all plants carry synergy between their effects on the body and their healing effects on the mind, we can start to heal deep-rooted and generational traumas. As a physical medicine Fireweed can help rebalance the toxic bacteria in the gut, encouraging the good flora to flourish. In this respect colonization can bring balance. As mentioned previously, we see this positive aspect of colonization in the wild as this pioneer plant rapidly moves into damaged areas to bring renewal. On a metaphysical level Fireweed can bring the imprints of our colonial past buried deep within our ancestral cells to the surface to be transmuted into the more balanced perspective of nonseparation or interconnectedness. The invader becomes the invaded who becomes the invader, over and over through lifetimes and time lines until we decide to break the cycle. We have all been the oppressor and the oppressed, we have all been colonized in different ways, and Fireweed can help move us out of this victim or destructive pattern back to alignment with the cosmic pattern of divine order. There is no need to perpetuate this destructive pattern, which can literally be lifted out of the cells by this peacemaker of a plant. The process can take a while; it is not instant, so old thought patterns and feelings of victimhood or oppression can be felt as they pass through the energy field on their way out. Fireweed is bringing balance to these perhaps inherited traumas and clearing the way for a more expanded awareness to arise. This balanced perspective then filters through to our external world, and so any clearing that you do on this level you do for the collective. Your inner work literally changes the external world; we never truly heal only for ourselves.

The spirit of Fireweed is another plant spirit that takes on the appearance of the culture through which it has been most appreciated and worked with. To my husband it appears as a Native American medicine man, complete with skins, feathers, and rattle. I experience this spirit as movement, like a fresh, warm summer breeze bringing messages of hope and freedom.

Trauma Release Meditation

Relief from trauma can be sought through meditation, whether you are wanting to release an upsurge in emotion during a protocol with Fireweed or to start to move old patterns of pain or discomfort. Trauma disconnects us from the body; it disconnects us from our internal signals of safety and security. With this in mind, be very gentle with yourself during the following meditation.

This meditation is a classic psychotherapeutic technique used to delve into the emotions trapped in the body. Set your space, ensuring you are comfortable and will not be disturbed. Open a sacred space for yourself, light a candle, and call in the plant spirits you already know to guard and protect your healing space. You will find that creating sacred space allows you to feel held and permits deeper exploration and therefore a more powerful healing meditation.

Find a comfortable spot outside next to a patch of fireweed, take five to six drops of the essence, or drink some fireweed tea. Connect to the spirit of Fireweed and ask it to bring release and renewal.

Calm your mind and drop into your heart awareness as outlined in chapter 1.

Bring your awareness to a part of your body that feels natural and comfortable for you. You might play a musical instrument and so have a positive relationship with your hands, or you might be appreciative of your legs that take you everywhere you want to go. Whatever part of your body you are comfortable with, rest here for a few minutes and observe the ease of positive thoughts that flow back and forth between you and that part of your body.

Then slowly move your attention to a difficult emotion or pain or discomfort in the body. Feel this for just a minute and then move back to the comfortable part of your body again.

Keep moving your attention back and forth between these two places. This reexperiencing of the two extremes of feeling can bring both into a place of neutrality. We do not always need to go into the story behind our trauma or issues, although this is often helpful; we can bring energetic balance and therefore harmony by repeated experiencing of the issue with its opposite.

Once you feel a sense of equilibrium between difficulty and comfort and these two extremes are not so present for you, gently bring yourself back to the room.

You may also experience insights, clarity, and a new perspective on the issue and trauma you are dealing with, releasing the power it holds over you.

Fig. 16.1. *Artemisia absinthium*

16

Integrating Shadow with the Spirit of Wormwood

WITH THE GREEN WITCH we venture onto the poison path and into the realm of native psychoactive plants. It is therefore advised to work with this plant only as an essence, a tea, or an incense and only after you have worked with more than five other plant spirits, including Mugwort. Wormwood and mugwort are members of the *Artemisia* family, and mugwort is an ideal introduction to the plant spirit world from this evocative yet cooperative species. Wormwood is a powerful plant and one that requires respect and a strong mind; becoming familiar first with her sister who is equally as powerful but is a more gentile teacher is advisable.

I don't know why such a hardy plant as wormwood is difficult to find in the wild today; it is easy to grow and even small plants in plastic pots can survive very cold winters when left outside. Young plants grow into sturdy and large bushes in the space of one season. The leaves of this beautiful plant have a dreamy bluish hue, and its high content of volatile oils make this a very potent medicine plant with a particularly distinct odor.

One of the most bitter plants in the world with a preponderance for clearing physical and etheric parasites, Wormwood likes to get her hands dirty and wanders the shadows in search of what lurks there. She takes on the jobs that no one else wants and is the messenger that always runs the risk of being shot. You either love her, or you don't.

You either appreciate the sublime beauty in her difficult and uncom-promising work, or you turn away and pretend you never even heard of Wormwood. Like many plants in the psychoactive group, Wormwood is a true shadow plant; her spirit can penetrate levels of existence that others fear to tread. It is her courting of the illusory and the surreal that earns her classification by Dale Pendell as a rhapsodica and why the ine-briant made predominantly from wormwood, absinthe, became popular with bohemian artists and authors of days gone by.[1]

Despite being grouped into the poisonous plant category, the green witch is actually very safe to consume over a short period of time. I do Dr. Hulda Clark's parasite cleanse every couple of years for eighteen days with black walnut, cloves, and wormwood. After this length of time, it is advised not to consume these plants again for at least three weeks to allow any toxins from these potent plants to be flushed out of the liver and body. The same applies with wormwood tea. This is why plant essences are such a great medicine to continue our work with the plant spirit as they only contain the bioresonance of the plant and not the chemical constituents.

Wormwood's predominant element is air; she has an affinity with the mind as reflected in the Old English and Old Saxon name for this plant, *wormod,* roughly translated as "defend the mind."[2] One would imagine that the name wormwood refers to the gut-parasite-clearing qualities of the plant, but this is not the case. A three-week protocol with only the essence allows Wormwood to show you the conditionings and unhelpful energies that influence your thoughts, blocking access to reality. We view the world through the lens of our preconceived ideas and beliefs about past experiences. We view others through the same filter and make judgments about their motivations based on seemingly similar situations in the past. She cleanses the mind and cuts through the illusions that bind our perceptions. She purifies the surface world so that the truth of the shadow can come to light.

Not everyone is ready to see the truth of reality or the real moti-vations of the people around them, hence Wormwood's reputation as a tough teacher. This is why we recommend Wormwood for those on the warrior healer path, for those healers who know the depths to which their own healing and cleansing need to go to be at the top of their game. Fine-tuning our thought processes helps us wriggle free of the indoctrinations that society and culture impose on us and safely expands our consciousness into the realms required for deeper healings to take place. For the cultivation of the warrior mind, we need courage to accept aspects of ourselves that we feel are not pleasant, such as our base emotions or our true motivations. We must refine our thought patterns down to the minutiae of their energy framework to weed out anything contradictory to unconditional love.

Precision is a key attribute to the spirit of our green witch, as she looks very closely and homes in on the details. The spirit of Wormwood has been a great teacher of mine while I was learning psychic surgery. She showed me how to be both quick and detailed in my work, honing both my visioning skills and faith in my ability at the same time. Like many of the *Artemisias,* working with this plant on a regular basis will develop and strengthen clairvoyance abilities, which is so necessary for shamanic healing.

A note and reminder of ethics: If you abuse your powers of seership by looking into the energy fields of others without permission, your gift will diminish through a buildup of karmic sediment in the energy field and a violation of natural law. It is contrary to the law of free will to influence the minds of others in any way without their permission. The line between what we call black magic and white magic is whether you are intentionally influencing other sentient beings (embodied and unembodied), bending them to your will without their permission. The energy of this action registers as a psychic attack in another's energy field. Love potions created by morally questionable witches are the perfect example of creating something to have a particular influencing effect on someone else without his or her agreement. Dowsing on others without their permission has the same detrimental effect and the same karmic debt accumulation for yourself. If you extend this basic understanding out to how our society is run, you will easily observe the ancient mind control magic still being exerted on us since the time of the Reformation by the Protestant Church. We are so used to it that a whole nation can be spelled into voting a certain way to keep a party in power and hardly anyone notices. Plant spirit healing is taking back sovereignty of your energy field and your mind, but with it comes great responsibility as you step outside the status quo and see beyond the illusions. Are you truly ready for that?

With her ruling planet being Mars, the teachings of the spirit of Wormwood are very direct. I once came across an unhelpful energy in my field that had been sent consciously by somebody else. I needed to know how I had allowed this energy in to better understand the doorway or the weakness in my mind and energy field. I asked Wormwood to show me the nature of the energy, and what I saw at first I dismissed out of disbelief. I then asked Wormwood again to show me the nature of the energy. Lady Wormwood appeared right in front of me with a very human face, just inches from mine, and said, "So you didn't already see?" Startled by her directness I was also humbled by my arrogance and denial of her power. Wormwood teaches in a direct and effective way, choosing the path of least resistance for your teachings. She has no time to mess around; she just says it how it is.

My husband, Davyd, also finds her teachings very blunt. Before we went to the Ecuadorian Amazon, he grew many wormwood plants to make antiparasite medicine to take with us. He thought he had seeded them too late, and so they were not very big when he needed to harvest. Knowing a local nursery had a huge wormwood bush, he asked them if he could harvest some of theirs, and they agreed. Upon arrival at the nursery, he found the plant covered in black aphids, common to the *Artemisia*. He left empty-handed and a little downcast. In his next meditation Wormwood told him how stupid he was that he didn't even see that he had an almost 100 percent germination rate on the packet of wormwood seeds he had planted, and he actually had approximately two hundred small plants, plenty to make the medicine we needed. She was not amused by his idiocy, apparently!

Repeated diets with Wormwood have taken my relationship deeper each time and how she appears to me in spirit form has also evolved. At the start of the COVID-19 pandemic of 2020, I went on a Wormwood diet to see the shadows of the macro, to expose the truth, and to see how Wormwood would respond to this outbreak and the associated energies. For three weeks I took the parasite cleanse dosage of wormwood every day, and I gradually sank into what I call a shamanic space where my consciousness expands easily into other realms and I can see the interconnectedness of the external and internal worlds. When I called to her, Wormwood started to appear to me as a much more wrathful spirit, floating above my bed one night like the ghost in the Edwardian novel *The Woman in Black* by Susan Hill. Quite scary. But she was also extremely beautiful, wrapped in green flowing robes and only partially visible from the shadow around her. She was my perfect ally for this time as truths, untruths, and partial truths were rampant throughout society and the media. She taught me new ways to deal with the vampiric energies coming our way, such as the force behind the mandatory vaccinations and the stripping of our human rights that took place at that time.

She also appears in various guises to Davyd, sometimes as a small green sprite-like being, sometimes as a silvery nature spirit. During the first years of his acquaintance with her, she appeared as a Victorian sleuth detective, embodying and expressing the energies of the period in which she had a lot of human interaction. Wormwood was famous in the Victorian era for the aforementioned absinthe drink, which coincides with stories such as Dracula and Frankenstein being published. I wonder if there is any coincidence that at a time when dark metaphysical phenomena were at the forefront of the collective mind of society, absinthe was a popular drink. Who knows, but the point being that plant spirits shape-shift into forms that express the essence of the time during which they are working closely with humans.

A friend once told me that the darkness doesn't laugh, and she was right; it is one of our most precious defenses and defining features of being human. So to balance all of this serious, painstaking, and fear-facing work, Wormwood has a great sense of humor. The molecular structure of wormwood's active ingredient thujone is remarkably similar to tetrahydrocannabinol, the psychoactive ingredient in cannabis, which could account for the giddiness and silliness, which is a feature of a plant diet with Wormwood. She provides the perfect antidote to shadow work. As a serious Virgo, when I diet with her I find myself playing silly pranks on my husband, much to his delight, as he is much more of a playful person than me and enjoys this often-hidden side of my personality being brought out. Joy is a form of protection without the need for separation that protective barriers around our energy field can engender. Raising our spirits automatically protects us from lower vibrational energies by moving us out of their frequency of reality. Our minds are lifted to the upper realms after doing our work in the murky lower worlds. Balance is required to ensure we do not dwell in polarity, to remind us that life does not always need to be taken so seriously.

Precaution: Wormwood is not recommended for pregnant and breastfeeding women, for epileptics, and for people on certain medications, such as warfarin. Do check with your preferred health care adviser before ingesting Artemisia absinthium.

Shadow Integration Meditation

The shadow aspect of the self is the driving force behind negative thoughts and behavior. Coming from Jungian psychology, it is a useful metaphor to assist us in understanding the unseen forces behind our personality and behavioral patterns. Carl Jung describes the shadow as follows:

> The shadow is a moral problem that challenges the whole ego-personality, for no one can become conscious of the shadow without considerable moral effort. To become conscious of it involves recognizing the dark aspects of the personality as present and real. This act is the essential condition for any kind of self-knowledge, and it therefore, as a rule, meets with considerable resistance.[3]

When we are triggered by certain words or when we project anger onto others, these are shadow behaviors emanating from blind spots in our psyche. These behaviors are usually exhibited to protect us from the pain of admitting that we have shortcomings or that we might be wrong. We hide our pain where we can't see it and hope that others can't either. The objective in our healing work is to bring conscious awareness to all aspects of the self in order to move out of polarity and into balanced awareness. In this regard, shadow work and integration are key.

A lunar cycle protocol with Wormwood is advised during which the following meditation can be employed. During this meditation we are going to travel into the deep psyche and meet a shadow aspect of ourselves. This journeying technique I learned from Celtic historian Caitlin Matthews; it has been adapted by the spirit of Wormwood to become a portal through which the spirit of *Artemisia absinthium* can share her wisdom with you. Before you commence it is advisable to check that you are ready and prepared to bring conscious awareness to something you have for so long preferred to lock away. Make sure you are in a grounded and open state of mind. It is also imperative that you are in a state of equanimity so that you can accept anything you encounter and not push it even further into the unconscious. The following affirmation can also be used to balance the mind in preparation: *I am open to any aspect of myself that wants to make itself known and welcome it with clarity and love.*

Begin by making yourself comfortable where you will not be disturbed. Ideally, sit facing the air direction of east.

Take your wormwood medicine of either the essence or tea and allow yourself to drop into coherence with it as it pervades your body and energy system.

Ask the spirit of Wormwood to be at your side and to guide you through the door that you find yourself standing in front of.

Wormwood gently opens the door only to reveal another one. You step through the first door and close it behind you.

Wormwood then opens the second door, and you both step through only to see another one.

More doors keep appearing, one after another, until Wormwood opens one into a small cavern where she will present an aspect of your shadow self.

This may appear in symbol, as a person, or as an object. If you don't understand what the image is telling you, then ask Wormwood to reveal its hidden meaning right now. Be open to receiving unambiguous clarity. Whatever immediately appears to you is Wormwood's message, avoid allowing your conceptual mind to create something by giving it time. Wormwood is quick and direct. If it helps you can step into the cavern in darkness and when you are ready ask Wormwood to turn the light on to reveal her message. Whatever is there in front of you is what she is revealing.

Once you have received the information and accepted this hidden aspect of yourself, thank Wormwood and leave via the doorways through which you arrived.

You may not fully understand what you have seen. You can therefore continue your meditation on this aspect of your shadow to see how you can integrate it, make it an ally against further shadow, and adjust your thoughts or behaviors to prevent it from growing into a stronger shadow, which can influence you from the unknown depths of the psyche.

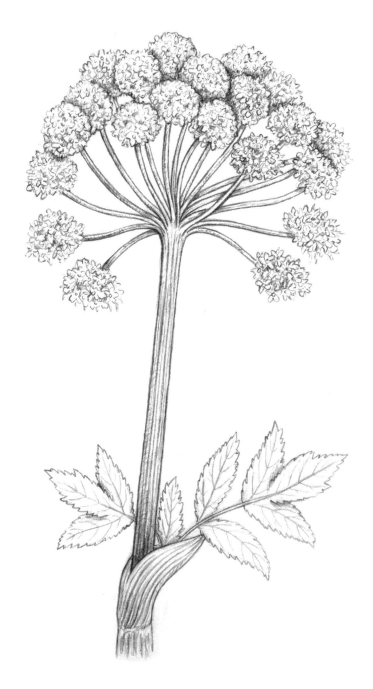

Fig. 17.1. *Angelica archangelica*

17

Awakening Your
Inner Divinity with
the Spirit of Angelica

WHO ARE YOU? Where are you from? What are you doing here? Ask yourself these questions not from a "this life" perspective but from an eternal spirit perspective, as an eternal being evolving through many lifetimes, time lines, and dimensions. Perhaps your current life has been challenging and has required much of your attention, leaving you no space to even consider this aspect of yourself. But as humanity moves into a new era, it is time for all of us to find answers to these questions so that we can step into a new level of wholeness and into true multi-dimensionality. Rudolf Steiner speaks of humanity's dual existence as temporal and eternal, driven to recognize our eternal side and create something higher:

> Here we arrive at the eternal dualism which lives in man, the perpetual antagonism between the temporal and the eternal. Through the eternal he has become something quite definite, and out of this, he is to create something higher. He is both dependent and independent. He can only participate in the eternal Spirit whom he contemplates, in the measure of the compound of elements which that eternal Spirit has effected within him. And it is just on this account that he is called upon to fashion the eternal out of the temporal.

The spirit works within him, but works in in a special way. It works out of the temporal. It is the peculiarity of the human soul that a temporal thing should be able to work like an eternal one, should grow and increase in power like an eternal thing. This is why the soul is at once like a god and a worm. Man, owing to this, stands in a mid-position between God and animals. This growing and increasing force within him is his daimonic element,—that within him which pushes beyond himself.[1]

Getting to the core of your being might need a bit of guidance and support; your true magnificence has been hidden for quite a long time. Welcome *Angelica archangelica* into your sacred space if you are ready to take this journey of self-discovery and awaken your eternal spirit.

In many ancient traditions, magical systems, and mythological legends, the objective of the seeker is the unification of the conceptual mind with the nonconceptual, the eternal aspect of our consciousness existent on a much higher plane of consciousness than the corporeal self. From Egyptian and Norse mythology to alchemy, the great work that all aspirants undertake is the awakening to our divine self. Within the Vedic tradition the crown and soul star chakras are the gateways and connections to this level of awareness. I emphasize again that *higher* simply means "finer or subtler"; it is not higher in respect to the ground level of Earth. As the name suggests, *Angelica archangelica* is a very high vibrational plant; its resonant frequency is in alignment with those of the fifth dimension and above, with the crown and soul star chakras and perhaps chakras that exist beyond in finer realms. The fifth dimension does blend into the higher fourth dimension so is still associated with emotions yet ones of a more transcendent nature. It is to this place and even higher that Angelica connects us. The hollow stem of this radiant plant is a conduit to the subtle realms, to our higher selves, to our inner divinity, and this is the focus of our work with this celestial ally.

Angelica archangelica of the Apiaceae family is not wild or native to the UK but to Europe and up as far north as Iceland and Greenland. The wild species in the UK is *Angelica sylvestris,* which can be found around lakes and riverbanks. It is the *archangelica* species that is reputed for its culinary and medicinal qualities and the one we turn to for our inner work here. In the right conditions angelica can grow up to seven feet tall with beautiful umbels of dainty pale cream and green flowers, which feed a multitude of insects. Its roots emerge from a deep red bulb, which resembles a human heart and which has a distinct and sweet aroma as well as many medicinal benefits. The leaf stems unfurl from its central stem, spreading beautiful large five-lobed and serrated green leaves whose inner fire leaves a tingly sensation on the tongue when nibbled. It truly is a plant of heavenly beauty. It is also remarkably easy to grow, and I recommend everyone to cultivate an angelica in your garden; this experience alone is heart opening and brings purifying protection to the house and garden.

The essential oil of angelica is renowned for its potency and is known as the messenger of the soul in traditional herbal alchemy, having long been known for its affiliation with divine forces and transcendent dimensions. The names and pantheon of the angels and archangels is Judaic and not from the British tradition; equivalent light beings would be the high elves. Often associated with the sun, due to the angles or vectors of their radiating luminous fiery energy, these beings come into our realm resembling rays of sunlight. Gold is the metal of the sun and the alchemical symbol of spirit, as we come full circle back to Angelica and arrive at its association with Archangel Mikael.

The epoch we live in right now is presided over by Archangel Mikael and will continue for another 380 years. According to Steiner there is a rotational system every few hundred years or so (it varies for each archangel) of a different archangel being the guiding principle of the era. The *age of Gabriel* went from 1510 to 1879, and from 1879 to approximately 2400 is the *age of Mikael.* According to occultists Archangel Oriphiel will then take over.[2] It makes sense that the protector of humans and the illumination of human consciousness,

Archangel Mikael, would be the guardian during this era of great change and transformation in human consciousness. Never before in living memory have we had the opportunities for growth that we have today. We have immediate access to most wisdom traditions and can experience almost any other culture we wish, and many are blessed with the time and resources to explore our passions and dreams. Yet many are not willing to make the sacrifices necessary for a truly spiritual life in service to others and the planet. Our comfortable lives easily compromise our motivations and true intentions. Our disconnect from spirit has misled our understanding of how the universe flows within us, and so we refuse to place our trust entirely in the abundance of reality outside the perceived money making system society operates in. Spiritual pursuits are often undertaken to be monetized or to establish a place in the spiritual supermarket. This hollow existence is the malady of the modern human and yet can be transformed and enlivened through the spirit of Angelica.

The spirit of Angelica appeared to me as a diamond-shaped peach-colored light that was in constant flux, creating the appearance of dancing. This spirit feels neither feminine nor masculine, as I would imagine gender plays no role on the angelic plane. It was fluid, graceful, yet strong and direct. The first time I met the Angelica spirit, it gently brought to my mind a dream I had not actually remembered in a waking state. I stood on the edge of the harbor of my hometown in Cornwall with the sun glinting across the water. Angelica asked me if I remembered what happened next. I admitted I did not, but as soon as the dream started to play out again, I knew deep in my soul that I had indeed had the dream before and this was a remembrance. As the wind blew gently across my face, two silhouettes emerged from the sea in front of me. They were filled with or made from stars and had glowing auras about them. I asked them who they were, and they said they were merfolk and proceeded to give me a message about my origins and the trajectory of my eternal spirit. This information dropped into my awareness as a gnosis, a gut feeling of undeniable truth, and it changed my life in an instant. An ancient aspect of myself had been reawakened, and I felt fuller and more alive than I had ever felt in my life. I experienced soul retrieval of my eternal self, healing a core wound within of deep perceived disconnect from the unseen realms of Earth. My yearning to go home was simply a longing to return back to myself, back to my home, Earth, and to my original ancestors. The effect of the healings with this plant spirit can be profound and powerful, assisting us into alignment with our ancient, divine, and even mythological selves. This plant can fill the empty space left by our true self as we fall from the heights of our divine nature. The force and direct focus of the high elves and the divine realms penetrates deep into our core, peeling away the layers that hide our deepest wounds. As a mirror into the physical world, the angelica herb is a useful expectorant for bronchial issues, again assisting issues relating to *espiritus,* the breath or spirit.

The *Angelica archangelica* plant is the embodied spirit of the frequency of Archangel Mikael as it passes through our realm. With his powerful sword of light, he cuts through the illusions that bind us to the trappings of the ahrimanic forces of modern life and highlights the detrimental influences holding us back, reminding us of the unconditional love that dwells at the center of all sentient beings. Angelica works with our core wounds. Angelica's renown for banishing lower vibrational beings and energies is recorded in folklore, as it was said to break curses, hexes, and detrimental spells. It was used for exorcism and as a powerful protector against evil. Smoking the leaves is said to cause visions, although I have never tried this myself.[3]

Angelica could be placed in the fiery south of your medicine wheel, aligning yourself to all of its transformational, protective, and angelic forces. Performing a healing ceremony on one of the cross-quarter festivals, such as Beltane, Imbolc, or Samhain, can add potency to inner work. Research the associated energies and transference of elements associated with these points in the year and design your ritual accordingly. Complementary planetary alignments can also be considered. The more intention you build into your intention and ritual, the more potential is held within its performance.

The Truth of You Meditation

The perfect setting for this meditation is underneath a mature angelica plant in a quiet and private location. If this is not possible, then your usual place of peace is fine. It is advisable to work with the essence or a tea of angelica and to take it before you commence. It may take you some time to establish your handle with angelica and therefore to be properly able to perform this meditation; however, once you have made a vibratory or visionary connection with the plant spirit, you are ready to walk this road less traveled.

Use the dropping the mind into the heart meditation in chapter 1 to calm the mind and bring awareness into the area of the heart, where the messages and impulses of spirit can be heard.

Connect yourself to your handle of angelica and through it to its spirit. Know its resonance in your heart. Ask to connect to its light of awareness and the unconditional love of its eternal spirit.

Feel a sense of spaciousness within the heart, and imagine a glowing violet light that grows stronger with each in breath. Bathe in the beauty and power of this divine light. As the light amplifies you may see a beautiful being of light looking back at you, graceful, strong, and compassionate.

Look into the eyes of this divine being and drink in the beauty of its divine spirit. As you receive its wise energy, realize that it is your own eternal spirit, your higher or divine self. Trust this moment and remember its strength. Know the light of your own essential nature and the truth of who you are.

When you feel you have stayed in this illumined state long enough, gently bring yourself back to the room, anchoring your experience upon your return.

Fig. 18.1. *Sambucus nigra*

18

Dying Consciously with the Spirit of Elder

WHEN WE CONSIDER the conscious intelligence of plants, we cannot overlook the wave of psychedelic teacher plants that have flooded the Western psyche during the last twenty years. Despite the issues that arise with anything that becomes popular in the Western world, these plants have come to us for a reason. They are free-thinking beings that work in alignment with Mother Earth, within the balance of nature, and like all the plants, they have been on this planet millennia longer than we have; they are much more advanced on their evolutionary path. The shamans who work with the spirits of these plants say that the younger brothers and sisters of the West have forgotten their connection to spirit and to Earth and their connection to their higher consciousness and to their eternal spirit, and so they are destroying themselves as well as the planet. Psychoactive or master plants (there are myriad names for them) offer a direct experience of the nonphysical planes; they open our doorways of perception to the unity consciousness that lies behind mundane experience. Whenever there is an imbalance in nature, Mother Nature responds with a counterforce, to bring balance back to the ecosystem. When bee colony numbers decline, dandelions, clover, and other flowers proliferate the following spring to support the bees, making it easier for them to find nectar. As we are also nature, the same is true for us: the plants and trees are coming to us more strongly at this point in time to bring balance back to the chronic imbalances that we have created in the world. A Kichwa shamanic teacher I know once noted that he serves much smaller doses of the medicinal plants that he works with compared to a year or two ago. His observations are that the plants are getting stronger because we need them, and they know it. Pam Montgomery, my plant spirit healer teacher, commented that some of the native plants she works with are stepping forward in their own evolution to assist us in ours.

Psychedelic plants are today also known as entheogens, meaning "that which generates God," which I find quite unhelpful. Giving these plants such a status above others fosters the belief that only these plants can give us that spiritual experience we so crave in our disconnected lives. It suggests that God will only work through certain plants, a concept diametrically opposed to the experience of the plant medicines themselves. It detracts from the deeper understanding that all plants are teacher plants; all plants are a direct conduit to source, to the origins of life, and can lead us to the deeper meaning of our own life. At the same time, many traditions have considered these master plants as sacraments. Religious groups, spiritual movements, and indigenous cultures, such as some Native Americans with peyote[1] and Rastafarianism with cannabis, employ these plants for spiritual purposes, seeking answers to life's most profound questions and exploring their place in the universe. Indeed, the persecution of the witches in Europe during the fifteenth to seventeenth centuries can be viewed as a rooting out by the church of the remaining pagan plant rituals and uses. The witches of the Middle Ages were known to work with psychoactives and plants categorized as poisonous plants, such as mandrake (*Mandragora officinarum*), deadly nightshade (*Atropa belladonna*), and wormwood (*Artemisia absynthium*). While I do not recommend working with the two former plants listed here, as they are lethal if you do not know how to work with them, I mention them to highlight the fact that taking consciousness-altering substances is in our ancestry and history; it is in our blood.

Many of the psychoactive plants are illegal today due to an unfounded classification system that places them alongside man-made and addictive substances, such as heroin and cocaine, while at the same time two of the most addictive and lethal drugs, alcohol and processed tobacco, are legal. I do not believe that our medicine plants should be legalized and placed into the greedy and unsanctimonious pockets of the government but declassified and taken out of any political arena to be put back into the free environment of nature where they belong. Many believe that the war on consciousness is the reason why many of our visionary plants are illegal, that their power to wake us up to the reality of life and to our own free-thinking mind is contrary to the plan of the ones who govern us. What these plants actually do, though, is teach us how to die.

One of these psychoactive plants is ayahuasca, a medicinal brew from the Amazon rainforest whose name means "vine of the soul" or "vine of the dead." It is not just a single plant but a combination of the *Banisteriopsis caapi* vine along with one of many other plants such as chacruna (*Psychotria viridis*), which contains the powerful psychoactive dimethyltryptamine (DMT). *Banisteriopsis* contains an MAO inhibitor, which when combined with the DMT creates a compound identical to the organic tryptamine in our brain. This facilitates the opening of our psychic and energetic channels to encounter ourselves in a more self-reflective way and to perceive other levels of reality, to experience what it is like to die.

Confusion arises within the initiate and experiencer because generally we have no idea where the land of the dead is. We have been conditioned to think that it is up in the heavens somewhere and New Age thought has compounded our Christian background by promoting escapist cosmic concepts, further moving us away from our earthly bodies before we have even learned how to truly live here in this body and on this planet. In the native understanding of the British Isles, the land of our ancestors is located in the Otherworld, deep within the soul forces of Earth. If the connection to our ancestors is our blood and bones, then this is the same earth element as the land that nourishes us and upon which we walk. Earth herself does not only have an earth body but, just like us, also has many dimensions and levels of consciousness within her. Our interiority is that of Earth's and vice versa. Our ancestors return back to Earth from whence they came.

What underlies the biochemical reaction induced by psychoactive plants and works through it are the spirits of them. Ayahuasca is often called Mother Ayahuasca for the nurturing she offers and the wisdom that she imparts. What is often overlooked in our uninitiated perceptions is that this brew can be programmed or attuned with whatever magic or intention the shaman wishes, and this has led to destructive and disempowering uses of this medicine. This plant comes from South America where shamanism is not necessarily related to spirituality but to survival, shamanic war being commonplace between tribes and villages. Tit-for-tat battles between shamans means what we would call black magic is experienced on a daily basis. The spirit of Ayahuasca is neutral yet has both powerful healing and destructive capabilities.

In the West this power should only be carried by those with many years of training and those with a pure mind and heart. As a guideline, ten years of training is a good benchmark for working with plants before teaching or holding a healing space for others. In many Amazonian lineages ten years is standard, and within the druidic tradition each of the three branches of Druidry—the Bard, Ovate, and Druid levels—require ten years to master. There is a danger with this most complicated of karmic medicines for it not to be treated with the respect it deserves. How can we, when we have forgotten the true meaning of sacred in our culture? If participants in these medicines do not have a spiritual practice or even a meditation practice, their seeking of truth can be thwarted by the egotism, self-centeredness, and pride that they have not got under control within themselves. The ego becomes spiritualized, and delusions of awakening and power overtake the mind.

We do not need to plunder the resources of our rainforests to satisfy a legion of truth seekers when the native plants and trees of our own lands can be just as powerfully healing and sometimes just as psychedelic. It is all about how you approach them, hence a meditation practice and traditional working context is extremely valuable. Speaking from many years of direct experience of both the master plant and native common plant worlds, the plant in the British Isles that is very similar to ayahuasca in its teachings is the elder tree, *Sambucus nigra*.

Elder, a common native and short-lived tree, is actually a shrub. Although it prefers wetlands and riverbanks, it can be found almost anywhere and is easily recognizable. The elements of both air and earth can be seen in the physical structure of elder: its flowers arranged in bunches spread facing the sky while the deep redness of the berries demonstrates the earthy qualities of her medicine. Traditionally, the flowers and berries are associated with the medicine of Elder, and her vast treasure chest of healing gifts is well documented in herbal books. We all know what an amazing healer of the common cold she is, but this fame is so belittling to the truly magical powers that Elder possesses. Her affinity to blood gives the first clue to the potential of her metaphysical healing.

We are the blood of our ancestors: their blood runs through our veins and our hearts beat thanks to the life we have inherited from them. When Elder purifies blood she is healing ancestral wounds, traumas, and imbalances. Often when people spend time working with Elder, deep-rooted emotional issues are activated, the origin of which could be several generations back and can therefore be obscured or difficult to understand. These issues are flushed out during a process of rebalancing. A healing crisis, where old issues are activated and come to the surface for clearing, can be concerning for people who want a quick allopathic fix. If an issue suddenly gets worse when working with a plant, misunderstanding about the healing process can arise. If we stop taking the medicine, the issue will still be there because the plant has not had time to finish its job and work the issue through the many energetic layers required for true healing, so it is best to allow the plant to finish what it started. This method is highly enlightening if you are on a spiritual path as we become more conscious through embodiment.

The spirit that works through Elder is a wise crone who helps us take a step back from any situation and see it from a wiser and more objective angle, allowing us to be more receptive to other avenues or options. Psychoactive plants in a similar way reflect our mind back at us so that we can see in detail how we operate, even breaking down one thought into its individual influencing parts. Illuminating our mental processes in this way helps us to see where the sliver of self-sabotage sneaks in or to reveal the influence of victim mentality in our communications.

In many wisdom traditions and religions is the concept of reincarnation, a phenomenon that is both misunderstood and misinterpreted, mainly due to the valley of forgetfulness, so to speak, that we travel through to arrive in this realm. In Buddhism the cycle of existence is based upon the concept of cause and effect, that nothing can happen or be produced without causes and conditions. Yet these causes and conditions stretch over eons and many lifetimes, so they are very hidden. The nature of our suffering is also made manifest through this process, past transgressions forming the impetus for further actions of a similar nature. Our tendency to remain in a polarized state of mind, either grasping at something we desire or avoiding something we don't want, creates suffering of many types due to our ignorance of the reality that we are already enough, everything we need is already within us. When we die it is our attachments to the things we grasp at that pulls us back for another round of earthly life. Karma is the result of every action we take, whether through body, speech, or mind from a polarized perspective. We create cycles within cycles over eons and lifetimes since beginningless time, which is why karma is known as a very hidden and complex phenomena. Both Ayahuasca and Elder teach us about these life cycles as these plant teachers open our psychic channels and lift the veils so that we can witness the origins of our disease and blockages, wherever they exist, in time, space, or some other dimension. Both medicines initiate us into the spirit world so that we can experience what the afterlife would be like for us if we died right now. What aspects of ourselves would we meet in the bardo (the state in between lives as described by the Buddhists)? Which soul fragments do we still need to retrieve to leave this realm whole? Which of our inner demons or aspects of our shadow do we need to integrate to die consciously?

Dying consciously can be seen as one of the main objectives of our inner work. The more we awaken to our true nature and to the present moment, the better chance we have of transcending cyclic existence and having the awareness to choose our next reincarnation here on Earth or decide to go somewhere else. One of the highest yoga tantras is the art of lucid dreaming (see mugwort chapter 7) or dream yoga, the highest realization of which is to die consciously. If we can become consciously aware in our dreams and therefore unattached to our physical body (our biggest attachment in life), which is a very achievable state, then our chances of remaining conscious as we enter the afterlife, having left our physical body at death, is much more likely. Rather than being swept along on the currents of karma with no control or awareness of where we are going, we can consciously direct the course of our postlife interdimensional travels. There is more than one heaven and many dimensions to experience. Working with plants not only for dream work but to have direct experiences of the spirit realm before we die is of great advantage to us. If the experience is one of an initiatory nature, which both Elder and Ayahuasca are capable of facilitating, the experience can be powerful enough for us to lose all fear of death. As the saying goes, to fully live we must first die, and this means dying to the old fearful self and stepping into realization of one's eternal being.

This brings us to perhaps the most important teaching of the medicine wheel. In many of the ancient wisdom traditions and within the secret teachings of the mystery schools is the key to exiting this earthly realm successfully, transcending the cycle of reincarnation and achieving immortality. Once the individual has managed to awaken his or her eternal self within conscious awareness and has achieved consciousness within the dream, the individual can learn how to correctly exit this plane of existence upon death.

The external world we inhabit right now is seen as the third dimension, Earth, symbolized by the cube within the platonic solids and the square within magical ritual. The cube and square are made from 90-degree angles. The flat cross of the medicine wheel is created from four 90-degree angles, not only indicating the four directions but indicating how this realm is made, its underlying geometric structure.

The 90-degree angle therefore creates the physical realm; it is intrinsic in its architecture. In the teachings of the sacerdotal class of the Egyptian dynasties and within the Native American wisdom is the instruction that upon death, once we have exited the body, we do not head toward the light but make a 90-degree turn and leave this realm to avoid the reincarnation loop. We follow the energetic framework of this reality to find our way out. The 90-degree angle turn also features in advanced out-of-body experience techniques such as ones practiced by Robert Monroe.[2] Sandra Corcoran, a shamanic teacher and author of *Shamanic Awakening,* who spent thirty years studying under various indigenous elders and who is trained as a dream decoder, suggests that shamans knew of practices that did not even require the individual to die physically to cross into other dimensions, which echoes Tibetan accounts of the rainbow body. She recounts the following:

> According to Grandmother Twylah, a Seneca Wolf Clan elder, (the Seneca were part of the Iroquois Six Nations Confederacy), when the ancient race known as the EL-ders left this planetary vibration, they exited at right angles with total conscious awareness, while maintaining their physical body structure. Through understanding how to shift frequencies and access multi-dimensional states, which they perceived as instructions imparted from various Star Nations, and practiced through forms of movement, sound, plant medicine, meditation and/or working in the dream state, the EL-ders understood how to expand their 3-D perceptive state, enabling them to shift beyond this reality.

Dying consciously is seen as the most important aspect of most wisdom and spiritual practices. Master plants are not here to help us conquer this life and become happy, successful, and wealthy in this life, as is often thought, but to conquer death. There is a 90-degree angle between the earth and air elements on the medicine wheel. Elder who holds these two elements powerfully within her medicine therefore holds the 90-degree angle within her inner energetic framework. She can teach us how to die, and this is why she is known as the tree of death.

We have forgotten how to die in the West, how to treat our dead, and how to ensure all soul fragments are retrieved from all directions before the deceased cross the veil. Death rituals were once adhered to in these lands, and having trained in Celtic funeral rites, I can understand why Elder is such a blessed ally for both the preparation for our own death and our assisting with the death of others. When we work shamanically with plants, we are engaging with their spirits and therefore with the spirit world. The combination of Elder's air and earth elements means she is a direct conduit to the spirit realm. Elder not only prepares us but knows the way back to the land of the ancestors and actually escorts lost earthbound spirits through to the Otherworld when we die. She is a powerful psychopomp who can release traumas from the wombs of women before carrying them over and shape-shift into motherly aspects to reassure the spirit that they are safe. Elder is the tree of death in the Ogham alphabet and is often found growing under the tree beyond death, the yew. Together they work in harmony, as the yew holds the portal to the land of our ancestors and Elder escorts us through.

Elder is known as a tree of initiation, and for the trainee healer or budding shaman, she can give us a taste of death, take us very close to it or even through the veil and bring us back again in order to awaken inner strength and other qualities that we are lacking for our work and life. During my initiation with Elder, she took away most of my Earth energy: that energy was hardly registering in my pulse, and I spent weeks in bed with no motivation to do anything. As a plant healer dedicated to the nature path and a triple Virgo, my earth energy defines me, or so I thought. Elder took away all of my power, everything that I thought I was, and made me look at myself to see who I was underneath this identity. What was I at a soul level if I didn't have any of my spirit team, have any of my magic, or if I didn't have any connection to Earth? In a defining moment, after weeks of languishing in the darkness, I remembered my inner light. I stepped into the light of my spirit and remembered that we are all beings of pure light simply trying to find our way back home, out of the maze and back to our light body, back to the expanded awareness of love that we are. This sounds very simple when I write it here, but it was a profound moment of integration of the most powerful force that we know, love. I was taken to the brink of death in order to release my fear of it and with that came a new level of respect for the greatest initiation of our life, the moment we leave our body.

The exercise for this chapter is not necessarily a meditation or journey but more of a ritual of empowerment that will have profoundly beneficial effects on your life and ultimately on your death. It is a shamanic practice given to me by High Chief Iarueri Rawi and shamanic healer David Leesley. I have adapted it here to work with the spirit of Elder as she will be your guide as you integrate over the following months. You will be calling back soul fragments that are ready to return to you from each of the six directions. We scatter soul fragments through many time lines and dimensions as we journey from lifetime to lifetime, experiencing trauma, loss, and grief. These holes in the integrity of our soul consciousness create blockages to living and dying consciously. By reclaiming aspects of ourselves, we start to become whole, and eventually these soul fragments integrate into our conscious awareness, illuminating inner wisdom and potentially spiritual lineages from previous lives.

This practice can be performed either outside with an elder tree or inside with your medicine wheel altar. If working with an outside tree, make sure you can access the tree on all sides. If this is difficult, you can also stand to one side of the tree and face each direction from one spot. Please ensure you make offerings to Elder Mother before you begin; she is literally a wise elder who needs respect. If working indoors with the medicine wheel, then have some elder essence, some elderflower tea, or your preferred form of her medicine before you begin. You will be standing and facing each of the four directions in turn, so make sure you have space to move wherever you are and check your directional orientation on the land before you begin. Whether we decide to work clockwise around the wheel or anticlockwise is a matter of preference. I feel that clockwise sends energy out into the world and widdershins or counterclockwise draws it in. For this exercise, we will therefore rotate counterclockwise around the wheel and the tree.

After imbibing the elder medicine, connecting to your elder handle, and asking for her guidance and assistance, stand facing the east direction or face outward on the east side of the elder tree. With strong conviction call back all of your soul fragments from any time line or dimension from the direction of north. Simply state: I call back all of my soul fragments that are ready to return from any time line or dimension from the direction of north. Grant that this is done now. Wait a few minutes or until you feel a shift, perhaps a sigh, then turn to face the west.

In the west direction reclaim your soul fragments stating: I call back all of my soul fragments that are ready to return from any time line or dimension from the direction of west. Grant that this is done now. Wait a few minutes or until you feel a shift, then turn to face the south.

Repeat the same process in the south, adapting the command accordingly, and then the east.

Then turn to face the center of the medicine wheel or toward the tree, and call to the below direction followed by the above direction.

Once you feel the internal shift, then sit down in peaceful meditation in whichever direction of the wheel you feel drawn to.

At this point you may ask Elder to show you beneath her magical branches an aspect of yourself that has returned so that you may know it. There may be more than one soul aspect and it may surprise you, trust your intuition and trust whatever you see. We are often shown the aspects of ourselves that are useful to our healing or beneficial to our life and spiritual path in some way.

You may prefer to sit and meditate after each direction, connecting to and witnessing any soul fragments or higher self aspects returning to you from each direction in turn.

Journal your insights, feelings, and thoughts about this process as you will find returning to it later will give great insight into the course of your life after empowering it with wholeness.

Fig. 19.1. *Taxus baccata*

19

Gone Beyond with the Spirit of Yew

ONE OF THE MOST ENIGMATIC aspects of the yew is the quality of light under its twisted hanging branches. It can be a bright sunny day, but step under a yew, and purple-hued twilight envelops you. It feels like stepping into another world. Rest awhile here and the yew will draw you in through entrainment of your heart to it; it looks straight into the core of your being and understands what makes you tick. Through a deep stillness that holds you safe, its mysterious presence stirs feelings of remembrance that you have known it all your lives, and perhaps you have.

Taxus baccata has a fearful reputation as the poisonous tree of the dead (the word *taxus* is Latin for "toxic"). Planted in churchyards to watch over the entombed, it has long-held renown as a portal to the Underworld. Yet as the tree beyond death in the Ogham alphabet, we are given a hint as to its multidimensional essence and its vast consciousness, which spans eons of time. The *Taxus* genus of conifers is believed to have evolved from *Palaeotaxus rediviva,* which dates back 200 million years.[1] It has survived ice ages and numerous cataclysms to stand as one of the 0.1 percent of all known earthly species that has survived into the present day.

Here in Wales we are blessed to be on the receiving end of its expansive time line, and we live among the most condensed population of ancient yews on the planet. Mainly found in churchyards today but not always, yews often grow in circles or groves, known to be venerated by the Druids and perhaps even planted by them. The trees existed long before the churches that sit in their center; the power of a yew circle did not go unnoticed. Today, as the decline of the church means the selling off of many of its grounds, the yews are in great danger to property developers who are not aware of the importance of this tree to our heritage and connection to our ancestors. The Ancient Yew Group has campaigned for many years to protect these ancient trees, so do seek them out online if you feel called as one of the warriors of the yew and honor this most blessed of trees.

There is no knowing to what age a yew tree can grow; the hollowing of its trunk means the standard method of counting a tree's rings to determine its age cannot be applied in this case. We can only guesstimate based on the esoteric wisdom of the tree. According to yew shaman Michael Dunning, the yew always seeks a womb-like space within its interiority to function effectively. If a yew is left to its own devices, its branches curve down and run along the ground, creating a central womb-like space around the trunk. Most yews in churchyards have their branches cut back above ground level for health and safety, and so as the yew ages, it starts to hollow in its trunk instead, to ensure it maintains its gestating space from which can emerge its transformational qualities. This space is a portal, a creatrix, a luminous void. It is the feminine interior from which life emerges.

The first time I meditated under a yew, I had no idea about this integral aspect of it, yet I was drawn down into a cavern beneath its roots. My consciousness was simply held in darkness. After a while I simply asked, So now what? Nothing. I just sat there waiting until I realized this was not a space for anything to happen in the usual way; it was simply a space of pure potentiality. As soon as this awareness dropped in, I was pushed up through the ground as a new tree, standing firm and strong in the Middle World, ready to face the upcoming large event I was running in London. A secret and defining feature of the conscious intelligence of the yew is that it is both the tree and the seed at the same time. The tree itself is the seed of potentiality and the gateway to nondual awareness. It was only through the Yew Mysteries teachings with Michael that I started to understand how this magnificent tree is not only the tree of the afterlife but the tree of rebirth also.

Yew calls its warriors to it and leaves its footprints through your life as it draws you ever closer. These signs of its guidance are subtle and span many years so can easily be missed if you're not paying attention. Upon returning to the UK after living overseas for fifteen years, we thought we would look for a place to live in Somerset. But after many weeks of searching, we could not find anywhere we liked, and then an invitation from a friend to visit her in Wales arrived. She was living in a large house in the countryside, and she was drawn there by an old yew tree in the garden that was over five hundred years old. When we arrived she had organized a lunch for us with two of her friends, Dr. Patrick MacManaway and Lynne Allbutt. Patrick became our geomancy teacher and a trusted friend. Lynne also became a dear friend and is well known for her barefoot run across Wales in two days. It was Lynne who introduced us to the amazing yew circle at Pencelli, and through a series of coincidences and connections, we were introduced to the yew shaman, Michael Dunning. At that time, he was looking to bring his body of work, the Yew Mysteries, back to the British Isles, as he was residing in North America. We became long-term students of Michael, supported him in establishing the Yew Mysteries school in the UK, and were part of the first group of yew tree initiates to complete the Yew Mysteries teachings in, perhaps, thousands of years. Michael's work is profound and comes directly from his own time under a yew in Scotland where he was healed of a chronic illness while at the same time ancestral beings who worked through the portal of Yew transmitted a lost and ancient body of teachings to him. My Yew Mysteries initiation coincided with me moving into a house that sits directly under an ancient yew in the energetic center of Wales in a small village called Abbeycwmhir. It is in this hidden hamlet that the last true and sovereign Prince of Wales, Llywelyn ap Gruffydd (ca. 1223–1282), the grandson of the celebrated Llywelyn the Great, is buried within the grounds of a cistercian abbey.

And it is here that my practical teachings with the yew really started and where I wrote this book.

As the footprints of Yew reveal themselves upon the course of one's life, it naturally leads to the contemplation of destiny and fate. The debate between fate and free will rages on as New Age theories and egotism overlay confusion and complexity onto what is essentially a rather straightforward natural law. Let's start at the beginning, the birth of the universe. All esoteric and wisdom teachings conclude that the universe we inhabit emerged from a single source through the power of the word, that is, through the unfoldment of the elements giving space to frequency. But what gave the impetus for the unfoldment in the first place? What ignited the beginning, if there is indeed one? The one who initiates birth is the Great Mother. Everything is born of woman, so it can only be from the universal feminine principle that Earth is born and from the womb of Mother Nature that we are born. As we see through close inspection of plants and through the Fibonacci sequence, our universe is fractal, so if we emerged from the womb, so did the universe. Micro as a reflection of the macro and vice versa. Everything flows from one state of being to another through the portal of the creatrix. Matriarchal civilizations of the ancient past attest to this. Every atom and every resulting thing, such as a stone or an animal, has its own trajectory through this world, the course of its life running along its own thread within the great tapestry, propelled by causes, conditions, and interdependence on everything around it. Nature is the Great Mother; they are one and the same. Nature cycles in its motion along its filaments. Nature is therefore fated. The hand of Mother Fate guides each phenomenal thing toward its destiny, that which it was always meant to be. A piece of rock may look static, but it is in an ever-evolving state, dying to its old state (perhaps as part of a cliff) and being reborn to another (reducing to dust).

In Hindu cosmology this web of threads of all contained within the seen and unseen realms is Indra's net. In the pagan cosmology of the British Isles, this is the Web of Wyrd, the web of dreams spun by the three Norns. This great matrix of life is always the same within its wholeness but ever changing and evolving within itself. It is both one and many at the same time. Of course, it has to be this way. Otherwise, the expression of life would not be able to function; everything would remain static and lifeless. We need paradox for this world of duality to exist. Yet while duality exists, and we can perceive everything as separate individual objects and things in this world, including ourselves, so the opposite must exist. If unity and nonduality did not exist, then we would not perceive the opposites in the world, and through common perception everything has an opposite. I did say earlier that this was a straightforward concept, and once you feel into this aspect of reality, you will wonder why you hadn't seen it before. According to Buddhist philosophy everything exists but not in the way we think it does: things are not separate and independent. Everything arises dependently upon everything else; nothing is inherently existent. It is a different way of saying that everything has emerged from the one source, the great void, emptiness, the womb, and so everything will always be connected in some way. Nothing can change without affecting everything else, and this is also the basis of the laws of karma from that tradition.

So where does that leave us human beings, searching for our inner truth and perhaps the purpose of our life so that we can feel fulfilled before we die? The choice is simple: Do you follow your self-interested desires and strive for fulfillment as a reflection of what others expect, think, or believe? Do you chase satisfaction outside yourself through money and status, seek validation from others? Or do you exercise your one aspect of free will and recognize your fate and consciously move toward your destiny? This is the only true act of free will that I perceive we have. Ultimately, we are all trying to remember our oneness with the divine principle, our truth, the light that shines within each of us. Is it our fate to achieve this or our choice? It is our choice, yet whichever way we choose, it was always our fate anyway; we cannot escape the great web, the Great Mother Fate. When I first started meditating on this concept, my anxiety shot up, my ego kicked into overdrive trying to hold on to some sense of self, desperately clinging to the perception of security within control over what happens to me. After a while the emotional turmoil receded and a deep sense of peace crept over me like a soothing blanket. I could actually let go. By surrendering to fate I can let go of striving to be anything, of striving to achieve anything or any sense of competition. This is not to say I felt defeated or that I was now going to drop out of society through the sense of not having to participate anymore. What it actually did was empower me to allow my truth of the present moment to express itself better through me. For fate does not mean that you are destined for a life of slavery on this prison planet; that is only one perspective. Recognizing fate means we recognize the river of life that we are standing in and we flow toward truth. We flow back toward the truth of who we are, and eventually all beings will do this as it is part of the great cycle of fate. For fate is not only something that is done to us but something we do to life. We are not separate from this natural law; we are one and the same with it. We are individual yet part of the whole. She is the weaver and we are the web; she is the needle and we are the thread. With this deep realization comes an acceptance of our uniqueness and oneness at the same time. Yew strips away all sense of the egoic "I am" and indeed strips away many delusions we have about who we think we are and takes us right back to our originality of simply being. It is at this point that we can see the association between the yew and karmic Saturn. The cycles of karma are expansive and can span many lifetimes, an often-overlooked fact about how karma works. It rarely manifests in the same lifetime; it is largely a hidden phenomenon. Yew knows how to bring karmic awareness, immanence, and transcendence into being.

I have seen many courses, workshops, and advertisements for readings claiming to tell you who you truly are. While no one other than yourself can discover the unique tapestry of your own eternal spirit, otherwise it has no useful reality, what does "your true self" mean anyway? We can conceptually know that we are made of the same stuff as the stars and our essence is universal; this is the unity perspective. Yet where does our individual self sit within that notion? We don't just dissolve and disappear into the ocean once we remember we are the ocean; we retain the memory of being a drop of water while at the same time being part of the ocean. Our eternal spirit has traversed the great web of the universe perhaps for eons, collecting many experiences of being many different types of beings and people. These memories are logged somewhere within our blueprint, within the depth consciousness of the mind. Our true self is the essence of all that we have known; it is the direct experience of all that is, and it is possible to bring all of that collated wisdom into conscious awareness once again or at least be able to tap into it in just the right moment when it is required.

The Awen of the Welsh Druids, the Sambhogakaya of the Mahayana Buddhists, the *ka* body of the Egyptians, and the great work of the alchemists all point us toward the immortal aspect of ourselves, which is our direct connection to all that is, to the source of all life. Conceptualizing this aspect of our inner world already puts this divine and all-encompassing aspect of our being into a conceptual box, yet in reality it is beyond words. Only through direct experience of this level of consciousness can we experience it, and this takes dedication. It is not weekend workshops, online courses, or reading books that will expand your awareness to this depth. It is only through application, practice, and endurance within whichever system or method you choose, and I hope you choose the plant path as nature is one of the only sources of uncorrupted truth left in this world.

The yew tree awakens potent aspects of the eternal self that are ready to come forth, and that aspect can be from any time line or dimension. If a Viking lifetime was particularly powerful, then the memory of the wisdom attained in that lifetime can awaken on the inner planes in this life. If the eternal self spent a long time in the Otherworld where the healing arts were part of the experience, then as a healer in this life that aspect of the self can awaken for the greatest good of all. These aspects of the eternal spirit will only awaken if they are in alignment with the divine plan of this life. They will not awaken if we operate from a place of duality or ego. If we get lost in these stories also, then we have strayed from the path of balance.

The yew is the tree beyond death because we have to die to all of the old within us, all of the conditionings, all of the conditional love, all of the concepts we had about ourselves and what we deserve. It is only when binds and conceptual boxes have been dropped that the truth of the self can be reborn into conscious awareness. Many people have achieved inner peace to this level of profundity; however, you will not see them shouting about it on social media. It is too precious to be debased in such a way. It is the wish-fulfilling jewel that forms the basis of self-mastery, and only those who have gone beyond the confines of society and are willing to question and change their sense of self-definition, those driven by spiritual seeking above mere survival or achievement, will even come close to finding it.

The earth star chakra of our inner world holding collective and individual memory, the yew is the embodiment of the world tree, the Yggdrasil about which our world turns, and so the last meditation in this book is not a meditation at all. There is nothing to do with Yew; there is only to be. The only way to experience the profundity of a yew is to go and breathe under one. Find a yew where you will not be disturbed and just be. You may notice after a while that the yew is breathing you; you are not the one breathing. Yew breathes the breath of life into us; so just surrender to your fate.

Plant Diet Working Example

SO HOW DO WE PULL all of these instructions and aspects of our required healing together to effectively transform both our inner and outer worlds for the greater good? Below is a guide for working with a plant diet to awaken the eternal spirit through ritual, plant spirits, and meditation.

Setting the Intention

To step onto the medicine wheel and begin a healing journey, we can either have a particular issue in mind that we need to work through or we can allow the plants themselves to bring our awareness to an issue that needs work. Oftentimes, our issues are buried deep, beyond our conscious awareness, so even though we may be aware that, for example, anger is a long-standing issue for us, we may have no idea why we carry it or where it came from. In this regard, it is always best to pray to the universe, the Great Spirit, or the plant kingdom for assistance. Request that a plant that can help you work through your mental, emotional, physical, or spiritual issue be brought to your awareness. There may already be a plant or tree that you have been drawn to recently, or as you state your prayer, one might immediately pop into your mind. Over the following week you may notice oaks everywhere you go, or dandelions might keep popping into your awareness. You will know within the time frame you have set for your plant diet which plant you will be working with for the start of your healing journey.

Find Out about the Plant

Working blind with a plant, knowing little about its healing qualities, can be a wondrous and self-validating way to discover it. The minimum requirements are that you check that it is edible, that it has no contraindications for any medication you may be on, and that its medicines are available to either purchase or make.

You may already know about the plant and its healing gifts and so instinctively know that it is the right plant to work with for your intentions. From this place you can explore where and how it grows, how it heals the physical body, and so on and start to investigate its energetic makeup. You could consult plant books, and there are also some great plant identification apps that might be useful.

Bring the Medicine

At this stage you need to decide what type of plant diet you want to do and how deep you want to dive. An essence protocol for a lunar cycle might be enough. You might have a week off work and can set aside the time to go deep with the plant every day through meditations, journey work, and multiple medicines. You may wish to take it slowly and set aside a few months to get to know the plant through its spring and summer cycle and how its changing energies affect your own. In the Amazon shamans will diet with a plant in relative solitude for up to a year. There are no set rules for the time frame, the type of plant diet, or the depth of your work; the only caveat is that you set the container and stick to it.

You could make your own herbal remedies to work with as outlined in chapter 5. If you purchase any medicines, make sure you energetically cleanse them through blessing them or asking the spirit to come back into the medicine. Factory-produced medicines or even medicines produced by someone else will have energies and intentions instilled into them that might not be in alignment with your own intentions. Handlers of the medicine can also transmit unhelpful energies. In this case, simply place the remedy under a tree for the night or use your intention (your own magic) to remove anything dead, toxic, or dying from in, on, or around the medicine. Grant that this is done now.

Starting the Plant Diet

To begin the plant diet, a small ritual or blessing for your journey, an offering to the plant, or a prayer placed on your medicine wheel will open the space and the portal for your healing journey. You may wish to actually open the space by calling in all the directions; if you do so, ensure that you also close the space in the same way at the end of your set time frame. You may wish to place the plant or tree (a small potted one!) in the center of your medicine wheel in the place of pure potential. Placing the plant in the west, for example, will call on the water element of the plant if you feel it is an aspect of emotional imbalance you are working on. Again, there are no set rules here; simply be guided by your intuition.

As you daily take your essence, hydrosol, oxymel, or whichever remedies and combination of remedies you have decided upon, allow yourself to spend time getting to know the plant, its handle, and how it works within and through you. Dream with it, dance with it, journey with it, draw with it. Get to know your handle. Allow its medicine to work through you on all levels. The plant spirit knows the time frame you've set for your diet; it therefore knows the healing process it is taking you through. This is why it is important to ensure you stick to your time frame. Quite often insights and healings come through during the final day or hours of the diet, so even if you have been feeling you are not getting anywhere or that the plant isn't working, stick with it. The plant spirit will at some point bring to the surface the issues or imbalances that are out of alignment, sometimes with startling clarity and at other times in gentle ways. Everything that happens to you during your plant diet, including everything in your external world, must be viewed through the lens of the plant. You might have an argument with your loved one, in which case you need to examine and explore your perspective. Investigate the emotions that arose for you and how you behaved during the argument. Looking at those aspects of the person that really annoyed you will give you a deeper understanding of yourself. Or you might have a profound encounter with a bird or animal; in which case, also investigate its shamanic medicine as it may have a message for your healing journey. The plant spirit will elicit experiences and insights to bring conscious awareness to the cause of your issue along with the healing remedy itself.

The Medicine Wheel Map

Your healing journey may start with a blank medicine wheel as you slowly get to know the directional energies and elements, along with the plants and trees you diet with, over time. Filling in the blanks of your map may take some time, years perhaps, but there is no rush. Even in its basic shape, the wheel still serves to anchor intentions, hold space for your meditations, and plot your progress through the healing process or through the year. Working with the wheel aligns us to the cyclical nature of life and brings realism to the healing path. We cannot expect one plant to answer all our life issues; however, we can return time and again to the map to help us go ever deeper into the psyche and guide the way into all our elemental imbalances. The medicine wheel is a lamp on the path of the ever present to help us avoid losing the thread of our journey or the pull of our eternal spirit. Over time, as we do more inner work, we realize that we are the medicine wheel; it is alive within us. The universe is both within and without.

Ending the Plant Diet

It is essential that you close any sacred space that you may have opened at the start of your plant diet and to give gratitude to your new plant ally for all of the insight, guidance, and protection it has offered you during your healing process. You might not have all of the answers you wanted, and your intentions may not have been answered in quite the way you envisaged, but you will be a new and different person, with an expanded consciousness and a deeper understanding of the self.

It is advisable after the plant diet to review it. Hopefully, you kept a journal of your process to facilitate the retrospective view. It might be an option to meditate with a psychoactive plant such as cannabis to connect more fully to your higher self and receive more and deeper insights and understandings of your healing journey. However you choose to end your plant diet, meditating on its ebb and flow will allow the teachings of the plant spirit to continue to live within you and to enliven your spiritual progress. This is ancient future technology that will support you through the great transition of the ages.

Notes

Introduction. A Guide to the Path of Plant Consciousness

1. Peck, *The Road Less Traveled*, 102.
2. Hughes, *Celtic Plant Magic*, 32.

Chapter 1. Returning to the Plant Spirit Path

1. Fidler, *Restoring the Soul of the World*, chap. 4.
2. Morell, *An Historical and Critical View*, 103.
3. Beament, "People 'Need Connection with Nature.'"
4. Anandamurti, *Yoga Psychology*.
5. HeartMath, "Unlock the Power of Your Heart" (website).

Chapter 2. The World of Spirit

1. Artisson, *The Witching Way of the Hollow Hill*.

Chapter 3. Meditation and Shamanic Journeying

1. Govinda, *Creative Meditation and Multidimensional Consciousness*, 96.
2. O'Donohue, *Anam Cara*, 65.
3. Knight, *Experiences of the Inner Worlds*, 64.
4. Matthews and Matthews, *Encyclopedia of Celtic Wisdom*, 350.

Chapter 4. The Way of the Ethical Warrior

1. Dalai Lama, *Stages of Meditation*, 38.
2. Trungpa, *The Sacred Path of the Warrior*, 132.
3. Thrangu, *Tilopa's Wisdom*.

Chapter 5. The Plant Spirit Path to Self-Realization

1. Matthews and Matthews, *Walkers between Worlds,* 154.
2. Drury, *The Dictionary of the Esoteric,* 195.
3. Beyer, *Singing to the Plants,* 82.
4. Lipton, "The Jump from Cell Culture to Consciousness."

Chapter 6. Becoming the Plant Medicine Wheel

1. Rinpoche, *Healing with Form, Energy, and Light,* 76.
2. Popham, *Evolutionary Herbalism,* 304.
3. Steiner, *Christianity as Mystical Fact,* 47.
4. Rinpoche, *Healing with Form, Energy, and Light,* 45.
5. Steiner, "The Astral World and Devachan," lecture 3.
6. Pythagoras, "Pythagoras Quotes" (website).

Chapter 7. Developing Inner Vision with the Spirit of Mugwort

1. Artisson, *The Witching Way of the Hollow Hill,* 147.

Chapter 8. Inner Wisdom with the Spirit of Oak

1. Stringer, "The Origin and Evolution of *Homo sapiens.*"
2. Mills, *The British Oak,* 17.

Chapter 10. Balancing and Healing with the Spirit of Nettle

1. Rinpoche, *Healing with Form, Energy, and Light.*

Chapter 11. Breaking Old Habits with the Spirit of Dandelion

1. Matthews and Matthews, *Walkers between Worlds,* 194.
2. William, *Medical Medium Liver Rescue,* 5.

Chapter 12. Emotional Balance with the Spirit of Alder

1. Boyer, *Under the Witching Tree,* 151.

Chapter 13. Alchemical Transformation with the Spirit of Lady's Mantle

1. Wood, *The Earthwise Herbal Repertory*, 329.
2. Kynes, *Complete Book of Correpsondences*, 446.
3. Bertrand and Bertrand, *Womb Awakening*, chap. 5.

Chapter 14. Uncovering Hidden Memories with the Spirit of Rosemary

1. Cunningham, *Encyclopedia of Magical Herbs*, 219.

Chapter 16. Integrating Shadow with the Spirit of Wormwood

1. Pendell, *Pharmakopoeia*, 103.
2. Pendell, *Pharmakopoeia*, 105.
3. Jung, *Aion*, 8.

Chapter 17. Awakening Your Inner Divinity with the Spirit of Angelica

1. Steiner, *Christianity as Mystical Fact*, 48–49.
2. Steiner, *The Archangel Michael*, chap. 1.
3. Cunningham, *Encyclopedia of Magical Herbs*, 34.

Chapter 18. Dying Consciously with the Spirit of Elder

1. Roberts, *Spiritual Growth with Entheogens*, xiii.
2. Monroe, *Journeys Out of the Body*, 220.

Chapter 20. Gone Beyond with the Spirit of Yew

1. Hageneder, *Yew*, 14.

Bibliography

Anandamurti, Shrii Shrii. *Yoga Psychology.* Translated by Acarya Vijayananda Avadhuta and Jayanta Kumar. Calcutta, India: Ananda Marga, 1990.

Artisson, Robin. *The Witching Way of the Hollow Hill.* Green Valley Lake, Calif.: Pendraig, 2009.

Beament, Emily. "People 'Need Connection with Nature'." Ecologist: Informed by Nature (website), February 27, 2020.

Bertrand, Azra, and Seren Bertrand. *Womb Awakening: Initiatory Wisdom from the Creatrix of All Life.* Rochester, Vt.: Bear & Co., 2017.

Beyer, Stephan V. *Singing to the Plants: A Guide to Mestizo Shamanism in the Upper Amazon.* Albuquerque: University of New Mexico Press, 2010.

Boyer, Corinne. *Under the Witching Tree.* Portland, Ore.: Llewellyn, 2020.

Bruton-Seal, Julie, and Matthew Seal. *Hedgerow Medicine: Harvest and Make Your Own Herbal Remedies.* Shropshire, UK: Merlin Unwin Books, 2008.

———. *Wayside Medicine: Forgotten Plants and How to Use Them.* Shropshire, UK: Merlin Unwin Books, 2017.

Corcoran, Sandra. *Shamanic Awakening: My Journey between the Dark and the Daylight.* Rochester, Vt.: Bear & Co., 2014.

Cunningham, Scott. *Encyclopedia of Magical Herbs.* 2nd ed. Portland, Ore.: Llewellyn, 2012.

Dalai Lama. *Stages of Meditation.* New York: Random House, 2001.

Drury, Nevill. *The Dictionary of the Esoteric.* London: Watkins, 2004.

Fidler, David. *Restoring the Soul of the World: Our Living Bond with Nature's Intelligence.* Rochester, Vt.: Inner Traditions, 2014.

Govinda, Lama Anagarika. *Creative Meditation and Multidimensional Consciousness.* Crows Nest, Australia: Unwin Paperbacks, 1977.

Hageneder, Fred. *Yew: A History.* Cheltenham, UK: History Press, 2011.

Hall, Manly P. *The Secret Teachings of All Ages*. New York: Dover, 2019.

Hughes, Jon G. *Celtic Plant Magic: A Workbook for Alchemical Sex Rituals*. Rochester, Vt.: Destiny Books, 2003.

Jung, Carl G. *Aion: Researches into the Phenomenology of the Self*. Vol. 9, part 2, of *Collected Works of C. G. Jung*, translated by Gerhard Adler and R. F. C. Hull. New York: Bollingen, 1959.

Knight, Gareth. *Experiences of the Inner Worlds*. Cheltenham, UK: Skylight Press, 2010.

Krishnamurti, Jiddu. *Total Freedom: The Essential Krishnamurti*. New York: HarperOne, 1996.

Kynes, Sandra. *Complete Book of Correspondences*. Portland, Ore.: Llewellyn, 2019.

Leesley, David. *Kassoso: When Myth Becomes Reality*. Cornwall, UK: Penwith Press, 2014.

———. *Return of the White Serpent*. Cornwall, UK: Penwith Press, 2012.

Lipton, Bruce. "The Jump from Cell Culture to Consciousness." *Integrative Medicine: A Clinician's Journal* 16, no. 6 (December 2017): 44–50.

Matthews, Caitlin, and John Matthews. *Encyclopedia of Celtic Wisdom*. Rockport, Maine: Element Books, 1994.

———. *Walkers between Worlds: The Western Mysteries from Shaman to Magus*. Rochester, Vt.: Inner Traditions, 2003.

Mills, Archie. *The British Oak*. Frome, UK: Butler Tanner & Dennis, 2013.

Monroe, Robert A. *Journeys Out of the Body*. Faber, Va.: Souvenir Press, 2010.

O'Donohue, John. *Anam Cara: Spiritual Wisdom from the Celtic World*. New York: Bantam Books, 1999.

Peck, M. Scott. *The Road Less Traveled: A New Psychology of Love, Traditional Values and Spiritual Growth*. London: Arrow Books, 1990.

Pendell, Dale. *Pharmakopoeia: Plant Powers, Poisons and Herbcraft*. Berkeley, Calif.: North Atlantic Books, 2010.

Popham, Sajah. *Evolutionary Herbalism: Science, Spiritualiity, and Medicine from the Heart of Nature*. Berkeley, Calif.: North Atlantic Books, 2019.

Roberts, Thomas B. *Spiritual Growth with Entheogens: Psychoactive Sacramentals and Human Transformation*. Rochester, Vt.: Park Street Press, 2012.

Rinpoche, Tenzin Wangyal. *Healing with Form, Energy and Light: The Five Elements in Tibetan Shamanism, Tantra and Dzogchen*. Ithaca, N.Y.: Snow Lion, 2003.

Steiner, Rudolf. *Christianity as Mystical Fact and the Mysteries of Antiquity.* 3rd rev. ed. New York: G. P. Putnam, 1914.

———. *The Archangel Michael: His Mission and Ours; Selected Lectures and Writings.* Edited by Christopher Bamford. Hudson, N.Y.: Anthroposophic Press, 1994.

———. "The Astral World and Devachan." Three lectures given in Berlin, 1908.

Stewart, R. J. *The Underworld Initiation: A Journey Towards Psychic Transformation.* Wellingborough, UK: Aquarian Press, 1985.

Stringer, Chris. "The Origin and Evolution of *Homo sapiens.*" *Philosophical Transactions of the Royal Society B: Biological Sciences* 371, no. 1698 (July 2016).

Thrangu, Khenchen. *Tilopa's Wisdom: His Life and Teachings on the Ganges Mahamudra.* Ithaca, N.Y.: Snow Lion, 2019.

Trungpa, Chögyam. *Shambhala: The Sacred Path of the Warrior.* Boston: Shambhala, 1984.

William, Anthony. *Medical Medium Liver Rescue.* Carlsbad, Calif.: Hay House, 2018.

Wood, Matthew. *The Earthwise Herbal Repertory: The Definitive Practitioner's Guide.* Berkeley, Calif.: North Atlantic Books, 2016.

Index

Page numbers in *italics* refer to illustrations.

Great Pyramid, author's experience at, xv
Green Man, 23
Gruffydd, Llywelyn ap, 245
guidance and insight journey, 150–52
Guyett, Carole, xvii, 80, 174
Gwydion, 80

habits, breaking old, 174–82
handle, 75–76
Hanh, Thich Nhat, 43
Hawthorn, 33, 83, 123–24
    and the heart, 156–62
    and myth, 159–61
    precautions regarding, 161
    tincture, 156–57
healing, 88. *See also* plant spirit healing
    defined, 12, 85–90
    holistic approach to, 87–88
    and knowing causative experience, 60, 89
healing and balancing meditation, 169–71
healing frequencies, 89
heart, 16–19
    broken, 158
    Hawthorn and the, 155–62
    role of, 155–56
heart-body perception, 17
herbalism, required knowledge of, 74–75
herb-Robert, 31
Hermetica, 176
Hinduism, consciousness in, 36
Holly, 147
Holly King, 147
Hughes, Jon G., 3
humanity, being fully human, 74
humility, 149

iboga, xvii, 31
identity, necessity of establishing, 2
illness, underlying cause of, 30, 86–87
imagination, usefulness of, 45
imbalance, 66, 100
immortality, 28
impulses from plants, interpreting, 41
indigenous cultures, their understanding of plants, 9–10
inheritance, genealogical, 150
inner eye, 24
inner sensation meditation, 78–79
inner vision, the spirit of Mugwort and, 38–42, 130–42
inner wisdom, and the spirit of Oak, 145–52
intentions, setting, 77–78, 251–52
interconnection, 122
interdependent origination, 70
intuition, 39

journal-keeping, 41, 85
journeys with plant spirits. *See individual plants;* shamanic journeying
Jung, Carl, 218
Juniper, 148–49

karma, 236, 247, 248
kinesiology, 39
kingship, 146–47
Knight, Gareth, 38
know thyself, in plant spirit healing, 90

Lady's mantle, 101, 190
    and alchemical transformation, 191–97
    author's diet with, 195
    precautions regarding, 196